IN ASSOCIATION WITH

✕ SQA

HODDER GIBSON

Model Papers

WITH ANSWERS

PLUS: Official SQA 2015
Past Paper With Answers

Higher for CfE
English

Model Papers & 2015 Exam

HODDER
GIBSON
AN HACHETTE UK COMPANY

This book contains the official SQA 2015 Exam for Higher for CfE English, with associated SQA approved answers modified from the official marking instructions that accompany the paper.

In addition the book contains model papers, together with answers, plus study skills advice. These papers, some of which may include a limited number of previously published SQA questions, have been specially commissioned by Hodder Gibson, and have been written by experienced senior teachers and examiners in line with the new CfE Higher syllabus and assessment outlines, Spring 2014. This is not SQA material but has been devised to provide further practice for Higher examinations in 2015 and beyond.

Hodder Gibson is grateful to the copyright holders, as credited on the final page of the Answer Section, for permission to use their material. Every effort has been made to trace the copyright holders and to obtain their permission for the use of copyright material. Hodder Gibson will be happy to receive information allowing us to rectify any error or omission in future editions.

Hachette UK's policy is to use papers that are natural, renewable and recyclable products and made from wood grown in sustainable forests. The logging and manufacturing processes are expected to conform to the environmental regulations of the country of origin.

Orders: please contact Bookpoint Ltd, 130 Park Drive, Milton Park, Abingdon, Oxon OX14 4SE. Telephone: (44) 01235 827720. Fax: (44) 01235 400454. Lines are open 9.00–5.00, Monday to Saturday, with a 24-hour message answering service. Visit our website at www.hoddereducation.co.uk. Hodder Gibson can be contacted direct on: Tel: 0141 848 1609; Fax: 0141 889 6315; email: hoddergibson@hodder.co.uk

This collection first published in 2015 by
Hodder Gibson, an imprint of Hodder Education,
An Hachette UK Company
2a Christie Street
Paisley PA1 1NB

Typeset by Aptara, Inc.

Printed in the UK

A catalogue record for this title is available from the British Library

ISBN: 978-1-4718-6073-7

3 2 1

2016 2015

Introduction

Study Skills – what you need to know to pass exams!

Pause for thought

Many students might skip quickly through a page like this. After all, we all know how to revise. Do you really though?

Think about this:

"IF YOU ALWAYS DO WHAT YOU ALWAYS DO, YOU WILL ALWAYS GET WHAT YOU HAVE ALWAYS GOT."

Do you like the grades you get? Do you want to do better? If you get full marks in your assessment, then that's great! Change nothing! This section is just to help you get that little bit better than you already are.

There are two main parts to the advice on offer here. The first part highlights fairly obvious things but which are also very important. The second part makes suggestions about revision that you might not have thought about but which WILL help you.

Part 1

DOH! It's so obvious but …

Start revising in good time

Don't leave it until the last minute – this will make you panic.

Make a revision timetable that sets out work time AND play time.

Sleep and eat!

Obvious really, and very helpful. Avoid arguments or stressful things too – even games that wind you up. You need to be fit, awake and focused!

Know your place!

Make sure you know exactly **WHEN and WHERE** your exams are.

Know your enemy!

Make sure you know what to expect in the exam.

How is the paper structured?

How much time is there for each question?

What types of question are involved?

Which topics seem to come up time and time again?

Which topics are your strongest and which are your weakest?

Are all topics compulsory or are there choices?

Learn by DOING!

There is no substitute for past papers and practice papers – they are simply essential! Tackling this collection of papers and answers is exactly the right thing to be doing as your exams approach.

Part 2

People learn in different ways. Some like low light, some bright. Some like early morning, some like evening / night. Some prefer warm, some prefer cold. But everyone uses their BRAIN and the brain works when it is active. Passive learning – sitting gazing at notes – is the most INEFFICIENT way to learn anything. Below you will find tips and ideas for making your revision more effective and maybe even more enjoyable. What follows gets your brain active, and active learning works!

Activity 1 – Stop and review

Step 1

When you have done no more than 5 minutes of revision reading STOP!

Step 2

Write a heading in your own words which sums up the topic you have been revising.

Step 3

Write a summary of what you have revised in no more than two sentences. Don't fool yourself by saying, "I know it, but I cannot put it into words". That just means you don't know it well enough. If you cannot write your summary, revise that section again, knowing that you must write a summary at the end of it. Many of you will have notebooks full of blue/black ink writing. Many of the pages will not be especially attractive or memorable so try to liven them up a bit with colour as you are reviewing and rewriting. **This is a great memory aid, and memory is the most important thing.**

Activity 2 – Use technology!

Why should everything be written down? Have you thought about "mental" maps, diagrams, cartoons and colour to help you learn? And rather than write down notes, why not record your revision material?

What about having a text message revision session with friends? Keep in touch with them to find out how and what they are revising and share ideas and questions.

Why not make a video diary where you tell the camera what you are doing, what you think you have learned and what you still have to do? No one has to see or hear it, but the process of having to organise your thoughts in a formal way to explain something is a very important learning practice.

Be sure to make use of electronic files. You could begin to summarise your class notes. Your typing might be slow, but it will get faster and the typed notes will be easier to read than the scribbles in your class notes. Try to add different fonts and colours to make your work stand out. You can easily Google relevant pictures, cartoons and diagrams which you can copy and paste to make your work more attractive and **MEMORABLE**.

Activity 3 – This is it. Do this and you will know lots!

Step 1

In this task you must be very honest with yourself! Find the SQA syllabus for your subject (www.sqa.org.uk). Look at how it is broken down into main topics called MANDATORY knowledge. That means stuff you MUST know.

Step 2

BEFORE you do ANY revision on this topic, write a list of everything that you already know about the subject. It might be quite a long list but you only need to write it once. It shows you all the information that is already in your long-term memory so you know what parts you do not need to revise!

Step 3

Pick a chapter or section from your book or revision notes. Choose a fairly large section or a whole chapter to get the most out of this activity.

With a buddy, use Skype, Facetime, Twitter or any other communication you have, to play the game "If this is the answer, what is the question?". For example, if you are revising Geography and the answer you provide is "meander", your buddy would have to make up a question like "What is the word that describes a feature of a river where it flows slowly and bends often from side to side?".

Make up 10 "answers" based on the content of the chapter or section you are using. Give this to your buddy to solve while you solve theirs.

Step 4

Construct a wordsearch of at least 10 × 10 squares. You can make it as big as you like but keep it realistic. Work together with a group of friends. Many apps allow you to make wordsearch puzzles online. The words and phrases can go in any direction and phrases can be split. Your puzzle must only contain facts linked to the topic you are revising. Your task is to find 10 bits of information to hide in your puzzle, but you must not repeat information that you used in Step 3. DO NOT show where the words are. Fill up empty squares with random letters. Remember to keep a note of where your answers are hidden but do not show your friends. When you have a complete puzzle, exchange it with a friend to solve each other's puzzle.

Step 5

Now make up 10 questions (not "answers" this time) based on the same chapter used in the previous two tasks. Again, you must find NEW information that you have not yet used. Now it's getting hard to find that new information! Again, give your questions to a friend to answer.

Step 6

As you have been doing the puzzles, your brain has been actively searching for new information. Now write a NEW LIST that contains only the new information you have discovered when doing the puzzles. Your new list is the one to look at repeatedly for short bursts over the next few days. Try to remember more and more of it without looking at it. After a few days, you should be able to add words from your second list to your first list as you increase the information in your long-term memory.

FINALLY! Be inspired...

Make a list of different revision ideas and beside each one write **THINGS I HAVE** tried, **THINGS I WILL** try and **THINGS I MIGHT** try. Don't be scared of trying something new.

And remember – "FAIL TO PREPARE AND PREPARE TO FAIL!"

Higher English

The course

The Higher English course aims to enable you to develop the ability to:

- listen, talk, read and write, as appropriate to purpose, audience and context
- understand, analyse and evaluate texts, including Scottish texts, as appropriate to purpose and audience in the contexts of literature, language and media
- create and produce texts, as appropriate to purpose, audience and context
- apply knowledge and understanding of language.

The basics

The grade you finally get for Higher English depends on three things:

- The two internal Unit Assessments you do in school or college: "Analysis and Evaluation" and "Creation and Production"; these don't count towards the final grade, but you must have passed them before you can get a final grade.
- Your Portfolio of Writing – this is submitted in April for marking by SQA and counts for 30% of your final grade.
- The two exams you sit in May – that's what this book is all about.

The exams

Reading for Understanding, Analysis and Evaluation

- exam time: 1 hour 30 minutes
- total marks: 30
- weighting in final grade: 30%
- what you have to do: read two passages and answer questions about the ideas and use of language in one of them (25 marks), and then compare the ideas in both passages (5 marks)

Critical Reading

- exam time: 1 hour 30 minutes
- total marks: 40 (20 marks for each Section)
- weighting in final grade: 40%
- what you have to do: Section 1: read an extract from one of the Scottish Texts which are set for Higher and answer questions about it; Section 2: write an essay about a work of literature you have studied during your course.

1 Reading for Understanding, Analysis and Evaluation

Questions which ask for understanding (e.g. questions which say "Identify ... " or "Explain what ... " etc.)

- Keep your answers fairly short and pay attention to the number of marks available.
- Use your own words as far as possible. This means you mustn't just copy chunks from the passage – you have to show that you understand what it means by rephrasing it in your own words.

Questions about language features (e.g. questions which say "Analyse how ... ")

- This type of question will ask you to comment on features such as Word Choice, Imagery, Sentence Structure and Tone.
- You should pick out a relevant language feature and make a valid comment about its impact. Try to make your comments as specific as possible and avoid vague comments (such as "It is a good word to use because it gives me a clear picture of what the writer is saying"). Remember that you will get no marks just for picking out a word, image or feature of a sentence structure – it's the comment that counts.
- Some hints:
  - **Word choice:** Always try to pick a single word and then give its connotations, i.e. what it suggests.
  - **Sentence structure:** Don't just name the feature – try to explain what effect it achieves in that particular sentence.
  - **Imagery:** Try to explain what the image means literally and then go on to explain what the writer is trying to say by using that image.
  - **Tone** This is always difficult – a good tip is to imagine the sentence or paragraph being read out loud and try to spot how the words or the structure give it a particular tone.

The last question

- Make sure you follow the instruction about whether you're looking for agreement or disagreement (or possibly both).
- When you start on Passage 2, you will have already answered several questions on Passage 1, so you should know its key ideas quite well; as you read Passage 2, try to spot important ideas in it which are similar or different (depending on the question).
- Stick to **key ideas** and don't include trivial ones; **three** relevant key ideas will usually be enough – your task is to decide what the most significant ones are.

2 Critical Reading

Section 1 – Scottish Text

The most important thing to remember here is that there are two very different types of question to be answered:

- Three or four questions (for a total of 10 marks) which focus entirely on the extract.
- One question (for 10 marks) which requires knowledge of the whole text (or of another poem or short story by the same writer).

The first type of question will often ask you to use the same type of close textual analysis skills you used in the Reading part of your Analysis and Evaluation Unit. The golden rules are to read each question very carefully and do exactly as instructed, and to remember that (just like the "Anlaysis" questions in the Reading for Understanding, Analysis and Evaluation paper) there are no marks just for picking out a word or a feature – it's the comment that matters.

The second type of question requires you to discuss common features (of theme and/or technique) in the extract and elsewhere in the writer's work. You can answer this question with a series of bullet points or by writing a mini-essay, so choose the approach you feel most comfortable with.

Finally, a bit of advice for the Scottish Text question: when you see the extract in the exam paper, don't get too confident just because you recognise it (you certainly should recognise it if you've studied properly!). And even if you've answered questions on it before, remember that the questions in the exam are likely to be different, so stay alert.

Section 2 – Critical Essay

A common mistake is to rely too heavily on ideas and whole paragraphs you have used in practice essays and try to use them for the question you have chosen in the exam. The trick is to come to the exam with lots of ideas and thoughts about at least one of the texts you have studied and use these to tackle the question you choose from the exam paper. You mustn't use the exam question as an excuse to trot out an answer you've prepared in advance.

Structure

Every good essay has a structure, but there is no "correct" structure, no magic formula that the examiners are looking for. It's **your** essay, so structure it the way **you** want. As long as you're answering the question all the way through, then you'll be fine.

Relevance

Be relevant to the question **all of the time** – not just in the first and last paragraphs.

Central Concerns

Try to make sure your essay shows that you have thought about and understood the central concerns of the text, i.e. what it's "about" – the ideas and themes the writer is exploring in the text.

Quotation

In poetry and drama essays, you're expected to quote from the text, but never fall into the trap of learning a handful of quotations and forcing them all into the essay regardless of the question you're answering. In prose essays, quotation is much less important, and you can show your knowledge more effectively by referring in detail to what happens in key sections of the novel or the short story.

Techniques

You are expected to show understanding of how various literary techniques work within a text, but simply naming them will not get you marks, and structuring your essay around techniques rather than around relevant ideas in the text is not a good idea.

Good luck!

Remember that the rewards for passing Higher English are well worth it! Your pass will help you get the future you want for yourself. In the exam, be confident in your own ability. If you're not sure how to answer a question, trust your instincts and just give it a go anyway – keep calm and don't panic! GOOD LUCK!

Model Paper 1

Whilst this Model Paper has been specially commissioned by Hodder Gibson for use as practice for the Higher (for Curriculum for Excellence) exams, the key reference documents remain the SQA Specimen Paper 2014 and SQA Past Paper 2015.

> Please note that in the Reading for Understanding, Analysis and Evaluation sections, these model papers use passages from previous Official SQA Papers, but with different questions in line with assessment criteria for the new Higher. There are three Model Papers, but for reasons of space, the third Model Paper does not cover the Scottish Text element.

HODDER
GIBSON
LEARN MORE

National
Qualifications
MODEL PAPER 1

English
Reading for Understanding,
Analysis and Evaluation

Date — Not applicable

Duration — 1 hour 30 minutes

Total marks — 30

Attempt ALL questions.

Write your answers clearly in the answer booklet provided. In the answer booklet you must clearly identify the question number you are attempting.

Use **blue** or **black** ink.

Before leaving the examination room you must give your answer booklet to the Invigilator; if you do not, you may lose all the marks for this paper.

The following two passages focus on the First World War.

Passage 1

The first passage is taken from the introduction to Peter Parker's book "The Last Veteran", published in 2009. The book tells the life story of Harry Patch, who fought in the First World War, and eventually became the last surviving soldier to have fought in the trenches. He died in 2009, aged 111.

Read the passage below and attempt the questions which follow.

At 11 a.m. on Monday, 11th November 1918, after four and a quarter years in which howitzers boomed, shells screamed, machine guns rattled, rifles cracked, and the cries of the wounded and dying echoed across the battlefields of France and Belgium, everything suddenly fell quiet. A thick fog had descended that morning, and in the muffled landscape the stillness seemed
5 almost palpable.

For those left alive at the Front — a desolate landscape in which once bustling towns and villages had been reduced to piles of smoking rubble, and acre upon acre of woodland reduced to splintered and blackened stumps — there was little cause for rejoicing. The longed-for day had finally arrived but most combatants were too enervated to enjoy it. In the great silence,
10 some men were able to remember and reflect on what they had been through. Others simply felt lost. The war had swallowed them up: it occupied their every waking moment, just as it was to haunt their dreams in the future.

There have been other wars since 1918, and in all of them combatants have had to endure privation, discomfort, misery, the loss of comrades and appalling injuries. Even so, the First
15 World War continues to exert a powerful grip upon our collective imagination. In Britain the international catastrophe that was the First World War has been adopted as a peculiarly national trauma.

When remembering the War, the British continue to talk about a lost generation. The statistics are, of course, extraordinary: over thirty per cent of British men who were aged between
20 twenty and twenty-four in 1914 were killed in action or died of wounds; on the first day of the Battle of the Somme alone, 20,000 British soldiers were killed.

There is a sense that we have never quite recovered from this loss. Not only was the flower of British youth cut down in Picardy and Flanders, but an almost prelapsarian state of innocence was destroyed for ever between the years 1914–1918. Cast out of our pre-war Eden, where it
25 was somehow always perfect summer weather, we have ever after tended to look yearningly back rather than expectantly forward.

The War continues to occupy a tremendously large place in our sense of the world and its history. It has become a seemingly endless resource not only for historians, but for novelists, poets, dramatists, filmmakers and composers. The sounds and images of the First World War
30 are engraved on the national consciousness. We recognise them instantly: the foreign place names such as the Somme, Ypres and Passchendaele; the lines of men at the recruiting offices on 4th August 1914; the rows of crosses in war cemeteries; the scarlet poppies blowing in a landscape rendered unrecognisable by shellfire.

Our popular notion of the First World War is that it was indeed uniquely horrible; that it was
35 conducted by an incompetent High Command that repeatedly sacrificed thousands of men in

order to gain a few yards of churned earth; that it was characterised by "mud, blood and futility". There is, however, another view of the conflict: that not all the generals were callous incompetents, not all ordinary soldiers hapless and unwilling victims. Nowadays, revisionist historians insist that some of the battles were brilliantly planned and fought. They remind us
40 that we did, after all, win the war.

By giving an overview of campaigns and strategy, military historians can tell us what the war was about; although what really interests us is what the war was *like*. For that we have always turned to those who were there, notably the poets and memoirists, but latterly to those more ordinary people, the diminishing band of living witnesses. The gulf between military history
45 and personal experience was exemplified by the man who became Britain's Last Veteran, Harry Patch.

For Harry, the War was not about military intelligence or plan of attack. He may have forgotten exact dates and places but he knew what a battlefield was *like*. It was, he said, about wading around in filth with no opportunity to change your lice-ridden clothes for months. It was
50 about discomfort and exhaustion and fear and having your friends quite literally "blown to pieces". Revisiting the battlefields he commented, "Millions of men came to fight in this war. I didn't know whether I would last longer than five minutes. We were the Poor Bloody Infantry — and we were expendable. What a waste. What a terrible waste."

Adapted from the introduction to Peter Parker's book "The Last Veteran", 2009

Questions

1. Re-read lines 1–12.

    (a) By referring to **at least two features of language** in these lines, analyse how the writer conveys the destructive nature of the First World War. In your answer you should refer to such features as word choice, sentence structure and sound.   4

    (b) According to the writer, what effects did the war have on "those left behind"?   3

2. In lines 13–17, what does the writer suggest is surprising about the way people in Britain view the First World War?   3

3. Re-read lines 18–26.

    In your own words, identify **three** important ways the First World War affected Britain.   3

4. Analyse how the writer's use of language in lines 27–33 conveys how important the First World War has become to us.   4

5. By referring to lines 34–40, explain in your own words the two opposing views of the First World War.   4

6. Read lines 41–53.

    Evaluate the effectiveness of these two paragraphs as a thought-provoking and emotional conclusion to the passage as a whole. In your answer you should refer to ideas and language.   4

Passage 2

Publisher's note: Ellipses [...] are used in Passage 2 to indicate where the original article has been edited slightly. This does not affect your reading of the passage or the way the questions should be answered. At the copyright holder's request, Passage 2 differs very slightly from that used in the 2014 Higher English SQA exam, but this does not affect in any way the answering of any of the questions.

In the second passage below, the Scottish novelist and filmmaker William Boyd, writing in the New York Times newspaper in February 2012, looks at why the First World War continues to be of such interest to us.

Read the passage and attempt the question which follows. While reading, you may wish to make notes on the main ideas and/or highlight key points in the passage.

In France I live near a little village called Sadillac. It's no more than a cluster of houses, an old chateau, a church and a graveyard surrounded by a few farms and vineyards. The village probably hasn't changed much since the French Revolution; its population hovers around 100. By the graveyard is a simple obelisk with the names of the 30 or so young men from Sadillac
5 who died in the First World War, 1914–18. It's almost impossible to imagine the effect on this tiny community of these fatalities over four years. Every year on November 11th at 11 a.m. — the hour and the day of the 1918 armistice — villagers gather to participate in a short memorial service around the obelisk.

In 2014 it will be a hundred years since the First World War began and yet, by a strange
10 paradox, its presence — in novels, films and television — has never been greater. . . The last old soldier or sailor has died and almost all of the witnesses have gone, but the war exerts a tenacious hold on the imagination.

For us British, the memories, images and stories of 1914–18 seem to have a persistence and a power that eclipse those of the Second World War. I'm symptomatic of this urge to revisit the
15 conflict: my new novel will be my third with the First World War at its centre. When I wrote and directed a movie, 'The Trench', about a group of young soldiers in 1916 waiting for the Battle of the Somme to begin, I was obsessed with getting every detail right: every cap-badge worn and cigarette smoked, every meal eaten. It was as if I wanted the absolute verisimilitude to provide an authentic, vicarious experience so the viewer would be in a position to say, "So
20 this is what it was like, this is what they went through, how they lived — and died".

I think this is the key behind the enduring obsession with that war. To our modern sensibilities it defies credulity that for more than four years European armies faced one another in a 500-mile line of trenches, stretching from the Belgian coast to the border of Switzerland. The war was also fought in other arenas — in Galicia, Italy, the Bosporus, Mesopotamia, East and West
25 Africa, in naval battles on many oceans — but it is the Western Front and trench warfare that define the war in memory. It was a deadly war of attrition in which millions of soldiers on both sides slogged through the mud of No Man's Land to meet their deaths in withering blasts of machine-gun fire and artillery. And at the end of four years and with about nine million troops dead, the two opposing forces were essentially where they were when they started.

30 In France and Germany, the traumas of the Second World War have to a degree erased memories of the First. But in Britain, where almost a million servicemen died, it's still images of the trenches of the Western Front that are shown and that resonate on Remembrance Day. One of the reasons for this is, surely, the power of the poetry. The poets of the First World War . . . are taught in almost all British schools. I can remember Wilfred Owen's terrifying poem

35 "Dulce et Decorum Est", about a mustard-gas attack, being read aloud to us in the classroom when I was 10 or 11. One boy actually ran outside, he was so overcome and upset. The war poems shaped our earliest perceptions of the First World War and were swiftly buttressed by the familiar images of the trenches — it was the first war to be extensively filmed — and the histories of the futile, costly battles. . .

40 And finally, there were family stories. One hundred years is not so very long ago. My great-uncle Alexander Boyd was wounded and decorated at the Battle of the Somme. His brother, my grandfather William Boyd, was wounded a year later at Passchendaele, as the Third Battle of Ypres was known. Family legend and anecdote fuelled my interest in the war.

But there is another deeper, perhaps more profound reason why the war continues to
45 preoccupy us. It was a conflict between 19th-century armies equipped with 20th-century weapons — hence the unprecedented carnage. . . The tactics were 19th-century: advance on the enemy. But the enemy had 20th-century weapons of mass destruction: the battlefield was dominated by tanks, machine guns, howitzers, aircraft and poisonous gas. . .

No society today would accept the horrendous casualty count. At the beginning of the Battle
50 of the Somme, on July 1, 1916, the British Army suffered 60,000 dead and wounded — in one day. It was arguably the worst butcher's bill in military history. . . There is a very real sense in which the modern world — our world — was born between 1914 and 1918. Something changed in human sensibility. Soldiers wouldn't be willing to engage in such slaughter . . . The days of cannon fodder are over forever as a result of that war. . . After the First World War,
55 nothing in the world would ever be the same.

Adapted from an article in the New York Times newspaper, January 2012

Question

7. Both writers express their views about the First World War. Identify key areas on which they agree. In your answer, you should refer in detail to both passages.   5

You may answer this question in continuous prose or in a series of developed bullet points.

[END OF MODEL PAPER]

**National
Qualifications
MODEL PAPER 1**

English
Critical Reading

Date — Not applicable

Duration — 1 hour 30 minutes

Total marks — 40

SECTION 1 — Scottish Text — 20 marks

Read an extract from a Scottish text you have previously studied and attempt the questions.

Choose ONE text from either

Part A – Drama Pages 2–7

Part B — Prose Pages 8–17

Part C — Poetry Pages 18–28

Attempt ALL the questions for your chosen text.

SECTION 2 — Critical Essay — 20 marks

Attempt ONE question from the following genres — Drama, Prose, Poetry, Film and Television Drama, or Language.

Your answer must be on a different genre from that chosen in Section 1.

You should spend approximately 45 minutes on each Section.

Write your answers clearly in the answer booklet provided. In the answer booklet you must clearly identify the question number you are attempting.

Use **blue** or **black** ink.

Before leaving the examination room you must give your answer booklet to the Invigilator; if you do not, you may lose all the marks for this paper.

SECTION 1 — SCOTTISH TEXT — 20 marks

Choose ONE text from Drama, Prose or Poetry.

Read the text extract carefully and then attempt ALL the questions for your chosen text.

You should spend about 45 minutes on this Section.

PART A — SCOTTISH TEXT — DRAMA

Text 1 — Drama

If you choose this text you may not attempt a question on Drama in Section 2.

Read the extract below and then attempt the following questions.

The Slab Boys by John Byrne

In this extract, which is from near the end of the play, Lucille surprises everyone with her choice of partner for the Staffie.

(*Enter LUCILLE dressed for home*)

LUCILLE: Burton's Corner ... quarter to ... okay?

(PHIL *and* SPANKY *look towards each other*)

ALAN: Yeh ... right, Lucille.

5   PHIL & SPANKY: (*Together*) Eh??

LUCILLE: Are you sure you can get your Dad's M.G.?

ALAN: No problem ...

LUCILLE: And put some cream on that pimple ... I swear it's twice the size it was this morning.

10 ALAN: For God's sake ...

LUCILLE: (*To* PHIL) Sorry ... I couldn't've went through with it even if I had said, yeh ... you can see that, can't you? I mean to say ... look at him ... he's a skelf.

PHIL: You're looking at a skelf that's branching out, doll ...

LUCILLE: Aw, go to hell. And if I was you I wouldn't go home via Storey Street ...
15   that's where Bernadette's boyfriend's got his jew-jipsey parlour. He eats smouts like you for his breakfast! (*To* ALAN) If you're not there on the dot I'm going in by myself so be warned! (*Exits*)

ALAN: Listen, Heck ...

HECTOR: (*Bravely*) Don't worry about it, Alan ... I'm taking Willie Curry on my ticket.
20   Well, you guys, I better shoot off ... Willie's giving us a lift down the road. You can keep that fitch if you find it, anybody.

(*Changes into overcoat*)

SPANKY: Heh ... hold on, Hector ... you can't go just like that. What about that money we gave you?

MARKS

25 HECTOR: Aw, yeh ... a quid, wasn't it? No ... I'll just hold onto that, if youse don't mind. Help towards a skin graft for my ear and the down payment on a nylon overall like Jimmy Robertson's got. 'Night all ... (*Exits*)

SPANKY: The cocky little ...

(HECTOR *re-enters*)

30 HECTOR: And I'll be expecting some smart grinding from this department in the future. No palming me off with sub-standard shades, Farrell. Oh ... sorry to hear you lost your job, Phil. Not to worry ... you'll not find much difference now you're "officially" out of work. (*Takes Parker pen from* PHIL'S *pocket and hands it to* ALAN) See youse at the Staffie. (*Exits*)

35 ALAN: I better push off, too ... heavy night ahead. (*Changes for home*)

SPANKY: Christ, I even let him into the secrets of gum making ... what happens? He strolls off into the sunset with the dame hanging from his top lip. Yeh, I think you better push off, Archie ... go on ... beat it.

(ALAN *crosses to door ... stops*)

40 ALAN: (*to* PHIL) There's always next year, you know ...

PHIL: You heard ... beat it!

ALAN: Fine. I was going to say "sorry" but I can see you're doing a pretty good job of that on your own. See you at the Dance ... buy you a small beer perhaps? And I'll be seeing you on Monday ... Sparky ... so take it easy on the floor ...
45   watch out nobody steps on your fingers ... there's quite a bit of grinding to get through ... That cabinet out there's an embarrassment...

Questions

1. By referring to lines 1—17, explain what is revealed about Lucille's character.   2

2. Explain how Hector's new-found confidence is made clear in lines 19—34.   4

3. Analyse how Alan's speech in lines 42—46 conveys his attitude to Phil and Spanky.   4

4. By referring to this extract and elsewhere in the play, discuss the role of Lucille **or** Hector in *The Slab Boys*.   10

OR

Text 2 — Drama

If you choose this text you may not attempt a question on Drama in Section 2.

Read the extract below and then attempt the following questions.

The Cheviot, the Stag and the Black, Black Oil by John McGrath

ANDY   The motel — as I see it — is the thing of the future. That's how we see it, myself and the Board of Directors, and one or two of your local Councillors — come on now, these are the best men money can buy. So — picture it, if yous will, right there at the top of the glen, beautiful vista — The Crammem Inn, High Rise Motorcroft — all finished in natural, washable, plastic granitette. Right next door, the "Frying Scotsman" All Night Chipperama — with a wee ethnic bit, Fingal's Caff — serving seaweed-suppers-in-the-basket, and draught Drambuie. And to cater for the younger set, yous've got your Grouse-a-go-go. I mean, people very soon won't want your bed and breakfasts, they want everything laid on, they'll be wanting their entertainment and that, and wes've got the know-how to do it and wes have got the money to do it. So — picture it, if yous will — a drive-in clachan on every hill-top where formerly there was hee-haw but scenery.

Enter LORD VAT OF GLENLIVET, *a mad young laird.*

LORD VAT   Get off my land — these are my mountains.

ANDY   Who are you, Jimmy?

LORD VAT   Lord Vat of Glenlivet. I come from an ancient Scotch family and I represent the true spirit of the Highlands.

ANDY   Andy McChuckemup of Crammem Inn Investments Ltd., Govan, pleased for to make your acquaintance Your Worship. Excuse me, is this your field?

LORD VAT   You're invading my privacy.

ANDY   Excuse me, me and wor company's got plans to develop this backward area into a paradise for all the family — improve it, you know, fair enough, eh?

LORD VAT   Look here, I've spent an awful lot of money to keep this place private and peaceful. I don't want hordes of common people trampling all over the heather, disturbing the birds.

ANDY   Oh no, we weren't planning to do it for nothing, an' that — there'll be plenty in it for you ...

LORD VAT   No amount of money could compensate for the disruption of the couthie way of life that has gone on here uninterrupted for yonks. Your Bantu — I mean your Highlander — is a dignified sort of chap, conservative to the core. From time immemorial, they have proved excellent servants — the gels in the kitchen, your sherpa — I mean your stalker — marvellously sure-footed on the hills, your ghillie-wallah, tugging the forelock, doing up your flies — you won't find people like that anywhere else in the world. I wouldn't part with all this even if you were to offer me half a million pounds.

ANDY   A-ha. How does six hundred thousand suit you?

LORD VAT   My family have lived here for over a century; 800,000.

ANDY   You're getting a slice of the action, Your Honour — 650,000.

MARKS

LORD VAT   I have my tenants to think of. Where will they go? 750,000.

40 ANDY   We'll be needing a few lasses for staff and that ... 700,000 including the stately home.

LORD VAT   You're a hard man, Mr. Chuckemup.

ANDY   Cash.

LORD VAT   Done (*shake.*)

Questions

5. Look at lines 1—12.

   (i) Explain what impression is created of Andy's character in these lines.   2

   (ii) Choose **four** specific details of his plan and analyse how each one is made to sound comical.   4

6. By referring to lines 14—44, explain how the dramatist makes Lord Vat a figure of fun to the audience.   4

7. By referring to this extract and elsewhere in the play, discuss McGrath's use of caricatures and/or stereotypes in *The Cheviot, the Stag and the Black, Black Oil*.   10

OR

Text 3 — Drama

If you choose this text you may not attempt a question on Drama in Section 2.

Read the extract below and then attempt the following questions.

***Men Should Weep* by Ena Lamont Stewart**

In this extract, which is from near the end of Act 1, Jenny arrives home late.

[John comes in holding Jenny by the arm. She is about eighteen, made up boldly (for the nineteen-thirties): her lipstick is spread over her mouth, her coat and blouse undone, her hair tousled.]

JENNY: Leave me go!

5 *[She shakes herself free and she and John stand glaring at each other. Maggie is watching fearfully.]*

JENNY: Makin a bloomin fool o me in front o ma friend!

JOHN: Where hae you been till this time o night?

JENNY: That's nane o your business. I'm grown up noo.

10 JOHN: Don't you speak to me like that. I asked ye where ye'd been.

JENNY: An I tellt ye! Nane o your damned interferin business.

MAGGIE: Jenny! John!

[John takes Jenny by the shoulders and shakes her.]

JOHN: Where wis ye? Answer me!

15 JENNY: At the pickshers.

JOHN: The pickchers comes oot at hauf ten. Where wis ye efter?

JENNY: [sullen] Wi Nessie Tate an a coupla friends.

[He lets her go and she flops into a chair, glaringly sullenly at him and rubbing her shoulder.]

20 JOHN: I don't approve o yon Nessie Tait.

JENNY: That's a peety. I dae.

JOHN: Ye impident little bitch! What I ought tae dae is tak ma belt tae ye.

JENNY: Jist you try it!

JOHN: The next time you come in here at this time o night wi yer paint smeared a
25   ower yer face, I wull! Look at yersel!

[He drags her over to a mirror, then propels her, resisting, to the sink, where, holding her head under his arm, he scrubs off her make-up.]

JOHN: There! And in the future, you'll let yer hair grow tae the colour God meant it
         tae be an leave it that wey.

MARKS

Questions

8. By referring to lines 1—11, explain what impressions are created of Jenny's character.   **3**

9. By referring to lines 13—23, explain how the playwright creates a dramatic conflict between John and Jenny.   **4**

10. By referring to lines 24—29, explain how John's anger is conveyed to the audience.   **3**

11. By referring to this extract and elsewhere in the play, discuss the role of Jenny in *Men Should Weep*.   **10**

SECTION — SCOTTISH TEXT — 20 marks

Choose ONE text from Drama, Prose or Poetry.

Read the text extract carefully and then attempt ALL the questions for your chosen text.

You should spend about 45 minutes on this Section.

PART B — SCOTTISH TEXT — PROSE

Text 1 — Prose

If you choose this text you may not attempt a question on Prose in Section 2.

Read the extract below and then attempt the following questions.

The Crater by Iain Crichton Smith

They screamed again, in the sound of the shells, and they seemed to hear an answer. They heard what seemed to be a bubbling. "Are you there?" said Robert, bending down and listening. "Can you get over here?" They could hear splashing and deep below them breathing, frantic breathing as if someone was frightened to death. "It's all right," he said,
5   "if you come over here, I'll send my rifle down. You two hang on to me," he said to the others. He was terrified. That depth, that green depth. Was it Morrison down there, after all? He hadn't spoken. The splashings came closer. The voice was like an animal's repeating endlessly a mixture of curses and prayers. Robert hung over the edge of the crater. "For Christ's sake don't let me go," he said to the other two. It wasn't right that a
10   man should die in green slime.

He hung over the rim holding his rifle down. He felt it being caught, as if there was a great fish at the end of a line. He felt it moving. And the others hung at his heels, like a chain. The moon shone suddenly out between two clouds and in that moment he saw it, a body covered with greenish slime, an obscene mermaid, hanging on to his rifle while the
15   two eyes, white in the green face, shone upward and the mouth, gritted, tried not to let the blood through. It was a monster of the deep, it was a sight so terrible that he nearly fell. He was about to say, "It's no good, he's dying," but something prevented him from saying it, if he said it then he would never forget it. He knew that. The hands clung to the rifle below in the slime. The others pulled behind him. "For Christ's sake hang on to the rifle,"
20   he said to the monster below. "Don't let go." And it seemed to be emerging from the deep, setting its feet against the side of the crater, all green, all mottled, like a disease. It climbed as if up a mountainside in the stench. It hung there against the wall.

"Hold on," he said. "Hold on." His whole body was concentrated. This man must not fall down again into that lake. The death would be too terrible. The face was coming over the
25   side of the crater, the teeth gritted, blood at the mouth. It hung there for a long moment and then the three of them had got him over the side. He felt like cheering, standing up in the light of No Man's Land and cheering. Sergeant Smith was kneeling down beside the body, his ear to the heart. It was like a body which might have come from space, green and illuminated and slimy. And over it poured the merciless moonlight.

30   "Come on," he said to the other two. And at that moment Sergeant Smith said, "He's dead."

MARKS

Questions

12. By referring to lines 1–10, analyse how the writer uses sound to intensify the atmosphere.   4

13. By referring to lines 11–22, explain how the writer creates a nightmarish atmosphere.   4

14. By referring to lines 23–31, discuss what the sentence "And over it poured the merciless moonlight." (line 29) contributes to the conclusion of the extract.   2

15. By referring to the extract and to at least one other story by Iain Crichton Smith, discuss how he creates tension his stories.   10

OR

Text 2 — Prose

If you choose this text you may not attempt a question on Prose in Section 2.

Read the extract below and then attempt the following questions.

The Bright Spade by George Mackay Brown

One night there was a meeting in the ale-house. All the men of the island were there. They took counsel together about the impending famine. That same morning the old man of Cornquoy who lived alone, the fiddler, had been found dead in his chair, after he had been missed for a week. They broke down his door. The young dog was gnawing at the
5   corpse's thigh. Jacob got his fiddle the night he shrouded him, though he knew nothing about music. The fiddle, once a sweet brimming shell, hung at Jacob's wall like a shrivelled chrysalis. The old fiddler was as light as a bird to handle. He needed a narrow grave.

"The meal and the meat are done in the island," said Harald of Ness at the meeting. "I've
10 eaten nothing myself but a handful of cold potatoes every day for the past week. My suggestion is this, that seven of the strongest men among us cross between the hills to the shore and get a large supply of limpets and dulse from the rocks at low tide."

The men agreed that it would be necessary to do that.

The seven men chosen set off at dawn the next day. They were Harald of Ness, Adam of
15 Skarataing, Ezekiel of the Burn, Thomas and Philip of Graystones, Simon the blacksmith, and Walter of Muce. That same morning the worst blizzard of winter descended, great swirling blankets of snow out of the east. Tinkers saw the seven men between the hills going towards the shore, like a troop of spectres. They were never seen again until their bodies were dug from the drifts a week later.

20 For the second time that winter Jacob laid seven men together in the kirkyard. This time he would accept no payment at all for his services — "for," said he, "it seems I have done better this winter than anyone else in the island ...".

In March Francis Halcrow the coughing sailor who had been with John Paul Jones in the American Wars died at Braebuster. Jacob buried him for his set of Nantucket harpoons.

25 And then men brought out ploughs, harness, harrows. The implements were dull and rusty after the hard winter. Jacob's spade, on the other hand, was thin and bright with much employment. "God grant," he said to the spade, putting it away in his shed, "that I won't be needing you again till after the shearing and the lobster fishing and the harvest."

MARKS

Questions

16. By referring to lines 1—8, identify the narrator's tone and explain how it is created.   3

17. By referring to lines 9—13, explain what impressions the narrator creates of Harald Ness as a person.   2

18. Discuss the effect achieved by naming each one of the men who set off on the journey (lines 14—19).   2

19. By referring to lines 20—28, explain what is revealed about Jacob as a person.   3

20. By referring to the extract and to at least one other story by George Mackay Brown, discuss his use of symbolism in his stories.   10

OR

Text 3 — Prose

If you choose this text you may not attempt a question on Prose in Section 2.

Read the extract below and then attempt the following questions.

The Trick is to Keep Breathing by Janice Galloway

In this extract, Tony takes Joy out for the evening.

There I am in the mirror, inoffensive in a dress with a thick belt to show what remains of the curves. New stockings and slingbacks despite the time of year. Lack of practicality is sexy in women's clothes. The gravel and the crunch of brakes outside makes me stare harder. I try not to hear the different size of shoe thudding on the boards.

5   Hello? Anybody home?

I see Tony from the top of the stairs, holding up a bottle in white paper, green glass and a foil neck pushing up from the tissue like a clumsy orchid.

       Anticipation, he says. Always take it for granted I'm going to win.

The lips disappear into his beard and the teeth appear, very white and straight. It's
10 definitely Tony. He tells me I look lovely, a real picture. I want to tell him it's not me but I smile instead. He reaches out his hand and says it again.

       You look lovely. You really do.

The car is the wrong colour. It plays Country and Western Music as we ease onto the main road.

15   She's on form, he says. Should have seen her this afternoon.

The seat creaks with his weight: now we're round the corner, he relaxes.

       Called round on the off chance you were home but no such luck. Thought you weren't well? Anyway, she's looking good. Nearly as good as you.

He pats my leg.

20   Expect a treat tonight.

I know we're talking about a dog and try to think of something appropriate to say. In the pause, he sings along with the tape.

       When you're in love with a beautiful woman, it's hard

He looks sidelong to see my reaction, encouraging me to be cute. He keeps doing it
25 between the sentences.

       Maybe after the race we could go somewhere. On the town. Assume you haven't eaten. Could do with some more even if you have. Few more pounds and you'd be a stunner. How are things by the way? I always forget to ask. You never look ill to me so I forget to ask.

30   *Then somebody hangs up when you answer the phone*

       Just relax and listen to the music. This one's my favourite. Dr Hook. Classic. You don't mind if I run it again. You look great. Should wear a dress more often. Hiding your best assets.

He looks over again, his face melting on the double-take.

35   Christ what did you do to your hands?

I look and see the knuckles bruised and oozy. This is not feminine.

       A dopey voice says Oops. I tripped. Silly me.

I tell myself I am with Tony in his car. I tell myself all the way to Glasgow.

MARKS

Questions

21. By referring to lines 1—12, explain how Tony is portrayed as an unpleasant character.   **4**

22. By referring to lines 13—25, explain how the writer creates an uneasy atmosphere in the car.   **2**

23. Analyse how aspects of Tony's character are revealed in lines 26—38.   **4**

24. By referring to the extract and elsewhere in the novel, discuss Joy's relationships with men.   **10**

OR

Text 4 — Prose

If you choose this text you may not attempt a question on Prose in Section 2.

Read the extract below and then attempt the following questions.

Sunset Song by Lewis Grassic Gibbon

In this extract, which is from Part III (Seed-time), a disagreement arises at the wedding celebration.

Up at Rob's table an argument rose, Chris hoped that it wasn't religion, she saw Mr Gordon's wee face pecked up to counter Rob. But Rob was just saying what a shame it was that folk should be shamed nowadays to speak Scotch — or they called it Scots if they did, the split-tongued sourocks! Every damned little narrow dowped rat that you met put
5   on the English if he thought he'd impress you — as though Scotch wasn't good enough now, it had words in it that the thin bit scraichs of the English could never come at. And Rob said *You can tell me, man, what's the English for sotter, or greip, or smore, or pleiter, gloaming or glunching or well-kenspeckled? And if you said gloaming was sunset you'd fair be a liar; and you're hardly that, Mr Gordon.*

10   But Gordon was real decent and reasonable, *You can't help it, Rob. If folk are to get on in the world nowadays, away from the ploughshafts and out of the pleiter, they must use the English, orra though it be.* And Chae cried out that was right enough, and God! who could you blame? And a fair bit breeze got up about it all, every soul in the parlour seemed speaking at once; and as aye when they spoke of the thing they agreed that the
15   land was a coarse, coarse life, you'd do better at almost anything else, folks that could send their lads to learn a trade were right wise, no doubt of that, there was nothing on the land but work, work, work, and chave, chave, chave, from the blink of day till the fall of night, no thanks from the soss and sotter, and hardly a living to be made.

Syne Cuddiestoun said that he'd heard of a childe up Laurencekirk way, a banker's son
20   from the town he was, and he'd come to do farming in a scientific way. So he'd said at first, had the childe, but God! by now you could hardly get into the place for the clutter of machines that lay in the yard; and he wouldn't store the kiln long. But Chae wouldn't have that, he swore *Damn't, no, the machine's the best friend of man, or it would be so in a socialist state. It's coming and the chaving'll end, you'll see, the machine'll do all the*
25   *dirty work.* And Long Rob called out that he'd like right well to see the damned machine that would muck you a pigsty even though they all turned socialist tomorrow.

MARKS

Questions

25. By referring to lines 1—9, explain how the writer conveys the strength of Rob's feelings about language. 4

26. By referring to lines 10—18, explain how the writer conveys the harshness of life working the land. 2

27. By referring to lines 19—26, explain how the writer's use of language conveys the conflicting views about "scientific" farming methods. You should refer to at least two techniques, such as sentence structure, tone, word choice. 4

28. By referring to this extract and elsewhere in the novel, discuss to what extent *Sunset Song* is a celebration of a traditional way of life or an illustration of the inevitability of change. 10

OR

Text 5 — Prose

If you choose this text you may not attempt a question on Prose in Section 2.

Read the extract below and then attempt the following questions.

The Cone-Gatherers by Robin Jenkins

In this extract from Chapter One, Duror is secretly watching the cone-gatherers.

Hidden among the spruces at the edge of the ride, near enough to catch the smell of larch off the cones and to be struck by some of those thrown, stood Duror the gamekeeper, in an icy sweat of hatred, with his gun aimed all the time at the feebleminded hunchback grovelling over the rabbit. To pull the trigger, requiring far less force than to break a
5   rabbit's neck, and then to hear simultaneously the clean report of the gun and the last obscene squeal of the killed dwarf would have been for him, he thought, release too, from the noose of disgust and despair drawn, these past few days, so much tighter.

He had waited over an hour there to see them pass. Every minute had been a purgatory of humiliation: it was as if he was in their service, forced to wait upon them as upon his
10   masters. Yet he hated and despised them far more powerfully than ever he had liked and respected Sir Colin and Lady Runcie-Campbell. While waiting, he had imagined them in the darkness missing their footing in the tall tree and coming crashing down through the sea of branches to lie dead on the ground. So passionate had been his visualising of that scene, he seemed himself to be standing on the floor of a fantastic sea, with an owl and a
15   herd of roe-deer flitting by quiet as fish, while the yellow ferns and bronzen brackens at his feet gleamed like seaweed, and the spruce trees swayed above him like submarine monsters.

He could have named, item by item, leaf and fruit and branch, the overspreading tree of revulsion in him; but he could not tell the force which made it grow, any more than he
20   could have explained the life in himself, or in the dying rabbit, or in any of the trees about him.

This wood had always been his stronghold and sanctuary; there were many places secret to him where he had been able to fortify his sanity and hope. But now the wood was invaded and defiled; its cleansing and reviving virtues were gone. Into it had crept this
25   hunchback, himself one of nature's freaks, whose abject acceptance of nature, like the whining prostrations of a heathen in front of an idol, had made acceptance no longer possible for Duror himself. He was humpbacked, with one shoulder higher than the other; he had no neck, and on the misshapen lump of his body sat a face so beautiful and guileless as to be a diabolical joke.

MARKS

Questions

29. Analyse how the word choice in lines 1—7 conveys Duror's loathing for Calum.   2

30. By referring to lines 8—17, explain how the writer makes the reader aware of Duror's disturbed state of mind.   4

31. Analyse how the imagery in lines 18—29 gives insight into Duror's feelings.   4

32. By referring to this extract and elsewhere in the novel, discuss the importance of the conflict between Duror and Calum.   10

SECTION 1 — SCOTTISH TEXT — 20 marks

Choose ONE text from Drama, Prose or Poetry.

Read the text extract carefully and then attempt ALL the questions for your chosen text.

You should spend about 45 minutes on this Section.

PART C — SCOTTISH TEXT — POETRY

Text 1 — Poetry

If you choose this text you may not attempt a question on Poetry in Section 2.

Read the extract below and then attempt the following questions.

To a Mouse by Robert Burns

Thy wee-bit housie, too, in ruin!
It's silly wa's the win's are strewin!
An' naething, now, to big a new ane,
O' foggage green!
5 An' bleak December's winds ensuin,
Baith snell an' keen!

Thou saw the fields laid bare an' waste,
An' weary winter comin fast,
An' cozie here, beneath the blast,
10 Thou thought to dwell,
Till crash! the cruel coulter past
Out thro' thy cell.

That wee-bit heap o' leaves an' stibble,
Has cost thee mony a weary nibble!
15 Now thou's turn'd out, for a' thy trouble,
But house or hald,
To thole the winter's sleety dribble,
An' cranreuch cauld!

But Mousie, thou art no thy lane,
20 In proving foresight may be vain;
The best-laid schemes o' mice an' men
Gang aft agley,
An' lea'e us nought but grief an' pain,
For promis'd joy!

25 Still thou art blest, compar'd wi' me!
The present only toucheth thee:
But och! I backward cast my e'e,
On prospects drear!
An' forward, tho' I canna see,
30 I guess an' fear!

MARKS

Questions

33. By referring closely to lines 1—6, analyse the use of poetic technique to create sympathy for the mouse's situation.   2

34. Identify **two** key themes of the poem which are developed in lines 7—18 and explain how each is clarified by the poet's technique.   4

35. Discuss the mood created in lines 19—30. You should explain the key ideas of these lines and analyse the use of poetic technique to create mood.   4

36. By referring to this poem and at least one other by Burns, discuss his use of verse form.   10

OR

Text 2 — Poetry

If you choose this text you may not attempt a question on Poetry in Section 2.

Read the extract below and then attempt the following questions.

Mrs Midas **by Carol Ann Duffy**

It was late September. I'd just poured a glass of wine, begun
to unwind, while the vegetables cooked. The kitchen
filled with the smell of itself, relaxed, its steamy breath
gently blanching the windows. So I opened one,
5   then with my fingers wiped the other's glass like a brow.
He was standing under the pear tree snapping a twig.

Now the garden was long and the visibility poor, the way
the dark of the ground seems to drink the light of the sky,
but that twig in his hand was gold. And then he plucked
10 a pear from a branch — we grew Fondante d'Automne —
and it sat in his palm like a light bulb. On.
I thought to myself, Is he putting fairy lights in the tree?

He came into the house. The doorknobs gleamed.
He drew the blinds. You know the mind; I thought of
15 the Field of the Cloth of Gold and of Miss Macready.
He sat in that chair like a king on a burnished throne.
The look on his face was strange, wild, vain. I said,
What in the name of God is going on? He started to laugh.

I served up the meal. For starters, corn on the cob.
20 Within seconds he was spitting out the teeth of the rich.
He toyed with his spoon, then mine, then with the knives, the forks.
He asked where was the wine. I poured with a shaking hand,
a fragrant, bone-dry white from Italy, then watched
as he picked up the glass, goblet, golden chalice, drank.

MARKS

Questions

37. By referring to lines 1—6, analyse the use of poetic techniques to create an ordinary, everyday atmosphere.   4

38. By referring to lines 7—12, analyse the use of poetic techniques to convey the confusion beginning to arise in the speaker's mind.   2

39. Explain how, in lines 13—24, the poet conveys the strangeness of the husband's behaviour.   4

40. By referring to this poem and at least one other by Carol Ann Duffy, discuss how she creates and develops ideas and/or situations which are unusual or surprising.   10

OR

Text 3 — Poetry

If you choose this text you may not attempt a question on Poetry in Section 2.

Read the extract below and then attempt the following questions.

Last Supper by Liz Lochhead

Already she was imagining it done with, this feast, and
exactly
what kind of leftover hash she'd make of it
among friends, when it was just
5   The Girls, when those three met again.
What very good soup
she could render from the bones,
then something substantial, something extra
tasty if not elegant.

10   Yes, there they'd be, cackling around the cauldron,
spitting out the gristlier bits
of his giblets;
gnawing on the knucklebone of some
intricate irony;
15   getting grave and dainty at the
petit-gout mouthfuls of reported speech.

"That's rich!" they'd splutter,
munching the lies, fat and sizzling as sausages.
Then they'd sink back
20   gorged on truth
and their own savage integrity,
sleek on it all, preening
like corbies, their bright eyes blinking
satisfied
25   till somebody would get hungry
and go hunting again.

MARKS

Questions

41. By referring to lines 1—9, explain how the poet develops the metaphor of "this feast".   2

42. Analyse the use of sound in lines 10—16 to create a negative impression of "The Girls".   4

43. Analyse the use of poetic techniques in lines 17—26 to describe the people at the Supper.   4

44. By referring to this poem and at least one other by Liz Lochhead, discuss her ability to describe characters in a precise way.   10

OR

Text 4 — Poetry

If you choose this text you may not attempt a question on Poetry in Section 2.

Read the poem below and then attempt the following questions.

Assisi by Norman MacCaig

The dwarf with his hands on backwards
sat, slumped like a half-filled sack
on tiny twisted legs from which
sawdust might run,
5 outside the three tiers of churches built
in honour of St Francis, brother
of the poor, talker with birds, over whom
he had the advantage
of not being dead yet.

10 A priest explained
how clever it was of Giotto
to make his frescoes tell stories
that would reveal to the illiterate the goodness
of God and the suffering
15 of His Son. I understood
the explanation and
the cleverness.

A rush of tourists, clucking contentedly,
fluttered after him as he scattered
20 the grain of the Word. It was they who had passed
the ruined temple outside, whose eyes
wept pus, whose back was higher
than his head, whose lopsided mouth
said *Grazie* in a voice as sweet
25 as a child's when she speaks to her mother
or a bird's when it spoke
to St Francis.

MARKS

Questions

45. Analyse how the use of sound in lines 1—4 enhances the description of the dwarf.   **2**

46. Explain how the poet creates an ironic tone in lines 5—9.   **2**

47. Discuss what the speaker's statement "I understood/the explanation and/the cleverness." (lines 15—17) suggests about his feelings at that moment.   **2**

48. By referring closely to lines 20—27, explain what the poet means by describing the dwarf as a "ruined temple".   **4**

49. By referring to this poem and at least one other by Norman MacCaig, discuss his use of wry humour in his poetry.   **10**

OR

Text 5 — Poetry

If you choose this text you may not attempt a question on Poetry in Section 2.

Read the extract below and then attempt the following questions.

Hallaig **by Sorley MacLean**

In Screapadal of my people
where Norman and Big Hector were,
their daughters and their sons are a wood
going up beside the stream.

5   Proud tonight the pine cocks
crowing on the top of Cnoc an Ra,
straight their backs in the moonlight –
they are not the wood I love.

I will wait for the birch wood
10 until it comes up by the cairn,
until the whole ridge from Beinn na Lice
will be under its shade.

If it does not, I will go down to Hallaig,
to the Sabbath of the dead,
15 where the people are frequenting,
every single generation gone.

They are still in Hallaig,
MacLeans and MacLeods,
all who were there in the time of Mac Gille Chaluim:
20 the dead have been seen alive.

The men lying on the green
at the end of every house that was,
the girls a wood of birches,
straight their backs, bent their heads.

MARKS

Questions

50. Look at lines 1—12.

    (i) Identify **two** central concerns of the poem which are introduced in these lines.   2

    (ii) Analyse how the poet's use of symbolism develops either or both of these concerns.   4

51. By referring closely to lines 13—24, explain how the poet creates a fusion of past and present.   4

52. By referring to this poem and at least one other by Sorley MacLean, discuss how he explores ideas of tradition and/or heritage in his poetry.   10

MARKS

OR

Text 6 — Poetry

If you choose this text you may not attempt a question on Poetry in Section 2.

Read the poem below and then attempt the following questions.

The Thread by Don Paterson

Jamie made his landing in the world
so hard he ploughed straight back into the earth.
They caught him by the thread of his one breath
and pulled him up. They don't know how it held.
5   And so today I thank what higher will
brought us to here, to you and me and Russ,
the great twin-engined swaying wingspan of us
roaring down the back of Kirrie Hill

and your two-year-old lungs somehow out-revving
10   every engine in the universe.
All that trouble just to turn up dead
was all I thought that long week. Now the thread
is holding all of us: look at our tiny house,
son, the white dot of your mother waving.

Questions

53.   Analyse the poet's use of imagery in lines 1—4 to describe his feelings about Jamie at the time of his birth.   2

54.   By referring to lines 5—10, explain how the poet expresses his feelings now.   4

55.   Evaluate the effectiveness of the last sentence ("Now … waving.") as a conclusion to the poem.   4

56.   By referring to this poem and at least one other by Don Paterson, discuss his use of verse form to explore important themes.   10

[END OF SECTION 1]

SECTION 2 — CRITICAL ESSAY — 20 marks

Attempt ONE question from the following genres — Drama, Prose, Poetry, Film and Television Drama, or Language.

You may use a Scottish text but **NOT** the one used in Section 1.

Your answer must be on a different genre from that chosen in Section 1.

You should spend approximately 45 minutes on this Section.

DRAMA

Answers to questions on **drama** should refer to the text and to such relevant features as characterisation, key scene(s), structure, climax, theme, plot, conflict, setting ...

1. Choose a play in which a central character is slow to understand fully the seriousness of his or her behaviour.

    Explain how this situation has developed and discuss how the character's behaviour influences your overall assessment of him or her.

2. Choose a play which explores one of the following: the nature of heroism, the impact of self-delusion, the burden of responsibility.

    Discuss how the dramatist explores this central concern through her or his presentation of one or more than character.

3. Choose from a play a scene in which you consider a character makes a significant error of judgement.

    Briefly explain the nature of this error of judgement and discuss how this error and its consequences influence your understanding of character and/or theme in the play as a whole.

PROSE — FICTION

> Answers to questions on **prose fiction** should refer to the text and to such relevant features as characterisation, setting, language, key incident(s), climax, turning point, plot, structure, narrative technique, theme, ideas, description …

4. Choose from a novel or short story an incident in which a character makes a decision which you consider unexpected or unwise or unworthy.

    Explain the circumstances surrounding the decision and discuss its importance to your understanding of character and them in the text as a whole.

5. Choose a novel or short story in which loyalty or trust plays an important part.

    Discuss how the writer explores this idea in a way which adds to your understanding of the central concern(s) of the text as a whole.

6. Choose a novel or short story in which the vulnerability of a central character is apparent at one or more than one key point in the text.

    Explain the situation(s) in which the character's vulnerability emerges and discuss the importance of the vulnerability to your understanding of character and/or theme in the text as a whole.

PROSE — NON-FICTION

> Answers to questions on **prose non-fiction** should refer to the text and to such relevant features as ideas, use of evidence, stance, style, selection of material, narrative voice …

7. Choose a piece of **travel writing** which engages you not only intellectually but also emotionally.

    Explain how the writer successfully engages both your mind and your emotions.

8. Choose a work of **biography** or **autobiography** in which the writer brings more than one key incident vividly to life.

    Explain how the writer brings the incidents vividly to life and how they contribute to your understanding of the person involved.

9. Choose a work of **non-fiction** in which the writer expresses outrage or shock about an issue which you feel is important.

    Explain how the writer conveys the emotion and discuss to what extent this emotional approach enhances your understanding of the issue.

POETRY

> Answers to questions on **poetry** should refer to the text and to such relevant features as word choice, tone, imagery, structure, content, rhythm, rhyme, theme, sound, ideas ...

10. Choose a poem in which the poet presents an apparently ordinary situation or event in an extraordinary way.

   Discuss how the poet gives impact and meaning to an apparently ordinary situation or event.

11. Choose a poem which you find emotionally unsettling or intellectually challenging.

   Explain how the poem elicits this response from you and discuss how this contributes to your understanding of the central concern(s) of the poem.

12. Choose a poem in which **two or more** of the following techniques significantly enhance the impact of the poem: rhyme, rhythm, sound, imagery.

   Explain how the poet's use of your chosen techniques enhances your understanding of the poem as a whole.

FILM AND TELEVISION DRAMA

> Answers to questions on **film and television drama*** should refer to the text and to such relevant features as use of camera, key sequence, characterisation, mise-en-scène, editing, setting, music/sound, special effects, plot, dialogue, ...

13. Choose a film or television drama in which a central character's principles are put to the test.

   Explain how the character's principles are put to the test and discuss how her or his response illuminates a central concern of the text.

14. Choose a film or television drama in which a particular atmosphere is an important feature.

   Show how the film or programme makers create this atmosphere and discuss how it contributes to your appreciation of the text as a whole.

15. Choose a film or television drama which explores a crisis in a relationship or the break-up of a family.

   Discuss how the film or programme makers' exploration of the crisis or break-up contributes to your understanding of character and/or theme.

   * "television drama" includes a single play, a series or a serial.

LANGUAGE

Answers to questions on **language** should refer to the text and to such relevant features as register, accent, dialect, slang, jargon, vocabulary, tone, abbreviation ...

16. Choose some of the rhetorical devices which underpin success in speechmaking.

    By referring to one or more than one important speech, discuss the effectiveness of your chosen rhetorical devices.

17. Choose the language of live broadcasting, e.g. live news coverage, sports commentaries, award ceremonies.

    Identify some of the characteristics of this language and discuss to what extent it is effective in communicating the event to its target audience.

18. Choose aspects of language associated with a particular vocational group such as lawyers, doctors or engineers.

    Identify some examples of the language used within the group and discuss to what extent this shared language contributes to the effectiveness of the group's vocational activities.

[END OF SECTION 2]

[END OF MODEL PAPER]

HIGHER FOR CfE

Model Paper 2

Whilst this Model Paper has been specially commissioned by Hodder Gibson for use as practice for the Higher (for Curriculum for Excellence) exams, the key reference documents remain the SQA Specimen Paper 2014 and SQA Past Paper 2015.

Please note that in the Reading for Understanding, Analysis and Evaluation sections, these model papers use passages from previous Official SQA Papers, but with different questions in line with assessment criteria for the new Higher. There are three Model Papers, but for reasons of space, the third Model Paper does not cover the Scottish Text element.

HODDER
GIBSON
LEARN MORE

National
Qualifications
MODEL PAPER 2

**English
Reading for Understanding,
Analysis and Evaluation**

Date — Not applicable

Duration — 1 hour 30 minutes

Total marks — 30

Attempt ALL questions.

Write your answers clearly in the answer booklet provided. In the answer booklet you must clearly identify the question number you are attempting.

Use **blue** or **black** ink.

Before leaving the examination room you must give your answer booklet to the Invigilator; if you do not, you may lose all the marks for this paper.

HODDER
GIBSON
LEARN MORE

The following two passages focus on shopping and consumerism.

Passage 1

In the first passage Carol Midgley, writing in "The Times" newspaper, considers the attraction of shopping and the power of "consumerism".

Read the passage below and attempt the questions which follow.

This is a story about modern consumerism; it is being written inside a mall. From my vantage point on a wooden bench purposely designed to be uncomfortable and placed alongside a digital screen pulsing ever-changing adverts selling other outlets, other products, other ways here to spend, spend, spend, I can watch shoals of people hurrying in and out of stores
5   honouring the creed of the turbo-consumer: live to shop.

How did we get here? How did we get to a point where shopping became the premier leisure activity, where we gladly boarded the work-to-spend treadmill, the insatiable pursuit of "more", which resulted in there being, for example, 121 mobile phones for every 100 people in the UK? Does it even matter? Shopping doesn't kill anyone, it keeps the economy going and
10   provides one in six jobs. If it makes people happy, why not leave them to it?

Well, that's just it. Turbo-consumerism – the age of instant gratification and voracious appetite for "stuff" – cannot make us happy and it never will. Every time we are seduced into buying one product, another appears that is "new", "improved", better than the one you have. Turbo-consumerism is the heroin of human happiness, reliant on the fact that our needs are
15   never satisfied. A consumer society can't allow us to stop shopping and be content because then the whole system would die. Instead it has to sell us just enough to keep us going but never enough that our wants are satisfied. The brief high we feel is compensation for not having a richer, fuller life.

For years, shops, retail centres, giant malls have been taking over public spaces worldwide,
20   creating a mainstream monoculture. The pedestrianisation of city centres, though largely regarded as pro-citizen, is in fact primarily to maximise "footfall" and shoppers' "grazing time". This retail creep has ensured that, increasingly, there's not much else to do but shop. The more we consume, the less space there is to be anything other than consumers. The space to be citizens and make decisions equally and collectively about the world around us is
25   diminished. It may be a free country, but we simply have the freedom to shop. Kings as consumers, pawns as citizens.

Am I over-catastrophising the consumer phenomenon? In the Liverpool One shopping "experience", where I am sitting, a place teeming with shoppers despite the credit crunch, and punctuated by *Massive Reductions*! signs, people don't look particularly disempowered or
30   depressed. Purposeful, I suppose, but also strangely distracted, as if they do not notice the environment around them, merely the magnetic shop signs. I understand the siren call of TK Maxx and how a £3 top can mend a bad day. But the question is, why does it?

We can answer this question from the basis of evolutionary psychology. The human body is a practical tool for reproduction and survival, but it is also the advertising and packaging for our
35   genes and our "fitness indicators". When a modern woman buys a new dress or a man a Rolex watch they are really self-marketing, saying: "Look at me, I'm attractive, successful, fertile, healthy – mate with me." It isn't that we are materialistic; in a marketing-dominated culture we just don't know any other way to do it.

40 But here's the thing: much of this is simply not true. In reality, consumerism is a poor means of self-advertising because the vast majority of people don't notice or care what you are wearing. The fundamental consumerist delusion is that branded goods are the most effective way of signalling to others our "fitness". But even in a turbo-consumer world it's a fallacy that we care more about the artificial products displayed by people than their conversation, their wit, or their affection. Yet when mineral water advertised with a photo of a nearly nude

45 Jennifer Aniston sells for 870 times the price of tap water, then marketing dominates life on Earth. Marketers understand that they are selling the sizzle not the steak.

Back at the mall, I speak to two young shoppers staggering under the weight of their carrier bags. Will they go home now and put their feet up? "No, we're taking these bags home in a taxi," says one. "Then we're coming back to do another hour before the shops close."

Adapted from an article in The Times newspaper, July 2009

MARKS

Questions

1. Re-read lines 1—5.

    (a) Identify **two** ways the mall seems to encourage consumerism.   2

    (b) Analyse how the writer's use of language in these lines emphasises the intensity of consumerism in the mall.   2

2. Re-read lines 6—18.

    (a) Explain why, according to the writer, consumerism might be considered harmless but also unable to make us happy?   4

    (b) Analyse how the writer's use of imagery in lines 11—18 emphasises her criticism of consumerism.   3

3. By referring to **at least two** features of language in lines 19—26, analyse how the writer's use of language conveys her disapproval of the large amount of space that is now devoted to shopping. You should refer in your answer to such features as word choice, sentence structure, tone, imagery ...   4

4. To what extent does the writer's description of the shoppers in lines 27—32 suggest that the she believes she is "over-catastrophising the consumer phenomenon" (line 27)?   3

5. Re-read lines 33—46.

    Explain how, according to the writer, "evolutionary psychology" can explain our need for material goods, but why she thinks "much of this is simply not true".   4

6. Evaluate the final paragraph's effectiveness as a conclusion to the ideas of the passage as a whole.   3

Passage 2

In the second passage below, Will Hutton, writing in "The Guardian" newspaper, considers the same topic from a different point of view.

Read the passage and attempt the question which follows. While reading, you may wish to make notes on the main ideas and/or highlight key points in the passage.

My two daughters have been addicted to shopping for years. From big city luxurious shopping mall to idiosyncratic old clothes shop, they fall upon it greedily.   They are fully paid-up members of the allegedly futile and empty materialist culture: rootless, obsessive shoppers for whom filling up their shopping bags is a substitute for politics, community
5   participation, family or faith. Critics of this culture indulge in a collective mass tut-tutting: shopping and everything that goes with it are apparently symbolic of what is wrong with the modern age. Serious shoppers are "slaves to the market", enemies of collective action whose individualistic appetite is helping to homogenise our high streets while destroying our moral wellbeing.

10   Critics also deplore the outcome — industrialised shopping malls, mass advertising, the manipulation of desire by producers and retailers — as if the consumers at the other end of all this effort were just brainwashed dolts colluding unwittingly in the destruction of their spiritual life and the interpersonal relationships which are central to their happiness. Shopping on this scale and with this degree of commitment, critics believe, is a form of psychosis.

15   There is a partial truth in this condemnation, but it too quickly casts the individual shopper as an empty vessel morally corroded by the dark forces of anonymous markets. Critics of shopping are so busy delivering their views that they rarely have the time to surrender to savouring that moment when they might unexpectedly enhance their lives by finding another diverting item on which to spend money – in short, by shopping.

20   My experience of shopping in Hong Kong recently has made me realise that shopping is enormous fun and profoundly satisfying. I'd dashed in to buy cheap gifts for my family and had intended to spend no more than 30 minutes. Instead, I found myself drawn into the heady delights of shopping. Choosing between a cornucopia of famous watch brands, not one of which costs more than £4, is an experience I defy anybody not to enjoy. And on top of that,
25   you can pick and mix every detail: case, colour, buckle, strap. I was shopping as my daughters shop — giving myself over to the minutiae of the experience.

On three floors almost every shop you pass excites another taste or way you might express yourself. Binoculars and telescopes; pocket DVD players; walking sticks; silk wall hangings; leather belts; mirrors; porcelain figurines — it was endless. The bargain prices were an
30   invitation to the recognition that individuals have an infinity of wants, some of which we don't even know about or have forgotten; I fell upon the binoculars with all the delight of a child. Much of the pleasure is not even the buying; it is acquiring the knowledge of the immense range of goods that exist that might satiate your possible wants. Shopping, as my daughters tell me, is life-affirming.

35   I would even extend the argument to the shopping mall – the quintessential expression of the alleged degradation of shopping. Hong Kong proclaims itself the shopping capital of the world; its malls are marble-floored temples to consumption that make their British counterparts look tawdry. But instead of recoiling from the excess, I found it attractive. The effort made to present the goods well is an act of creativity in its own right. The collective impact throbs with
40   vitality.

MARKS

To condemn shopping as somehow degrading to those who take it seriously as a cultural expression of themselves is to obscure an important dimension of our lives. True happiness may be about the quality of our interpersonal relationships and wanting to belong to a just society; but it is also about the opportunity to express how we want to live through what we
45 buy. The genius of shopping is that it offers ordinary people the chance both to generate and to satisfy their multiple wants – as well as propelling our economy. Instead of the denigration of shopping culture it is time to recognise that the millions who love it are not stupid, being manipulated or slaves of markets – they are doing something important.

Adapted from an article in The Guardian newspaper, September 2005

Question

7. Both writers express their views about shopping. Identify key areas on which they disagree. In your answer, you should refer in detail to both passages.   5

You may answer this question in continuous prose or in a series of developed bullet points.

[END OF MODEL PAPER]

National
Qualifications
MODEL PAPER 2

English
Critical Reading

Date — Not applicable

Duration — 1 hour 30 minutes

Total marks — 40

SECTION 1 — Scottish Text — 20 marks

Read an extract from a Scottish text you have previously studied and attempt the questions.

Choose ONE text from either

Part A — Drama Pages 2–7

Part B — Prose Pages 8–17

Part C — Poetry Pages 18–29

Attempt ALL the questions for your chosen text.

SECTION 2 — Critical Essay — 20 marks

Attempt ONE question from the following genres — Drama, Prose, Poetry, Film and Television Drama, or Language.

Your answer must be on a different genre from that chosen in Section 1.

You should spend approximately 45 minutes on each Section.

Write your answers clearly in the answer booklet provided. In the answer booklet you must clearly identify the question number you are attempting.

Use **blue** or **black** ink.

Before leaving the examination room you must give your answer booklet to the Invigilator; if you do not, you may lose all the marks for this paper.

HODDER
GIBSON
LEARN MORE

SECTION 1 — SCOTTISH TEXT — 20 marks

Choose ONE text from Drama, Prose or Poetry.

Read the text extract carefully and then attempt ALL the questions for your chosen text.

You should spend about 45 minutes on this Section.

PART A — SCOTTISH TEXT — DRAMA

Text 1 — Drama

If you choose this text you may not attempt a question on Drama in Section 2.

Read the extract below and then attempt the following questions.

The Slab Boys by John Byrne

In this extract, Alan intervenes on Hector's behalf.

	HECTOR:	D'you like it, Alan?
	ALAN:	It's ... er ... (PHIL *threatens to snap pen*) ... really gadgey, Heck.
	HECTOR:	Will I go now and ask her? Will I? (*Heads for door*)
5	SPANKY:	(*Cutting him off*) Not just yet, Hector ... Remember you've still got to go and see Willie.
	HECTOR:	Yeh, but I can do that after I've asked Lucille ...
	PHIL:	No, Spanky's right, kiddo ... better go and see Willie first. It's important. Lucille'll not go off the boil. Here, I'll give you my coat to put on ... (*Takes off coat*)
10	HECTOR:	What do I want that for? I don't mind doing a bit of swanking now that my clothes are up to date.
	PHIL:	Yeh, but you don't want anybody else to get a preview, do you? Lessen the impact ... know what I mean? Get the coat on. (*Forces* HECTOR's *arms into sleeves*)
	SPANKY:	(*Pulling balaclava helmet from cupboard*) You better put this on and all ... it's draughty in Willie's room. (*Pulls helmet over* HECTOR's *head*) Cosy, eh?
15	HECTOR:	(*Slightly bamboozled*) Yeh, but will he not think I'm a bit happed up?
	PHIL:	That's just it. You've been down at Nurse. Influenza verging on pleurisy. She ordered you home but you decided to soldier on. He'll like that. Maybe not give you your ... (*Stops*)
	SPANKY:	(*Quickly*) Wireless back.
20	HECTOR:	I'm not expecting my wireless back. You know what he's like.
	SPANKY:	Well, you can't just expect it back cos you've got the flu, Heck ...
	PHIL:	Triple pneumonia, Spanks.
	HECTOR:	I'm all mixed up ... what've I got again?
	SPANKY:	Triple pneumonia ...
25	PHIL:	Double rupture ...
	HECTOR:	I'll away along then.

Page two

MARKS

	SPANKY:	Good man. All the best.
	PHIL:	Good luck, son … (*They shove* HECTOR *out the door*) You'll need it.

(*They hold onto each other laughing*)

30 ALAN: Well, I hope you're proud of yourselves … that was a pretty lousy trick to play!

SPANKY: Oh, was it, by jove?

PHIL: A trick, you cad! Take that! (*Bops* ALAN's *head a smack*)

ALAN: Hey, watch it! That was sore … Chuckit! Okay, so I'm speaking out of turn but that poor little bastard's gone off to Willie Curry's office thinking that underneath
35 that dustcoat and helmet he really does cut a dash … and he'll probably stop off on the way back to have a word with Lucille … doff the coat and hat and you know what'll happen then … she'll wet herself. Which will probably give you and your crummy friend a big laugh, won't it?

PHIL: Gosh and All Serene … the Fifth Form at St Dominic's. Listen, Steerforth Minor,
40 if it wasn't for me and Spanks there that 'poor little bastard' wouldn't have any pals. Yeh, that's right. So, we do take the piss … set him up a bit …

ALAN: More than a bit.

Questions

1. By referring to lines 1—29, explain how the audience is made to feel sorry for Hector.   4

2. Explain how the playwright's use of language in lines 30—32 allows Phil and Spanky to make fun of Alan.   2

3. By referring to lines 33—42, explain how the playwright emphasises the animosity between Alan and Phil.   4

4. By referring to the extract and elsewhere in the play, discuss the importance of the conflict between Phil and Alan in exploring at least one theme in the play.   10

OR

Text 2 — Drama

If you choose this text you may not attempt a question on Drama in Section 2.

Read the extract below and then attempt the following questions.

***The Cheviot, the Stag and the Black, Black Oil* by John McGrath**

In this extract, the roots of the Highland Clearances are explained.

(GAELIC SINGER *is singing a quiet Jacobite song in Gaelic*)

M.C.   It begins, I suppose, with 1746 – Culloden and all that. The Highlands were in a bit of a mess. Speaking — or singing — the Gaelic language was forbidden. (*Singing stops.*) Wearing the plaid was forbidden. (SINGER *takes off her plaid, sits.*) Things were all set for a change. So Scene One — Strathnaver 1813.

5

Drum roll. Page of book turned, a cottage pops up from in between the next two pages.

Enter two Strahnaver girls, singing.

GIRLS: Hé mandu's truagh nach tigeadh
Hé mandu siod 'gam iarraidh
10   Hé mandu gille's litir
He ri oro each is diollaid
Heman dubh hi ri oro
Hó ró hù ó

As they sing, a YOUNG HIGHLANDER *comes on, watches them, talks to audience.*

15   Y.H.   The women were great at making it all seem fine. But it was no easy time to be alive in. Sir John Sinclair of Caithness had invented the Great Sheep; that is to say, he had introduced the Cheviot to the North. Already in Assynt the Sutherland family had cleared the people off their land – and the people were not too pleased about it.

FIRST
WOMAN: Ach blethers —

SECOND
20   WOMAN: Cha chuir iad dragh oirnne co diubh. (They won't bother us here).

FIRST
WOMAN: The Countess has always been very kind to us.

Y.H.   Aye, and she's away in England.

FIRST
WOMAN.   Why wouldn't she be?

Y.H.   With her fancy palaces and feasts for Kings and fine French wines – and it's our rent
25   she's spending.

FIRST
WOMAN: Rent! You never pay any rent –

MARKS

30	Y.H.	Where would I get the money to pay rent? (*To audience.*) If it's not bad weather flattening the barley, it's mildew on the potatoes, and last year it was both together ... And now they're talking about bringing in soldiers to clear us off the land completely ...
	SECOND WOMAN:	Saighdearan? De mu dheidhinn saighdearan? (Soldiers — what do you mean, soldiers?)
	Y.H.	There were one hundred and fifty of them arrived in a boat off Lochinver.
	FIRST WOMAN:	Would you get on with some work?
35	SECOND WOMAN:	Seo-lion an cogan. (Here fill up the bucket)

They sing on, as Y.H. goes to a corner of the cottage to pee in the bucket. They watch him and laugh. Suddenly he panics, does up his trousers and rushes over.

	Y.H.	Here — there's a couple of gentlemen coming up the strath.
	FIRST WOMAN:	Gentlemen?
40	Y.H.	(*to audience*). The two gentlemen were James Loch and Patrick Sellar, factor and under-factor to the Sutherland estates.
	FIRST WOMAN:	Oh, look at the style of me ...
	Y.H.	(*handing them the bucket*). You might find a good use for this. (*Goes.*)

Questions

5. By referring to lines 1—18, explain how the playwright creates a relaxed mood.   4

6. By referring to lines 19—34, explain how the playwright conveys the difference in outlook between the Young Highlander and the Two Women.   4

7. Explain how the extract ends on a humorous note.   2

8. The staging of *The Cheviot, the Stag and the Black, Black Oil* is very different from that of a conventional play. By referring to the extract and to elsewhere in the play, discuss how effective you find this unconventional staging in exploring at least one key idea in the play.   10

OR

Text 3 — Drama

If you choose this text you may not attempt a question on Drama in Section 2.

Read the extract below and then attempt the following questions.

***Men Should Weep* by Ena Lamont Stewart**

In this extract, which is from near beginning of the play, Lily questions some of Maggie's assumptions.

	LILY:	Dae you think you're happy?
	MAGGIE:	Aye! I'm happy!
	LILY:	In this midden?
5	MAGGIE:	Ye canna help havin a midden o a hoose when there's kids under yer feet a day. I dae the best I can.
	LILY:	I ken ye do. I'd gie it up as hopeless. Nae hot water. Nae place tae dry the weans' clothes … nae money. If John wad gie hissel a shake …
	MAGGIE:	You leave John alane! He does his best for us.
10	LILY:	No much o a best. O.K. O.K. Keep yer wig on! Ye're that touchy ye'd think ye wis jist new merriet. I believe you still love him!
	MAGGIE:	Aye. I still love John. And whit's more, he loves me.
	LILY:	Ye ought to get yer photies took and send them tae the Sunday papers! "Twenty-five years merriet and I still love ma husband. Is this a record?"
	MAGGIE:	I'm sorry for you, Lily. I'm right sorry for you.
15	LILY:	We're quits then.
	MAGGIE:	Servin dirty hulkin brutes o men in a Coocaddens pub.
	LILY:	Livin in a slum and slavin efter a useless man an his greetin weans.
	MAGGIE:	They're *my* weans! I'm workin for ma ain.
	LILY:	I'm *paid* for my work.
20	MAGGIE:	So'm I! No in wages … I'm paid wi love. [*pause*] And when did you last have a man's airms roon ye?
	LILY:	*Men*! I'm wantin nae man's airms roon me. They're a dirty beasts.
	MAGGIE:	Lily, yer mind's twisted. You canna see a man as a man. Ye've got them a lumped thegither. Ye're daft!
25	LILY:	You're *saft*! You think yer man's wonderful and yer weans is a angels. Look at Jenny …
	MAGGIE:	[*instantly on the defensive*] There's naethin wrang wi Jenny!
	LILY:	No yet.

MARKS

Questions

9. Look at lines 1—15.

    (i) Explain what important aspects of Maggie's character are revealed in these lines.   4

    (ii) Explain one important aspect of Lily's character which is revealed in these lines.   2

10. Analyse how lines 16—28 are structured in such a way as to provide a lively dramatic exchange between Maggie and Lily.   4

11. By referring to the extract and to elsewhere in the play, discuss to what extent men in the play are presented as weak.   10

SECTION 1 — SCOTTISH TEXT — 20 marks

Choose ONE text from Drama, Prose or Poetry.

Read the text extract carefully and then attempt ALL the questions for your chosen text.

You should spend about 45 minutes on this Section.

PART B — SCOTTISH TEXT — PROSE

Text 1 — Prose

If you choose this text you may not attempt a question on Prose in Section 2.

Read the extract below and then attempt the following questions.

The Painter by Iain Crichton Smith

In this extract, the narrator describes the fight between Red Roderick and his father-in-law.

As Red Roderick was drunk perhaps the advantage given him by relative youth was to a certain extent cancelled. There was however no doubt that he wished to kill the old man, so enraged was he, so frustrated by the life that tortured him. As they swung their scythes towards each other ponderously, it looked at first as if they could do little harm, and
5   indeed it was odd to see them, as if each was trying to cut corn. However, after some time — while the face of the old man gradually grew more demoniac in a renewal of his youth — he succeeded at last in cutting his son-in-law's left leg so that he fell to the ground, his wife running towards him like an old hen, her skirts trailing the ground like broken wings.

But that was not what I meant to tell since the fight in itself, though unpleasant, was not
10   evil. No, as I stood in the ring with the others, excited and horrified, I saw on the edge of the ring young William with his paint-brush and canvas and easel painting the fight. He was sitting comfortably on a chair which he had taken with him and there was no expression on his face at all but a cold clear intensity which bothered me. It seemed in a strange way as if he were asleep. As the scythes swung to and fro, as the faces of the
15   antagonists became more and more contorted in the fury of battle, as their cheeks were suffused with blood and rage, and their teeth were drawn back in a snarl, he sat there painting the battle, nor at any time did he make any attempt to pull his chair back from the arena where they were engaged.

I cannot explain to you the feelings that seethed through me as I watched him. One
20   feeling was partly admiration that he should be able to concentrate with such intensity that he didn't seem able to notice the danger he was in. The other feeling was one of the most bitter disgust as if I were watching a gaze that had gone beyond the human and which was as indifferent to the outcome as a hawk's might be. You may think I was wrong in what I did next. I deliberately came up behind him and upset the chair so that he fell down head
25   over heels in the middle of a brush-stroke. He turned on me such a gaze of blind fury that I was reminded of a rat which had once leaped at me from a river bank, and he would have struck me but that I pinioned his arms behind his back. I would have beaten him if his mother hadn't come and taken him away, still snarling and weeping tears of rage. In spite of my almost religious fear at that moment, I tore the painting into small pieces and

MARKS

30 scattered them about the earth. Some people have since said that what I wanted to do was to protect the good name of the village but I must in all honesty say that that was not in my mind when I pushed the chair over. All that was in my mind was fury and disgust that this painter should have watched this fight with such cold concentration that he seemed to think that the fight had been set up for him to paint, much as a house exists or an old wall.

Questions

12. By referring to lines 1—8, explain how the narrator's account creates an ambiguous impression of how serious the fight is.   4

13. By referring to lines 9—18, analyse how the writer makes clear the contrast between William and the two fighters.   4

14. By referring to lines 19—34, describe in your own words why the narrator is so incensed at William.   2

15. By referring to the extract and to at least one other story by Iain Crichton Smith, discuss the impressions he creates of life in a small community.   10

OR

Text 2 — Prose

If you choose this text you may not attempt a question on Prose in Section 2.

Read the extract below and then attempt the following questions.

The Eye of the Hurricane by George Mackay Brown

In this extract, Captain Stevens tries to convince the narrator to buy him alcohol.

"Now, Barclay, about this cold of mine."

"Miriam says you haven't got a cold at all," I said.

"The little bitch," he said. "Did she go into your room? She had no right to be disturbing you. I'll speak to her about that. I expect she told you also that I have drinking bouts."

5 "She did," I said.

"Well," he said, "everybody knows. Can't do a thing about it, Barclay. It's a natural thing, like a storm, you just have to let it blow itself out, keep the ship headed into it. Do you understand that, Barclay?"

"I know nothing about it," I said.

10 "I thought writers are supposed to understand things," he said, "the quirks of human nature. That's what they're for. Don't take hard what I say, Barclay. I like you. I'm very glad you're living in this house. I'm just explaining the situation to you, setting the course through the storm, so that you can take your turn at navigating if the need arises. The best way you can help the voyage, Barclay, is just do what I say. I'm the skipper of this ship.
15 And the first thing I want you to do is open that drawer and you'll see a wallet."

"No," I said, and got to my feet.

"There should be four five-pound notes in it. Take one of them out."

"No," I said.

"Two bottles of navy rum from Wilson's, as quick as you can."

20 Charity is no hard-minted currency to be distributed according to whim, a shilling here and a sovereign there – it is the oil and wine that drop uncertainly through the fingers upon the wounds of the world, wherever the roads of pity and suffering cross. It might help this old man, as he said, if I stood close beside him on the bridge till this particular hurricane blew itself out. But I trusted the older wisdom of women. I had made a
25 promise to Miriam.

"No," I said.

"Very well, Mr Barclay," he said after a pause. "Let me see. At the moment you are paying me a rent of two pounds a week, I think. As from Monday next you will pay me four pounds a week. In fact, I think you should make arrangements to leave this house
30 before the end of the month. I find you an unsatisfactory tenant. Now get out."

All night, till I fell into a drowse around three o'clock in the morning, I heard him pacing back and fore, back and fore in his room, an ancient mariner in a ship of dark enchantment.

MARKS

Questions

16. By referring to the whole extract, explain the various methods the Captain uses to convince the narrator to buy him alcohol.   4

17. Analyse how the narrator uses imagery in lines 20—25 to explain his views on charity.   4

18. Explain what the last three lines suggest about the narrator's feelings for the Captain.   2

19. By referring to the extract and to at least one other story by George Mackay Brown, discuss how he creates confrontations between characters.   10

OR

Text 3 — Prose

If you choose this text you may not attempt a question on Prose in Section 2.

Read the extract below and then attempt the following questions.

The Trick is to Keep Breathing by Janice Galloway

In this extract, Joy meets 'Dr Three'.

The doctor is over an hour late. An entirely different man to Dr Two. But questions involve risk and I don't want to look picky. I follow him down the sea-coloured corridor to a room with no pictures and all the curtains closed. It smells like dog in the rain. Dr Three doesn't waste any time.

5   DR THREE   [Sitting] Well?

Leather elbow patches on his horrible jacket glint in the gloom. Behind the specs his eyes are all iris.

    PATIENT   [Mesmerised] Well what? I thought you would start.

    DR THREE   Start what? Start what? You asked to see me. You are the one who knows
10   what this is about.

    PATIENT   I've been here nearly a week.

    DR THREE   Yes. So what can I do for you?

    PATIENT   [Confused. Has forgotten and is trying to remember.] Treatment. I want
            to know about treatment.

15   DR THREE   [Leans back with an ominous creak] I don't know what sort of thing you
            expected. There's no set procedure for these things. You ask to see one of
            us when you feel you need to. So. Any other questions?

    PATIENT   I have to think. [Silence]

    DR THREE   Well?

20   PATIENT   [Nothing. Eyes filling up.]

    DR THREE   [Draw a long breath through the nose, leaning back on the chair] How long
            have you been here did you say?

    PATIENT   Nearly a week. I haven't seen anyone.

    DR THREE   [Sighing] I suppose you want a pass. [Silence] To go home for the
25   weekend? You should be going home on pass. Getting out of here and
            facing up to things on the outside. You can go out on pass any time you like,
            all right?

    PATIENT   No. I don't understand any of this.

    DR THREE   I don't know what that's supposed to mean.

30   PATIENT   It's too fast. You're rushing me.

    DR THREE   All right. Take your time. [Silence] Right then. Good day.

He taps the bundle of papers on his desk, then folds his arms. The interview is finished. PATIENT stands thinking maybe this is some kind of therapy.

    DR THREE   The interview is over.   [Opens a drawer. The stack of papers flake
35   dangerously. He pretends not to notice.]

MARKS

Questions

20. By referring to lines 1—7, explain how the writer establishes an unwelcoming atmosphere at the start of the extract.   3

21. By referring to lines 8—23, analyse how the exchange between the Patient and Dr Three highlights the lack of communication between them.   4

22. By referring to lines 24—35, explain how the Doctor's uncaring approach is made clear.   3

23. By referring to the extract and elsewhere in the novel, discuss how *The Trick Is To Keep Breathing* explores the way the individual is treated within the Mental Health system.   10

OR

Text 4 — Prose

If you choose this text you may not attempt a question on Prose in Section 2.

Read the extract below and then attempt the following questions.

***Sunset Song* by Lewis Grassic Gibbon**

In this extract, which is from Part IV (Harvest), Ewan has returned on leave from the army.

Drunk he had come from the station and more than two hours late. Standing at last in the kitchen in his kilts he'd looked round and sneered *Hell, Chris, what a bloody place!* as she ran to him. And he'd flung his pack one way and his hat the other and kissed her as though she were a tink, his hands on her as quickly as that, hot and questing and wise as
5   his hands had never been. She saw the hot smoulder fire in his eyes then, but no blush on his face, it was red with other things. But she smothered her horror and laughed, and kissed him and struggled from him, and cried *Ewan, who's this?*

Young Ewan held back, shy-like, staring, and just said *It's father.* At that the strange, swaying figure in the tartan kilts laughed, coarse-like, *Well, we'll hope so, eh Chris? Any*
10   *supper left – unless you're too bloody stand-offish even to have that?*

She couldn't believe her own ears. *Stand-offish? Oh, Ewan!* and ran to him again, but he shook her away, *Och, all right, I'm wearied. For Christ's sake let a man sit down.* He staggered to the chair she'd made ready for him, a picture-book of young Ewan's lay there, he picked the thing up and flung it to the other side of the room, and slumped down
15   into the chair. *Hell, what a blasted climb to a blasted place. Here, give us some tea.*

She sat beside him to serve him, she knew her face had gone white. But she poured the tea and spread the fine supper she'd been proud to make, it might hardly have been there for the notice he paid it, drinking cup after cup of the tea like a beast at a trough. She saw him clearer then, the coarse hair that sprang like short bristles all over his head, the neck
20   with its red and angry circle about the collar of the khaki jacket, a great half-healed scar across the back of his hand glinted putrescent blue. Suddenly his eyes came on her, *Well, damn't, is that all you've to say to me now I've come home? I'd have done better to spend the night with a tart in the town.*

She didn't say anything, she couldn't, the tears were choking in her throat and smarting
25   and biting at her eyelids, pressing to come, the tears that she'd sworn she'd never shed all the time he was home on leave. And she didn't dare look at him lest he should see, but he saw and pushed back his chair and got up in a rage, *God Almighy, what are you snivelling about now? You always were snivelling, I mind.* And out he went, young Ewan ran to her side and flung his arms round her, *Mother, don't cry, I don't like him, he's a tink, that*
30   *soldier!*

MARKS

Questions

24. Analyse how the writer's use of language in lines 1–15 emphasises the offensiveness of Ewan's behaviour.

    4

25. By referring to lines 16-23, analyse how the writer makes the reader aware of Chris's perception of Ewan.

    4

26. By referring to the whole extract, identify the change in young Ewan's reaction to his father.

    2

27. By referring to the extract and elsewhere in the novel, discuss the development of the relationship between Chris and Ewan.

    10

OR

Text 5 — Prose

If you choose this text you may not attempt a question on Prose in Section 2.

Read the extract below and then attempt the following questions.

The Cone-Gatherers by Robin Jenkins

In this extract, Calum witnesses the killing of a deer.

Calum no longer was one of the beaters; he too was a deer hunted by remorseless men. Moaning and gasping, he fled after them, with no hope of saving them from slaughter but with the impulse to share it with them. He could not, however, be so swift or sure of foot. He fell and rose again; he avoided one tree only to collide with another close to it; and all

5   the time he felt, as the deer must have, the indifference of all nature; of the trees, of tall withered stalks of willowherb, of the patches of blue sky, of bushes, of piles of cut scrubwood, of birds lurking in branches, and of the sunlight: presences which might have been expected to help or at least sympathise.

The dogs barked fiercely. Duror fired his gun in warning to those waiting in the ride.
10   Neil, seeing his brother rush into the danger, roared to him to come back. All the beaters, except Charlie in the rear, joined in the commotion; the wood resounded with their exultant shouts. Realising this must be the finish or kill, Graham, recuperating on the road, hopped back over the fence into the wood and bellowed loudest of all.

As Duror bawled to his dogs to stop lest they interfere with the shooting, and as the deer
15   hesitated before making the dash across the ride, Calum was quite close to them as, silent, desperate, and heroic, they sprang forward to die or escape. When the guns banged he did not, as Neil had vehemently warned him to do, fall flat on the ground and put his fingers in his ears. Instead, with wails of lament, he dashed on at demented speed and shot out onto the broad green ride to hear a deer screaming and see it, wounded in the breast and
20   forelegs, scrabbling about on its hindquarters. Captain Forgan was feverishly reloading his gun to fire again. Calum saw no one else, not even the lady or Mr. Tulloch, who was standing by himself about twenty yards away.

Screaming in sympathy, heedless of the danger of being shot, Calum flung himself upon the deer, clasped it round the neck, and tried to comfort it. Terrified more than ever, it
25   dragged him about with it in its mortal agony. Its blood came off onto his face and hands.

While Captain Forgan, young Roderick, and Lady Runcie-Campbell stood petrified by this sight, Duror followed by his dogs came leaping out of the wood. He seemed to be laughing in some kind of berserk joy. There was a knife in his hand. His mistress shouted to him: what it was she did not know herself, and he never heard. Rushing upon the
30   stricken deer and the frantic hunchback, he threw the latter off with furious force, and then, seizing the former's head with one hand cut its throat savagely with the other. Blood spouted. Lady Runice-Campbell closed her eyes. Captain Forgan shook his head slightly in some kind of denial. Roderick screamed at Duror. Tulloch had gone running over to Calum.

35   The deer was dead, but Duror did not rise triumphant; he crouched beside it, on his knees, as if he was mourning over it. His hands were red with blood; in one of them he still held the knife.

MARKS

Questions

28. Analyse how the sentence structure in lines 1–8 helps to convey how Calum is feeling.   2

29. By referring to lines 9–25, analyse how the writer's use of language creates a sense of "commotion" (line 11).   4

30. By referring to lines 26–37, explain how the reader is made aware of Duror's state of mind at this point.   4

31. By referring to the extract and elsewhere in the novel, discuss how the writer explores the theme of death in *The Cone-Gatherers*.   10

SECTION 1 — SCOTTISH TEXT — 20 marks

Choose ONE text from Drama, Prose or Poetry.

Read the text extract carefully and then attempt ALL the questions for your chosen text.

You should spend about 45 minutes on this Section.

PART C — SCOTTISH TEXT — POETRY

Text 1 — Poetry

If you choose this text you may not attempt a question on Poetry in Section 2.

Read the extract below and then attempt the following questions.

Tam o' Shanter by Robert Burns

In this extract, Tam manages to outrun the witches.

As bees bizz out wi' angry fyke,
When plundering herds assail their byke;
As open pussie's mortal foes,
When, pop! she starts before their nose;
5   As eager runs the market-crowd,
When 'Catch the thief!' resounds aloud;
So Maggie runs, the witches follow,
Wi' mony an eldritch skriech and hollo.

Ah, Tam! ah, Tam! thou'll get thy fairin!
10   In hell they'll roast thee like a herrin!
In vain thy Kate awaits thy comin!
Kate soon will be a woefu' woman!
Now, do thy speedy utmost, Meg,
And win the key-stane o' the brig;
15   There at them thou thy tail may toss,
A running stream they dare na cross.
But ere the key-stane she could make,
The fient a tail she had to shake!
For Nannie far before the rest,
20   Hard upon noble Maggie prest,
And flew at Tam wi' furious ettle;
But little wist she Maggie's mettle —
Ae spring brought aff her master hale,
But left behind her ain grey tail:
25   The carlin claught her by the rump,
And left poor Maggie scarce a stump.

Now, wha this tale o' truth shall read,
Ilk man and mother's son, take heed;
Whene'er to drink you are inclin'd,
30   Or cutty-sarks run in your mind,
Think! ye may buy the joys o'er dear —
Remember Tam o' Shanter's mare.

Page eighteen

MARKS

Questions

32. Analyse how the extended simile in lines 1—8 creates a vivid picture of what is happening.   3

33. By referring to lines 9—26, explain how Burns makes this part of the poem dramatic.   4

34. Discuss to what extent you think lines 27—32 are meant as a serious warning to the reader.   3

35. Referring to Tam o' Shanter and at least one other poem by Burns, discuss to what extent he passes judgements in his poetry.   10

OR

Text 2 — Poetry

If you choose this text you may not attempt a question on Poetry in Section 2.

Read the extract below and then attempt the following questions.

Anne Hathaway by Carol Ann Duffy

The bed we loved in was a spinning world
of forests, castles, torchlight, clifftops, seas
where he would dive for pearls. My lover's words
were shooting stars which fell to earth as kisses
5   on these lips; my body now a softer rhyme
to his, now echo, assonance; his touch
a verb dancing in the centre of a noun.
Some nights, I dreamed he'd written me, the bed
a page beneath his writer's hands. Romance
10   and drama played by touch, by scent, by taste.
In the other bed, the best, our guests dozed on,
dribbling their prose. My living laughing love –
I hold him in the casket of my widow's head
as he held me upon that next best bed.

MARKS

Questions

36. By referring to two techniques of poetry, analyse how the first sentence (lines 1—3) establishes the speaker's passion.   2

37. Explain how the poet uses references to writing in lines 3—10 to convey the speaker's feelings .   4

38. Evaluate the effectiveness of lines 11—14 as a conclusion to the poem.   4

39. Love is a common theme in Carol Ann Duffy's poetry. By referring to this poem and to at least one other by her, discuss how she explores the theme of love.   3̶ 10

OR

Text 3 — Poetry

If you choose this text you may not attempt a question on Poetry in Section 2.

Read the extract below and then attempt the following questions.

Some Old Photographs **by Liz Lochhead**

weather evocative as scent
the romance of dark stormclouds
in big skies over the low wide river
            of long shadows and longer shafts of light

5   of smoke
fabulous film-noir stills of Central Station
of freezing fog silvering the chilled, stilled parks
        of the glamorous past
        where drops on a rainmate are sequins
10   in the lamplight, in the black-and-white

your young, still-lovely mother laughs, the
hem of her sundress whipped up
by a wind on a beach before you were even born

all the Dads in hats
15   are making for Central at five past five
in the snow, in the rain, in the sudden what-a-scorcher,
in the smog, their
belted dark overcoats white-spattered by the starlings

starlings swarming
20   in that perfect and permanent cloud
above what was
never really this photograph
but always all the passing now
and noise and stink and smoky breath of George Square

25   wee boays, a duchess, bunting, there's a
big launch on the Clyde
and that boat is yet to sail

MARKS

Questions

40. By referring to more than one technique of poetry, explain how the poet creates a dream-like atmosphere in lines 1—10.   4

41. By referring to lines 11—18, explain how the poet reminds the reader that these photographs are old.   2

42. By referring to lines 19—24, explain what impression the poet creates of George Square.   2

43. Explain how the poet creates a sense of excitement in the last three lines of the poem.   2

44. Liz Lochhead's poems have sometimes been criticised for being overly nostalgic. By referring to this poem and to at least one other, discuss whether you think this is a fair criticism.   10

OR

Text 4 — Poetry

If you choose this text you may not attempt a question on Poetry in Section 2.

Read the extract below and then attempt the following questions.

Memorial by Norman MacCaig

Everywhere she dies. Everywhere I go she dies.
No sunrise, no city square, no lurking beautiful mountain
but has her death in it.
The silence of her dying sounds through
5   the carousel of language. It's a web
on which laughter stitches itself. How can my hand
clasp another's when between them
is that thick death, that intolerable distance?

She grieves for my grief. Dying, she tells me
10   that bird dives from the sun, that fish
leaps into it. No crocus is carved more gently
than the way her dying
shapes my mind. — But I hear, too,
the other words,
15   black words that make the sound
of soundlessness, that name the nowhere
she is continuously going into.

Ever since she died
she can't stop dying. She makes me
20   her elegy. I am a walking masterpiece,
a true fiction
of the ugliness of death.
I am her sad music.

MARKS

Questions

45. "The silence of her dying sounds through
the carousel of language. It's a web
on which laughter stitches itself." (lines 4—6)

Analyse how any **one** of these images conveys how the speaker has been affected by the death.   3

46. By referring to lines 9—17, explain how the poet uses contrast to reveal the persona's feelings.   4

47. By referring to lines 18—23, explain how the persona makes clear the impact the death has had on him.   3

48. By referring to this poem and to at least one other by Norman MacCaig, discuss his exploration of deeply emotional situations.   10

OR

Text 5 — Poetry

If you choose this text you may not attempt a question on Poetry in Section 2.

Read the poem below and then attempt the following questions.

***Shores* by Sorley MacLean**

If we were in Talisker on the shore
where the great white mouth
opens between two hard jaws,
Rubha nan Clach and the Bioda Ruadh,
5   I would stand beside the sea
renewing love in my spirit
while the ocean was filling
Talisker bay forever:
I would stand there on the bareness of the shore
10 until Prishal bowed his stallion head.

And if we were together
on Calgary shore in Mull,
between Scotland and Tiree,
between the world and eternity,
15 I would stay there till doom
measuring sand, grain by grain,
and in Uist, on the shore of Homhsta
in presence of that wide solitude,
I would wait there forever,
20 for the sea draining drop by drop.

And if I were on the shore of Moidart
with you, for whom my care is new,
I would put up in a synthesis of love for you
the ocean and the sand, drop and grain.
25 And if we were on Mol Stenscholl Staffin
when the unhappy surging sea dragged
the boulders and threw them over us,
I would build the rampart wall
against an alien eternity grinding (its teeth).

MARKS

Questions

49. By referring to lines 1—10, analyse how the poet conveys the power of natural features.

3

50. By referring to lines 11—20, explain how the poet conveys his commitment to the person he is addressing.

3

51. The last verse (lines 21—29) is structurally similar to the other two verses, but there are differences. By referring to both the similarities and the differences, evaluate the last verse as a conclusion to the poem as a whole.

4

52. By referring to this poem and to at least one other by Sorley MacLean, discuss the importance of landscape in his poetry.

10

OR

Text 6 — Poetry

If you choose this text you may not attempt a question on Poetry in Section 2.

Read the poem below and then attempt the following questions.

Two Trees by Don Paterson

One morning, Don Miguel got out of bed
with one idea rooted in his head:
to graft his orange to his lemon tree.
It took him the whole day to work them free,
5   lay open their sides, and lash them tight.
For twelve months, from the shame or from the fright
they put forth nothing; but one day there appeared
two lights in the dark leaves. Over the years
the limbs would get themselves so tangled up
10   each bough looked like it gave a double crop,
and not one kid in the village didn't know
the magic tree in Miguel's patio.

The man who bought the house had had no dream
so who can say what dark malicious whim
15   led him to take his axe and split the bole
along its fused seam, then dig two holes.
And no, they did not die from solitude;
nor did their branches bear a sterile fruit;
nor did their unhealed flanks weep every spring
20   for those four yards that lost them everything,
as each strained on its shackled root to face
the other's empty, intricate embrace.
They were trees, and trees don't weep or ache or shout.
And trees are all this poem is about.

MARKS

Questions

53. Explain how the poet makes the first verse (lines 1—12) sound like the start of a simple folk tale or parable.

4

54. Explain how lines 13—16 act as a link or turning point in the poem as a whole.

2

55. By referring to lines 17—24, explain how the poet subverts the idea that the poem is a parable or a tale with a message.

4

56. By referring to this poem and to at least one other by Don Paterson, discuss his use of symbolism to explore important themes.

10

[END OF SECTION 1]

SECTION 2 — CRITICAL ESSAY — 20 marks

Attempt ONE question from the following genres — Drama, Prose, Poetry, Film and Television Drama, or Language.

You may use a Scottish text but **NOT** the one used in Section 1.

Your answer must be on a different genre from that chosen in Section 1.

You should spend approximately 45 minutes on this Section.

DRAMA

> Answers to questions on **drama** should refer to the text and to such relevant features as characterisation, key scene(s), structure, climax, theme, plot, conflict, setting …

1. Choose a play in which a character shows signs of instability at one or more than one key point in the play.

   Explain the reason(s) for the character's instability and discuss how this feature adds to your understanding of the central concern(s) of the text.

2. Choose a play in which an important part is played by one of the following: crime, punishment, retribution.

   Explain how the dramatist explores the issue and discuss its importance to your understanding of character and/or theme in the play as a whole.

3. Choose from a play a scene which you find amusing or moving or disturbing.

   Explain how the scene provokes this response and discuss how this aspect of the scene contributes to your understanding of the play as a whole.

PROSE — FICTION

Answers to questions on **prose fiction** should refer to the text and to such relevant features as characterisation, setting, language, key incident(s), climax, turning point, plot, structure, narrative technique, theme, ideas, description ...

4. Choose a novel or short story in which envy or malice or cruelty plays a significant part.

   Explain how the writer makes you aware of this aspect of the text and discuss how the writer's exploration of it enhances your understanding of the text as a whole.

5. Choose a novel or short story in which a character is influenced by a particular location or setting.

   Explain how the character is influenced by the location or setting and discuss how this enhances your understanding of the text as a whole.

6. Choose a novel or short story in which the death of a character clarifies an important theme in the text.

   Explain how this theme is explored in the text and discuss how the death of the character clarifies the theme.

PROSE — NON-FICTION

Answers to questions on **prose non-fiction** should refer to the text and to such relevant features as ideas, use of evidence, stance, style, selection of material, narrative voice ...

7. Choose a piece of **travel writing** in which the writer's own personality emerges as a significant feature.

   Explain how the style of writing conveys a sense of the writer's personality and discuss to what extent this is important to your understanding of the key idea(s) of the text.

8. Choose a **non-fiction text** which is written in the specific form of a diary or a journal or a letter.

   Discuss to what extent the writer's exploitation of specific features of the chosen form is important in conveying key idea(s) of the text.

9. Choose a piece of **journalism** which, in your opinion, deals with a fundamental truth about human nature.

   Explain how the writer's presentation of key ideas enhances your understanding of this fundamental truth.

POETRY

> Answers to questions on **poetry** should refer to the text and to such relevant features as word choice, tone, imagery, structure, content, rhythm, rhyme, theme, sound, ideas ...

10.   Choose a poem which explores the pain of love or the pleasure of love or the power of love.

      Discuss how the poet's exploration deepens your understanding of the pain or the power or the pleasure of love.

11.   Choose a poem in which there is a powerful evocation of place.

      Discuss how the poet powerfully explores a specific place to explore an important theme.

12.   Choose a poem in which humour is used to convey a serious message.

      Discuss how the poet uses humour to convey the underlying seriousness of the poem.

FILM AND TELEVISION DRAMA

> Answers to questions on **film and television drama*** should refer to the text and to such relevant features as use of camera, key sequence, characterisation, mise-en-scène, editing, setting, music/sound, special effects, plot, dialogue, ...

13.   Choose a film or television drama which presents a mainly bleak vision of life.

      Explain how the film or programme makers convey the bleakness and discuss to what extent you feel the text offers any optimism.

14.   Choose a film or television drama in which the true nature of a major character is gradually revealed.

      Explain how the film or programme makers present the gradual revelation and discuss how this added to your appreciation of the text as a whole.

15.   Choose from a film or television drama a sequence in which a tense mood is created through at least two key filmic techniques such as mise-en-scène, montage, soundtrack ...

      Explain how the film or programme makers use these techniques to create a tense mood in the sequence and discuss the importance of the sequence to your appreciation of the text as a whole.

      * "television drama" includes a single play, a series or a serial.

LANGUAGE

Answers to questions on **language** should refer to the text and to such relevant features as register, accent, dialect, slang, jargon, vocabulary, tone, abbreviation …

16. Choose some of the ways language is evolving as a result of advances in communication technology.

By referring to specific examples, discuss to what extent these advances are improving or impeding communication.

17. Choose the language of persuasion used in advertising or in politics.

Discuss several ways in which the language you have chosen attempts to be persuasive.

18. Choose aspects of language associated with a particular group in society which shares a professional or leisure activity.

Identify some examples of the language used and discuss how these examples facilitate communication within the group.

[END OF SECTION 2]

[END OF MODEL PAPER]

HIGHER FOR CfE

Model Paper 3

Whilst this Model Paper has been specially commissioned by Hodder Gibson for use as practice for the Higher (for Curriculum for Excellence) exams, the key reference documents remain the SQA Specimen Paper 2014 and SQA Past Paper 2015.

Please note that, for reasons of space, this Model Paper offers practice in Reading for Understanding, Analysis and Evaluation, and in Critical Essay but does not offer further Scottish Set Text questions.

HODDER
GIBSON
LEARN MORE

National
Qualifications
MODEL PAPER 3

English
Reading for Understanding,
Analysis and Evaluation

Date — Not applicable

Duration — 1 hour 30 minutes

Total marks — 30

Attempt ALL questions.

Write your answers clearly in the answer booklet provided. In the answer booklet you must clearly identify the question number you are attempting.

Use **blue** or **black** ink.

Before leaving the examination room you must give your answer booklet to the Invigilator; if you do not, you may lose all the marks for this paper.

HODDER
GIBSON
LEARN MORE

The following two passages focus on video games.

Passage 1

In the first passage Steven Johnson, writing in The Times newspaper, considers whether video games are as bad for young people as is often claimed.

Read the passage below and attempt the questions which follow.

Reading books enriches the mind; playing video games deadens it — you can't get much more conventional than the conventional wisdom that kids today would be better off spending more time reading books, and less time zoning out in front of their video games.

5   For the record, I think that the virtues of reading books are great. We should all encourage our kids to read more. But even the most avid reader is inevitably going to spend his or her time with other media — games, television, movies, the internet. Yet the question is whether these other forms of culture have intellectual virtues in their own right — different from, but comparable to, reading. Where most critics allege a dumbing down, I see a progressive story: popular culture steadily, but almost imperceptibly, making our brains sharper as we soak in 10   entertainment usually dismissed as so much lowbrow fluff. I hope to persuade you that increasingly the non-literary popular culture is honing different mental skills that are just as important as the ones exercised by reading books.

The most powerful example of this trend is found in the world of video games. And the first and last thing that should be said about the experience of playing today's video games, the 15   thing you almost never hear, is that games are fiendishly, sometimes maddeningly, hard. The dirty little secret of gaming is how much time you spend not having fun. You may be frustrated; you may be confused or disorientated; you may be stuck. But when you put the game down and move back into the real world, you may find yourself mentally working through the problem you have been wrestling with, as though you were worrying a loose tooth.

20   So why does anyone bother playing these things? And why does a seven-year-old soak up, for instance, the intricacies of industrial economics in the game form of SimCity 2000, when the same subject would send him screaming for the exits in a classroom? To date, there has been little direct research into the question of how games get children to learn without realising that they are learning. But I believe a strong case can be made that the power of games to captivate 25   largely involves their ability to tap into the brain's natural reward circuitry. If you create a system in which rewards are both clearly defined and achieved by exploring an environment, you will find human brains drawn to those systems, even if they are made up of virtual characters and simulated sidewalks. In the game world, reward is everywhere. The gaming universe is literally teeming with objects that deliver very clearly articulated rewards: more 30   life, access to new levels, new equipment, new spells. Most of the crucial work in game design focuses on keeping players notified of potential rewards available to them, and how much these rewards are currently needed. Most games offer a fictional world where rewards are larger, and more vivid, and more clearly defined than life.

You may just want to win the game, of course, or perhaps you want to see the game's narrative 35   completed, or in the initial stages of play, you may just be dazzled by the game's graphics. But most of the time, when you're hooked on a game, what draws you in is an elemental form of desire: the desire to see the Next Thing. After all, with the occasional exception, the actual content of the game is often childish or gratuitously menacing. Much of the role play inside the gaming world alternates between drive-by shooting and princess-rescuing. It is not the 40   subject matter that attracts; it is the reward system that draws those players in, and keeps their famously short attention spans locked on the screen.

Page two

Playing down the content of video games shouldn't be seen as a cop-out. We ignore the content of many other activities that are widely considered to be good for the brain. No one complains about the simplistic, militaristic plot of chess games. We teach algebra to children
45 knowing full well that the day they leave the classroom 99 per cent of those kids will never again directly employ their algebraic skills. Learning algebra isn't about acquiring a specific tool; it's about building up a mental muscle that will come in handy elsewhere.

So it is with games. It's not what you're thinking about when you're playing a game, it's the way you're thinking that matters. Novels may activate our imagination and may conjure up
50 powerful emotions, but games force you to analyse, to choose, to prioritise, to decide. From the outside, the primary activity of a gamer looks like a fury of clicking and shooting. But if you peer inside the gamer's mind, the primary activity turns out to be another creature altogether: making decisions, some of them snap judgements, some of them long-term strategies.

Adapted from an article in The Times newspaper, May 2005

MARKS

Questions

1. Re-read lines 1–12.

   (a) Analyse how the writer's word choice in lines 1–3 emphasises the "conventional wisdom" that reading books is better than playing video games.

   2

   (b) Explain in your own words "the question" the writer asks in line 6 about "other forms of culture".

   2

   (c) **By referring to at least two features of language in lines 8–12** ("Where ... books"), analyse how the writer emphasises the contrast between his positive view of "other forms of culture" and the negative view held by "most critics". You should refer in your answer to such features as word choice, imagery, sentence structure ...

   4

2. By referring to lines 13–19, analyse how the writer conveys the difficulty of playing video games by his use of sentence structure **and** imagery.

   4

3. Re-read lines 20–33.

   Identify **three** reasons why "reward" is so important to the learning process involved in playing video games. Use your own words as far as possible.

   3

4. Re-read lines 34–47.

   Identify **two** criticisms and **two** defences the writer makes of video games.

   4

5. Re-read lines 48–54.

   (a) Explain in your own words the key distinction the writer makes between reading a novel and playing a video game.

   2

   (b) Analyse how the writer's use of language in lines 50–54 ("From ... strategies") conveys the contrast between what a gamer looks like from "the outside" and what is happening "inside the gamer's mind".

   4

Passage 2

In the second passage below, the politician and journalist Boris Johnson, writing on his own website, takes a different view about video games.

Read the passage and attempt the question which follows. While reading, you may wish to make notes on the main ideas and/or highlight key points in the passage.

It's the snarl that gives the game away. It's the sobbing and the shrieking and the horrible pleading — that's how you know your children are undergoing a sudden narcotic withdrawal. As the strobing colours die away and the screen goes black, you listen to the wail of protest from the offspring and you know that you have just turned off their drug, and you know that
5 they are, to a greater or lesser extent, addicts.

Millions of seven-to-fifteen-year olds are hooked, especially boys, and it is time someone had the guts to stand up, cross the room and just say no to Nintendo. It is time to garrotte the Game Boy and paralyse the PlayStation, and it is about time, as a society, that we admitted the catastrophic effect these blasted gizmos are having on the literacy and the prospects of young
10 males.

We demand that teachers provide our children with reading skills; we expect the schools to fill them with a love of books; and yet at home we let them slump in front of the consoles. We get on with our hedonistic 21st-century lives while in some other room the nippers are bleeping and zapping in speechless rapture, their passive faces washed in explosions and gore. They sit
15 for so long that their souls seem to have been sucked down the cathode ray tube.

They become like blinking lizards, motionless, absorbed, only the twitching of their hands showing that they are still conscious. These machines teach them nothing. They stimulate no ratiocination, discovery or feat of memory — though some of them may cunningly pretend to be educational. I have just watched an eleven-year-old play a game that looked fairly historical,
20 on the packet. Your average guilt-ridden parent might assume that it taught the child something about the Vikings and medieval siege warfare. Phooey! The red soldiers robotically slaughtered the white soldiers, and then they did it again, that was it. Everything was programmed, spoon-fed, immediate — and endlessly showering the player with undeserved praise, richly congratulating him for his bogus massacres.

25 The more addictive these games are to the male mind, the more difficult it is to persuade boys to read books. It's not that these young people lack the brains; the raw circuitry is better than ever. It's the software that's the problem. They have not been properly programmed, because they have not read enough. The only way to learn to write is to be forced time and again to articulate your own thoughts in your own words, and you haven't a hope of doing this if you
30 haven't read enough to absorb the basic elements of vocabulary, grammar, rhythm, style and structure; and young males in particular won't read enough if we continually capitulate and let them fritter their lives away in front of these drivelling machines.

So I say now: go to where your children are sitting in auto-lobotomy in front of the console. Summon up all your strength, all your courage. Steel yourself for the screams and yank out
35 that plug. And if they still kick up a fuss, then get out the sledgehammer and strike a blow for literacy.

Adapted from an article published on Boris Johnson's website in June 2006

Question

6. Both writers express their views about video games. Identify key areas on which they disagree. In your answer, you should refer in detail to both passages.   **5**

   You may answer this question in continuous prose or in a series of developed bullet points.

[END OF MODEL PAPER]

National
Qualifications
MODEL PAPER 3

**English Paper 2
Critical Reading**

Date — Not applicable

Duration — 1 hour 30 minutes

For reasons of space, this Model Paper contains Section 2 — Critical Essay only.

SECTION 2 — Critical Essay — 20 marks

Attempt ONE question from the following genres — Drama, Prose, Poetry, Film and Television Drama, or Language.

You should spend approximately 45 minutes this Section.

Write your answers clearly in the answer booklet provided. In the answer booklet you must clearly identify the question number you are attempting.

Use **blue** or **black** ink.

Before leaving the examination room you must give your answer booklet to the Invigilator; if you do not, you may lose all the marks for this paper.

SECTION 2 — CRITICAL ESSAY — 20 marks

Attempt ONE question from the following genres — Drama, Prose, Poetry, Film and Television Drama, or Language.

You may use a Scottish text but **NOT** the one used in Section 1.

Your answer must be on a different genre from that chosen in Section 1.

You should spend approximately 45 minutes on this Section.

DRAMA

Answers to questions on **drama** should refer to the text and to such relevant features as characterisation, key scene(s), structure, climax, theme, plot, conflict, setting ...

1. Choose a play in which a central character experiences rejection or isolation or loneliness.

    Explain how the dramatist makes you aware of the character's situation and discuss how it adds to your understanding of character and/or theme in the play as a whole.

2. Choose a play which features one of the following conflicts: traditional values versus modern thinking; duty versus self-interest; delusion versus self awareness.

    Explain how the dramatist presents this conflict and discuss how this contributes to your understanding of the play as a whole.

3. Choose a play in which the setting in time and/or place is an important feature.

    Explain how the dramatist exploits aspects of the setting in a way which enhances your understanding of the central concern(s) of the play as a whole.

PROSE — FICTION

> Answers to questions on **prose fiction** should refer to the text and to such relevant features as characterisation, setting, language, key incident(s), climax, turning point, plot, structure, narrative technique, theme, ideas, description …

4. Choose a novel or short story which explores loss or futility or failure.

    Discuss how the writer explores one of these ideas in a way you find effective.

5. Choose a novel or short story in which a particular mood is dominant.

    Explain how the writer creates this mood and discuss how it contributes to your understanding of the text as a whole.

6. Choose a novel or short story in which there is a character who is not only realistic as a person but who has symbolic significance in the text as a whole.

    Explain how the writer makes you aware of both aspects of the character.

PROSE — NON-FICTION

> Answers to questions on **prose non-fiction** should refer to the text and to such relevant features as ideas, use of evidence, stance, style, selection of material, narrative voice …

7. Choose a work of **non-fiction** in which vivid description is an important feature.

    Explain in detail how the vivid impression is created and discuss how it contributes to your appreciation of the text as a whole.

8. Choose a work of **biography** or **autobiography** which you feel is inspirational or moving.

    Explain how the writer evokes this response and discuss why you find the text inspirational or moving.

9. Choose a piece of **journalism** which presents difficult or challenging ideas in an accessible way.

    Explain what is difficult or challenging about the writer's ideas and discuss how she or he presents them in an accessible way.

POETRY

> Answers to questions on **poetry** should refer to the text and to such relevant features as word choice, tone, imagery, structure, content, rhythm, rhyme, theme, sound, ideas ...

10. Choose a poem which features a complex character.

    Explain how the complexity of the character is presented and discuss how significant this aspect of characterisation is to the impact of the poem.

11. Choose **two** poems which approach a similar theme in different ways.

    Explain the nature of these different approaches and discuss which approach leads, in your opinion, to the more pleasing poem.

12. Choose a poem which explores either the problems of growing older or the joys of being young.

    Explain how the poet presents these aspects and discuss to what extent she/ he succeeds in deepening your understanding of them.

FILM AND TELEVISION DRAMA

> Answers to questions on **film and television drama*** should refer to the text and to such relevant features as use of camera, key sequence, characterisation, mise-en-scène, editing, setting, music/sound, special effects, plot, dialogue, ...

13. Choose a film or television drama in which a character overcomes or gives way to temptation.

    Discuss how the film or programme makers use this situation to influence your response to the text as a whole.

14. Choose a film or television drama which contains a sequence you find disturbing or unsettling.

    Explain how the film or programme makers achieve this response and go on to discuss the importance of the sequence to your appreciation of the text as a whole.

15. Choose a film or television drama in which setting has a significant influence on mood and theme.

    Explain how the film or programme makers reveal this setting and discuss why it is so influential in terms of mood and theme.

    * "television drama" includes a single play, a series or a serial.

LANGUAGE

> Answers to questions on **language** should refer to the text and to such relevant features as register, accent, dialect, slang, jargon, vocabulary, tone, abbreviation ...

16. Choose some of the ways language differs across generations.

    Identify some of these differences and the factors which cause them. Go on to discuss to what extent this is advantageous to those involved.

17. Choose the spoken and/or written language used by people who exercise power effectively.

    Identify what is distinctive about the language and discuss why it is effective in influencing its audience.

18. Choose the technical language associated with a sport, a craft, a profession or one of the arts.

    By referring to specific examples, discuss to what extent you feel such language leads to clearer communication.

[END OF SECTION 2]

[END OF MODEL PAPER]

HIGHER FOR CfE

2015

X724/76/11

**English
Reading for Understanding,
Analysis and Evaluation — Text**

FRIDAY, 15 MAY

9:00 AM – 10:30 AM

Total marks — 30

Read the passages carefully and then attempt ALL questions, which are printed on a separate sheet.

The following two passages consider the negative impact of intensive farming.

Passage 1

Read the passage below and then attempt questions 1 to 8.

In the first passage, Isabel Oakeshott gives a disturbing account of her visit to Central Valley, California, an area where intensive farming is big business.

On a cold, bright November day I stood among a million almond trees and breathed in the sweet air. I was in Central Valley, California, in an orchard stretching over 700,000 acres. Before me was a vision of how the British countryside may look one day. Beyond the almond orchards were fields of pomegranates, pistachios, grapes and apricots. Somewhere in the distance were almost
5 two million dairy cows, producing six billion dollars' worth of milk a year.

It may sound like the Garden of Eden but it is a deeply disturbing place. Among the perfectly aligned rows of trees and cultivated crops are no birds, no butterflies, no beetles or shrubs. There is not a single blade of grass or a hedgerow, and the only bees arrive by lorry, transported across the United States. The bees are hired by the day to fertilise the blossom, part of a
10 multibillion-dollar industry that has sprung up to do a job that nature once did for free.

As for the cows, they last only two or three years, ten-to-fifteen years less than their natural life span. Crammed into barren pens on tiny patches of land, they stand around listlessly waiting to be fed, milked or injected with antibiotics. Through a combination of selective breeding, artificial diets and growth hormones designed to maximise milk production, they are pushed so
15 grotesquely beyond their natural limit that they are soon worn out. In their short lives they never see grass.

Could the British countryside ever look like this? If current trends continue, the answer is yes. Farming in Britain is at a crossroads, threatened by a wave of intensification from America. The first mega-dairies and mega-piggeries are already here. Bees are disappearing, with serious
20 implications for harvests. Hedgerows, vital habitats for wildlife, have halved since the Second World War. The countryside is too sterile to support many native birds. In the past forty years the population of tree sparrows has fallen by 97%.

With an eye to the future, Owen Paterson, the UK environment secretary, has been urging families to buy British food. Choosing to buy fewer imports would reduce the relentless pressure
25 British farmers are under to churn out more for less. Paterson's vision is of a more eco-friendly way of eating, based on locally-produced, seasonal fruit and vegetables and, crucially, British meat.

But, as I discovered when I began looking into the way food is produced, increasingly powerful forces are pulling us in the opposite direction. We have become addicted to cheap meat, fish
30 and dairy products from supply lines that stretch across the globe. On the plus side, it means that supermarkets can sell whole chickens for as little as £3. Things that were once delicacies, such as smoked salmon, are now as cheap as chips. On the downside, cheap chicken and farmed fish are fatty and flaccid. Industrially reared farm animals — 50 billion of them a year worldwide — are kept permanently indoors, treated like machines and pumped with drugs.

35 My journey to expose the truth, to investigate the dirty secret about the way cheap food is produced, took me from the first mega-dairies and piggeries in Britain to factory farms in France, China, Mexico, and North and South America. I talked to people on the front line of the global food industry: treadmill farmers trying to produce more with less. I also talked to their neighbours — people experiencing the side effects of industrial farms. Many had stories about
40 their homes plummeting in value, the desecration of lovely countryside, the disappearance of wildlife and serious health problems linked to pollution.

I wanted to challenge the widespread assumption that factory farming is the only way to produce food that everyone can afford. My investigation started in Central Valley, California, because it demonstrates the worst-case scenario — a nightmarish vision of the future for parts of
45 Britain if current practices continue unchecked. It is a five-hour drive south of San Francisco and I knew I was getting close when I saw a strange yellowish-grey smog on the horizon. It looks like the sort of pollution that hangs over big cities, but it comes from the dairies. California's bovine population produces as much sewage as 90 million people, with terrible effects on air quality. The human population is sparse, but the air can be worse than in Los Angeles on a
50 smoggy day.

Exploring the area by car, it was not long before I saw my first mega-dairy, an array of towering, open-sided shelters over muddy pens. The stench of manure was overwhelming — not the faintly sweet, earthy smell of cowpats familiar from the British countryside, but a nauseating reek bearing no relation to digested grass. I saw farms every couple of miles, all with several
55 thousand cows surrounded by mud, corrugated iron and concrete.

It may seem hard to imagine such a scene in Britain but it is not far-fetched. Proposals for an 8,000 cow mega-dairy in Lincolnshire, based on the American model, were thrown out after a public outcry. On local radio the man behind the scheme claimed that "cows do not belong in fields". It will be the first of many similar fights, because dairies are expanding and moving
60 indoors. The creep of industrial agriculture in Britain has taken place largely unnoticed, perhaps because so much of it happens behind closed doors. The British government calls it "sustainable intensification". Without fuss or fanfare, farm animals have slowly disappeared from fields and moved into hangars and barns.

Adapted from an article in The Sunday Times newspaper.

Passage 2

Read the passage below and attempt question 9. While reading, you may wish to make notes on the main ideas and/or highlight key points in the passage.

In the second passage, Audrey Eyton considers the reasons for the introduction of intensive farming and explains why it could be viewed as a mistake.

The founding fathers of intensive farming can claim, "It seemed a good idea at the time!" Indeed it did, in Britain, half a century ago. The post-war government swung into action with zeal, allocating unprecedented funds to agricultural research. The outcome was that the mixed farm, where animals grazed in the fields, was replaced by the huge factories we see today.

5 The aim in confining animals indoors was to cut costs. It succeeded. Indoors, one or two workers can "look after" hundreds of penned or tethered pigs, or a hundred thousand chickens. Great economies were made and thousands of farm workers lost their jobs. This new policy of cheap meat, eggs and cheese for everyone was completely in tune with the national mood, as Britain ripped up its ration books. It was also in tune with nutritional thinking, as nutritionists at
10 that time thought greater consumption of animal protein would remedy all dietary problems.

So factory farming marched on. And became more and more intensive. Where first there were one or two laying hens in a cage, eventually there became five in the same small space. The broiler chicken sheds expanded to cram in vast acres of birds. Many beef cattle were confined in buildings and yards. Until mad cow disease emerged, such animals were fed all kinds of
15 organic matter as cheap food. In the UK dairy cows still spend their summers in the fields, but many of their offspring are reared in the cruelty of intensive veal crate systems.

The aim of those early advocates of intensive farming was "fast food" — fast from birth to table. Again, they succeeded. Chicken, once an occasional treat, now the most popular meat in Britain, owes its low price largely to the short life of the bird. Today's broiler chicken has
20 become the fastest growing creature on earth: from egg to take-away in seven weeks. Most farm animals now have less than half of their pre-war lifespan. Either they are worn out from overproduction of eggs or milk, or have been bred and fed to reach edible size in a few short weeks or months.

But meat, eggs and dairy products have indeed become cheap, affordable even to the poor. All
25 of which made nutritionists exceedingly happy — until they discovered that their mid-century predecessors had made a mighty blunder. Before intensive farming brought cheap meat and dairy products to our tables, man obtained most of his calories from cereal crops and vegetables. The meat with which he supplemented this diet had a much lower fat content than intensively produced products. Now, however, degenerative diseases like coronary heart disease
30 and several types of cancer have been linked to our increased consumption of fatty foods. War-time Britons, on their measly ration of meat and one ounce of cheese a week, were much healthier.

With this knowledge, the only possible moral justification for intensive farming of animals collapses. The cheap animal production policy doesn't help the poor. It kills them. In addition,
35 the chronic suffering endured by animals in many intensive systems is not just a sentimental concern of the soft-hearted. It is a scientifically proven fact. Cracks are beginning to show in our long-practised animal apartheid system, in which we have convinced ourselves, against all evidence, that the animals we eat are less intelligent, less in need of space and exercise than are those we pat, ride or watch.

40 It is also a scientifically proven fact that intensive farming has caused the loss of hedgerows and wildlife sustained by that habitat, has polluted waterways, decimated rural employment and caused the loss of traditional small farms. We need to act in the interests of human health. We need to show humane concern for animals. We need to preserve what remains of the countryside by condemning the practice of intensive farming. We need to return the animals to
45 the fields, and re-adopt the environmentally friendly, humane and healthy system we had and lost: the small mixed farm.

Adapted from an article in The Observer newspaper.

[END OF TEXT]

Page five

[OPEN OUT]

DO NOT WRITE ON THIS PAGE

[BLANK PAGE]

DO NOT WRITE ON THIS PAGE

X724/76/21

English
Reading for Understanding, Analysis
and Evaluation — Questions

FRIDAY, 15 MAY

9:00 AM – 10:30 AM

Total marks — 30

Attempt ALL questions.

Write your answers clearly in the answer booklet provided. In the answer booklet you must clearly identify the question number you are attempting.

Use **blue** or **black** ink.

Before leaving the examination room you must give your answer booklet to the Invigilator; if you do not, you may lose all the marks for this paper.

MARKS

Attempt ALL questions
Total marks — 30

1. Read lines 1—5.

   Identify any **two** positive aspects of Central Valley, California, which are conveyed in these lines. Use your own words in your answer.   2

2. Read lines 6—10.

   By referring to at least **two** examples, analyse how the writer's use of language creates a negative impression of Central Valley.   4

3. Read lines 11—16.

   By referring to both word choice **and** sentence structure, analyse how the writer makes clear her disapproval of dairy farming methods used in Central Valley.   4

4. Read lines 17—19.

   Explain the function of these lines in the development of the writer's argument. You should make close reference to the passage in your answer.   2

5. Read lines 23—34.

   In your own words, summarise the differences between UK Government food policy and consumer wishes.   4

6. Read lines 35—41.

   Analyse how both imagery **and** sentence structure are used in these lines to convey the writer's criticism of industrial farming.   4

7. Read lines 42—55.

   Explain how the writer continues the idea that the Central Valley dairy farming is "nightmarish". Use your own words in your answer. You should make **three** key points.   3

8. Read lines 56—63.

   Evaluate the effectiveness of the final paragraph as a conclusion to the writer's criticism of industrial farming.   2

Question on both passages

9. Look at both passages.

   Both writers express their views about intensive farming.

   Identify **three** key areas on which they agree. You should support the points you make by referring to important ideas in both passages.

   You may answer this question in continuous prose or in a series of developed bullet points.   5

[END OF QUESTION PAPER]

National
Qualifications
2015

X724/76/12

**English
Critical Reading**

FRIDAY, 15 MAY

10:50 AM – 12:20 PM

Total marks — 40

SECTION 1 — Scottish Text — 20 marks

Read an extract from a Scottish text you have previously studied and attempt the questions.

Choose ONE text from either

Part A — Drama   Pages 2–11

or

Part B — Prose   Pages 12–21

or

Part C — Poetry   Pages 22–33

Attempt ALL the questions for your chosen text.

SECTION 2 — Critical Essay — 20 marks

Attempt ONE question from the following genres — Drama, Prose Fiction, Prose Non-fiction, Poetry, Film and Television Drama, or Language.

Your answer must be on a different genre from that chosen in Section 1.

You should spend approximately 45 minutes on each Section.

Write your answers clearly in the answer booklet provided. In the answer booklet you must clearly identify the question number you are attempting.

Use **blue** or **black** ink.

Before leaving the examination room you must give your answer booklet to the Invigilator; if you do not, you may lose all the marks for this paper.

SECTION 1 — SCOTTISH TEXT — 20 marks

Choose ONE text from Drama, Prose or Poetry.

Read the text extract carefully and then attempt ALL the questions for your chosen text.

You should spend about 45 minutes on this Section.

PART A — SCOTTISH TEXT — DRAMA

Text 1 — Drama

If you choose this text you may not attempt a question on Drama in Section 2.

Read the extract below and then attempt the following questions.

The Slab Boys by John Byrne

This extract is taken from Act 2 of the play. Phil has been dismissed from his job.

(*Enter PHIL.*)

SPANKY:	I thought you were away?
PHIL:	I went along for my wages . . . doll said she gave them to Jack.
JACK:	The monkey's got them . . .
5 SPANKY:	Catch. (*Flings packet to PHIL.*) 'S that you off, Jack-knife? Not fancy a hot poultice before you go?
JACK:	If you need a lift home, Alan, let me know . . . I'll try and arrange something . . .
ALAN:	Thanks.
10 (*Exit JACK.*)	
SPANKY:	(*To PHIL, who is opening his wage packet*) Your books?
PHIL:	Yeh . . . P45, the lot . . . (*Reads document:*) "Non-Contributory Pension Scheme" . . . what's that?
ALAN:	It means you haven't paid directly into . . .
15 PHIL:	Shuttit, you! I'm talking to my friend. Well?
SPANKY:	How should I know? I've got all these dishes to wash! Can you not give us a hand? There's hundreds of them.
PHIL:	You're forgetting something, Spanky. I don't work here any more.
SPANKY:	You never did, Phil.
20 PHIL:	Less of the sarcasm . . . (*Sarcastically*) Slab Boy.
SPANKY:	At least I still am one.
PHIL:	Yeh . . . how come? Me and Hector get the heave and you're still here washing dishes safe and secure. How d'you manage it, eh?
SPANKY:	Going to get out of my road? I've got work to do . . .
25 PHIL:	Work? Has Noddy there been getting to you?
SPANKY:	Why don't you can it, Phil? Me and the boy wants to get cleared up.

PHIL: Aw . . . it's "me and the boy" now, is it?

SPANKY: Yeh . . . what of it?

PHIL: I think I'm going to be sick.

30 SPANKY: Well, don't hang over the shades, there's gum in them already . . .

           (*PHIL grabs him. They confront one another. Enter CURRY.*)

CURRY: Still here, McCann? You can go any time, you know.

PHIL: I'm waiting for a phone call.

CURRY: Only urgent personal calls allowed . . .

35 PHIL: This is urgent. I'm waiting for word from the hospital.

CURRY: What's up . . . someone in the family ill?

PHIL: It's my maw.

CURRY: Oh, yes, of course. Were the lacerations severe? It can do a great deal of damage, plate glass . . .

40 PHIL: What?

CURRY: Plate glass . . . the stuff they have in shop windows.

PHIL: What d'you know about shop windows? Who told you about it?

CURRY: There was a bit in today's *Paisley Express* . . . "Ferguslie Park Woman in Store Window Accident" . . .

45 PHIL: It wasn't an accident. She meant to do it.

CURRY: Eh? But the paper said your mother was thrown through the window by a passing car . . .

PHIL: Well, they got it wrong, didn't they? There was a car there but it wasn't passing . . . it was parked. What she done was take a header off the roof . . .
50   straight through the Co. window . . . simple.

CURRY: From the roof of a car? She must've been badly injured.

PHIL: Not a scratch. They say it was the angle she jumped off the roof of the motor.

CURRY: Good God, it must've been a miracle.

55 PHIL: Nope . . . a Ford Prefect.

Questions

1. Look at lines 1—15.

    Explain fully the contrast in these lines between the attitude of Jack and Phil towards Alan.   **2**

2. Look at lines 16—31.

    By referring to at least two examples, analyse how the tension between Phil and Spanky is made clear.   **4**

3. Look at lines 32—55.

    By referring to at least two examples, analyse how language is used to convey the feelings of Phil and/or Curry.   **4**

4. In this extract, various aspects of Phil's character are revealed through humour. By referring to this extract and elsewhere in the play, discuss how humour is used to develop Phil's character.   **10**

Page five

[OPEN OUT FOR QUESTIONS]

DO NOT WRITE ON THIS PAGE

SQA EXAM PAPER 2015   **117**   HIGHER FOR CfE ENGLISH

OR

Text 2 — Drama

If you choose this text you may not attempt a question on Drama in Section 2.

Read the extract below and then attempt the following questions.

The Cheviot, the Stag and the Black, Black Oil by John McGrath

DUKE: The Queen needs men, and as always, she looks to the North.   My Commissioner, Mr Loch, informs me that the response so far has been disappointing.

Enter LOCH, *now an old man.*

5 LOCH: Disappointing?   A disgrace.   In the whole county of Sutherland, not one man has volunteered.

DUKE: I know you to be loyal subjects of the Queen.   I am prepared to reward your loyalty.   Every man who enlists today will be given a bounty of six golden sovereigns from my own private purse.   Now if you will all step up in an

10   orderly manner, Mr Loch will take your names and give you the money.

The DUKE *sits.   Silence.   Nobody moves.   The* DUKE *stands angrily.*

DUKE: Damn it, do you want the Mongol hordes to come sweeping across Europe, burning your houses, driving you into the sea? (LOCH *fidgets.*)   What are you fidgeting for Loch?   Have you no pride in this great democracy that we

15   English — er — British have brought to you?   Do you want the cruel Tsar of Russia installed in Dunrobin Castle?   Step forward.

Silence.   Nobody moves.

DUKE: For this disgraceful, cowardly conduct, I demand an explanation.

Short silence. OLD MAN *stands up in audience.*

20 OLD MAN: I am sorry for the response your Grace's proposals are meeting here, but there is a cause for it.   It is the opinion of this country that should the Tsar of Russia take possession of Dunrobin Castle, we could not expect worse treatment at his hands than we have experienced at the hands of your family for the last fifty years.   We have no country to fight for.   You robbed us of our country and

25   gave it to the sheep.   Therefore, since you have preferred sheep to men, let sheep now defend you.

ALL: Baa-aa.

The DUKE *and* LOCH *leave.* SOLDIER *beats retreat.*

MC: One man only was enlisted at this meeting.   No sooner was he away at Fort
30   George than his house was pulled down, his wife and family turned out, and put in a hut from which an old female pauper was carried a few days before to the churchyard.

          Out of thirty-three battalions sent to the Crimea, only three were Highland.

          But this was only a small set-back for the recruiters.   These parts were still
35   raided for men; almost as fast as they cleared them off the land, they later recruited them into the Army.   The old tradition of loyal soldiering was fostered and exploited with careful calculation.

MARKS

Questions

5. Look at lines 1—18.

    The Duke uses a variety of tones in his speeches to the people in these lines. By referring to at least two examples, analyse how language is used to create different tones.   4

6. Look at lines 17—27.

    Analyse how both the stage directions and dialogue convey the local people's defiance of the Duke.   4

7. Look at lines 29—37.

    Explain how the MC's speech brings this section of the play to an ironic conclusion.   2

8. Discuss how McGrath develops the theme of change in this extract and elsewhere in the play.   10

[Turn over

OR

Text 3 — Drama

If you choose this text you may not attempt a question on Drama in Section 2.

Read the extract below and then attempt the following questions.

***Men Should Weep* by Ena Lamont Stewart**

In this extract from Act 3, Jenny is paying a visit to Maggie and John's tenement home after a period of absence.

	Lily:	Jenny, whit're ye getting at?
	Jenny:	Mammy seems tae think they're letting Bertie hame; but they're no. *No here.* No tae this. Mammy, ye've tae see the Corporation for a Cooncil hoose.
5	Maggie:	A Cooncil house! A Cooncil hoose! Yer daddy's been up tae that lot til he's seek scunnert. Ye've tae wait yer turn in the queue.
	Jenny:	But if they kent aboot Bertie . . .
	Lily:	Is this whit brought ye back, Jenny?
10	Jenny:	It's whit gied me the courage tae come. Least . . . it was ma daddy's face . . . in the water; (*more to herself than the others*) there wis lights shimmerin on the blackness . . . it kind o slinks alang slow, a river, in the night. I was meanin tae let it tak me alang wi it.

Maggie gives a gasp.

	Maggie:	Whit kind o talk is this, Jenny? Did ye no think o us. Yer daddy an me?
15	Jenny:	Think o ye? Oh aye, Mammy, I thought o ye. But thinkin jist made me greet. I was that ashamed o masel . . . Isa and me, we were that rotten tae ye, the things we said.
	Maggie:	That's a bye, Jenny.
20	Jenny:	Naethin's ever *bye*, Mammy; it's a there, like a photy-album in yer heid . . . I kept seein ma daddy, the way he used tae sing tae me when I wis wee; I seen him holdin ma bare feet in his hands tae warm them, an feedin me bread an hot milk oot o a blue cup. (*Pause*) I don't know where you were, Mammy.
	Lily:	Ben the back room wi the midwife, likely. (*Pause*) It's as weel ye came tae yer senses; yon's no the way tae tak oot o yer troubles; a river. But ye're daein fine noo? Ye merriet?
25	Jenny:	No.
	Lily:	Oh. Livin in sin, as they ca it these days, eh?
	Jenny:	(*suddenly flaring up*) Aye, if ye want tae ca it sin! I don't. The man I'm livin wi is kind, an generous.
	Lily:	Oh aye. We can see that. We've had an eye-fu o yer wages o sin.
30	Maggie:	(*mournful*) Aw Jenny. I wisht ye'd earned it.
	Lily:	(*coarse laugh*) Oh, she'll hae earned it, Maggie. On her back.
	Maggie:	*Lily!*
	Lily:	So the Bible's a wrang, is it? The wages o sin's nae deith, it's fancy hair-dos an a swanky coat an pur silk stockins.

35 Jenny: You seem tae ken yer Bible, Auntie Lily. I never pretended tae. But I'm happy, an I'm makin *him* happy. We've a nice wee flat in a clean district, wi trees an wee gardens.

    Lily: A wee love-nest oot west! Great! Juist great — till yer tired business man gets tired o you an ye're oot on yer ear.

40 Jenny: Well, ye hevnae changed, Auntie Lily. I've got tae laugh at you.

    Lily: Laugh awa. I'm no mindin. I've kept ma self-respect.

    Jenny: Aye. An that's aboot a ye've got.

    Maggie: Oh, stop it! Stop it! (*Her hands to her head*) I wis that happy . . .

    Jenny: Mammy, I'm sorry. We'll sit doon properly an talk. (*She draws a couple of*
45   *chairs together, deliberately excluding Lily who moves off a little, but keeps within ear-shot and stands, back resting against the table — or the sideboard — watching.*) I've got plans for you.

    Maggie: Plans?

    Jenny: Aye. For getting yous a oot o this.

50 Maggie: Och Jenny, pet; you wis aye fu o dreams.

    Lily: Aye. Dreams. Fairy-tales. She went awa an impident wee bizzom an she's come back on Christmas Eve, kiddin on she's a fairy wi a magic wand.

    Jenny: (*She doesn't even look at Lily*) Listen, Mammy. We canna wait for a hoose frae the cooncil, it'll tak too lang; but mind! Ye've tae get ma daddy tae speak tae
55   them. (*Maggie nods*) So, while ye're waitin, ye're goin tae flit tae a rented hoose.

    Maggie: Jenny, ye need a lot o money tae flit!

    Jenny: I've got that. (*She opens her handbag and produces a roll of notes that makes*
60   *Maggie's eyes bulge. She gasps.*) There's plenty for the flittin and the key money forbye.

John comes in. He stops at the sight of Jenny and at first his face lights up: then his lips tighten.

MARKS

Questions

9. Look at lines 1—21.

    Explain two of Jenny's reasons for visiting the family home.   2

10. Look at lines 22—42.

    Analyse how Lily and Jenny's differing attitudes are shown.   4

11. Look at lines 43—62.

    Analyse the dramatic impact of at least two of the stage directions in these lines.   4

12. By referring to this extract and elsewhere in the play, discuss how Jenny's growing maturity is made clear.   10

[OPEN OUT FOR QUESTIONS]

DO NOT WRITE ON THIS PAGE

SECTION 1 — SCOTTISH TEXT — 20 marks

Choose ONE text from Drama, Prose or Poetry.

Read the text extract carefully and then attempt ALL the questions for your chosen text.

You should spend about 45 minutes on this Section.

PART B — SCOTTISH TEXT — PROSE

Text 1 — Prose

If you choose this text you may not attempt a question on Prose in Section 2.

Read the extract below and then attempt the following questions.

Mother and Son by Iain Crichton Smith

"It isn't my fault I haven't." He spoke wearily. The old interminable argument was beginning again: he always made fresh attacks but as often retired defeated. He stood up suddenly and paced about the room as if he wanted to overawe her with his untidy hair, his thick jersey, and long wellingtons.

5 "You know well enough," he shouted, "why I haven't my day's work. It's because you've been in bed there for ten years now. Do you *want* me to take a job? I'll take a job tomorrow . . . if you'll only say!" He was making the same eternal argument and the same eternal concession: "If you'll only say." And all the time he knew she would never say, and she knew that he would never take any action.

10 "Why, you'd be no good in a job. The manager would always be coming to show you what you had done wrong, and you'd get confused with all those strange faces and they'd laugh at you." Every time she spoke these words the same brutal pain stabbed him. His babyish eyes would be smitten by a hellish despair, would lose all their hope, and cloud over with the pain of the mute, suffering animal. Time and time again he would say to

15 her when she was feeling better and in a relatively humane mood: "I'm going to get a job where the other fellows are!" and time and time again, with the unfathomable and unknowable cunning of the woman, she would strike his confidence dead with her hateful words. Yes, he was timid. He admitted it to himself, he hated himself for it, but his cowardice still lay there waiting for him, particularly in the dark nights of his mind when

20 the shadow lay as if by a road, watching him, tripping behind him, changing its shape, till the sun came to shine on it and bring its plausible explanations. He spoke again, passing his hand wearily over his brow as if he were asking for her pity.

"Why should anybody laugh at me? They don't laugh at the other chaps. Everybody makes mistakes. I could learn as quickly as any of them. Why, I used to do his lessons for

25 Norman Slater." He looked up eagerly at her as if he wanted her to corroborate. But she only looked at him impatiently, that bitter smile still upon her face.

"Lessons aren't everything. You aren't a mechanic. You can't do anything with your hands. Why don't you hurry up with that tea? Look at you. Fat good you'd be at a job."

He still sat despairingly leaning near the fire, his head on his hands. He didn't even hear

30 the last part of her words. True, he wasn't a mechanic. He never could understand how things worked. This ignorance and inaptitude of his puzzled himself. It was not that he wasn't intelligent: it was as if something had gone wrong in his childhood, some lack of interest in lorries and aeroplanes and mechanisms, which hardened into a wall beyond which he could not go through — paradise lay yonder.

MARKS

35 He reached up for the tea absent-mindedly and poured hot water into the tea-pot. He watched it for a while with a sad look on his face, watched the fire leaping about it as if it were a soul in hell. The cups were white and undistinguished and he felt a faint nausea as he poured the tea into them. He reached out for the tray, put the tea-cup and a plate with bread and jam on it, and took it over to the bed. His mother sat up and took the

40 tray from him, settling herself laboriously back against the pillows. She looked at it and said:

"Why didn't you wash this tray? Can't you see it's all dirty round the edges?" He stood there stolidly for a moment, not listening, watching her frail, white-clad body, and her spiteful, bitter face. He ate little but drank three cups of tea.

Questions

13. Look at lines 1—22.

By referring to at least two examples, analyse how language reveals the nature of the relationship between mother and son.   4

14. Look at lines 27—28.

Identify the tone of the mother's words and analyse how this tone is created.   3

15. Look at lines 29—38.

By referring to at least two examples, analyse how language is used to convey the son's reaction to his mother's words.   3

16. By referring to this extract and to at least one other story, discuss how Iain Crichton Smith uses contrasting characters to explore theme.   10

[Turn over

OR

Text 2 — Prose

If you choose this text you may not attempt a question on Prose in Section 2.

Read the extract below and then attempt the following questions.

The Wireless Set **by George Mackay Brown**

One afternoon in the late summer of that year the island postman cycled over the hill road to Tronvik with a yellow corner of telegram sticking out of his pocket.

He passed the shop and the manse and the schoolhouse, and went in a wavering line up the track to Hugh's croft. The wireless was playing music inside, Joe Loss and his
5 orchestra.

Betsy had seen him coming and was standing in the door.

"Is there anybody with you?" said the postman.

"What way would there be?" said Betsy. "Hugh's at the lobsters."

"There should be somebody with you," said the postman.

10 "Give me the telegram," said Betsy, and held out her hand. He gave it to her as if he was a miser parting with a twenty-pound note.

She went inside, put on her spectacles, and ripped open the envelope with brisk fingers. Her lips moved a little, silently reading the words.

Then she turned to the dog and said, "Howie's dead." She went to the door. The
15 postman was disappearing on his bike round the corner of the shop and the missionary was hurrying towards her up the path.

She said to him, "It's time the peats were carted."

"This is a great affliction, you poor soul," said Mr. Sinclair the missionary. "This is bad news indeed. Yet he died for his country. He made the great sacrifice. So that we could
20 all live in peace, you understand."

Betsy shook her head. "That isn't it at all," she said. "Howie's sunk with torpedoes. That's all I know."

They saw old Hugh walking up from the shore with a pile of creels on his back and a lobster in each hand. When he came to the croft he looked at Betsy and the missionary
25 standing together in the door. He went into the outhouse and set down the creels and picked up an axe he kept for chopping wood.

Betsy said to him, "How many lobsters did you get?"

He moved past her and the missionary without speaking into the house. Then from inside he said, "I got two lobsters."

30 "I'll break the news to him," said Mr. Sinclair.

From inside the house came the noise of shattering wood and metal.

"He knows already," said Betsy to the missionary. "Hugh knows the truth of a thing generally before a word is uttered."

Hugh moved past them with the axe in his hand.

35 "I got six crabs forby," he said to Betsy, "but I left them in the boat."

He set the axe down carefully inside the door of the outhouse. Then he leaned against the wall and looked out to sea for a long while.

MARKS

"I got thirteen eggs," said Betsy. "One more than yesterday. That old Rhode Islander's laying like mad."

40 The missionary was slowly shaking his head in the doorway. He touched Hugh on the shoulder and said, "My poor man — "

Hugh turned and said to him, "It's time the last peats were down from the hill. I'll go in the morning first thing. You'll be needing a cart-load for the Manse."

The missionary, awed by such callousness, walked down the path between the cabbages
45 and potatoes. Betsy went into the house. The wireless stood, a tangled wreck, on the dresser. She brought from the cupboard a bottle of whisky and glasses. She set the kettle on the hook over the fire and broke the peats into red and yellow flame with a poker. Through the window she could see people moving towards the croft from all over the valley. The news had got round. The mourners were gathering.

50 Old Hugh stood in the door and looked up at the drift of clouds above the cliff. "Yes," he said, "I'm glad I set the creels where I did, off Yesnaby. They'll be sheltered there once the wind gets up."

"That white hen," said Betsy, "has stopped laying. It's time she was in the pot, if you ask me."

Questions

17. Look at lines 1—5.

    Explain how Mackay Brown creates both a sense of community life and the role of the wireless set within it. 2

18. Look at lines 6—22.

    (a) By referring to lines 6—15, analyse how the postman's attitude to Betsy is revealed. 2

    (b) By referring to lines 16—22, analyse how language is used to convey the different reactions of the missionary and Betsy to the news. 2

19. In lines 23—54, Mackay Brown reveals a contrast between the couple's real feelings and the missionary's perception of how they feel.

    By referring to at least two examples from these lines, analyse how the contrast is revealed. 4

20. In his writing, Mackay Brown explores the relationship between the island/small mainland community and the outside world. By referring to this extract and at least one other story by Mackay Brown, discuss how he does this. 10

[Turn over

OR

Text 3 — Prose

If you choose this text you may not attempt a question on Prose in Section 2.

Read the extract below and then attempt the following questions.

The Trick Is To Keep Breathing by Janice Galloway

In this extract, Joy is struggling to cope after the death of her partner, Michael.

Look

all I wanted was to be civilised and polite. I wanted to be no trouble. I wanted to be brave and discreet. This had to be the final stage of the endurance test and all I had to do was last out. I thought I was Bunyan's Pilgrim and Dorothy in The Wizard of Oz. But
5 the lasting out was terrible. I made appointments with the doctor and he gave me pills to tide me over when I got anxious. I got anxious when they didn't tide me over into anything different. He gave me more pills. I kept going to work. I was no nearer Kansas or the Celestial City. Then

I started smelling Michael's aftershave in the middle of the night. I would go to bed and
10 there it was, in a cloud all round my head. I thought if I could smell his aftershave he must be around somewhere. I saw him in cars, across the street, in buses, roaring past on strange motorbikes, drifting by the glass panel of my classroom door. I read his horoscope. How could he be having a difficult phase with money if he was dead? Of course he wasn't *dead*: just hiding. At night I sunk my face into his clothes and howled
15 at the cloth. A magazine article said it was fairly common and not as unhealthy as you'd think. Then I would go to bed and wait for the slow seep of aftershave through the ether. I knew he wasn't just a carcass liquefying in a wooden box but an invisible presence hovering in a cloud of Aramis above my bed. I also suspected I was lying. When I found the bottle, tipped on its side and leaking along the rim I knew for sure. I had put it there
20 myself ages ago so I could reach for it and smell his neck when I wanted to feel like hell in the middle of the night. Then I must have knocked it over and been too wilful to admit to what it was later. My own duplicity shocked me. I held onto the bottle for a week or so then threw it out.

My mother was right. I have no common sense. I don't know a damn thing worth
25 knowing.

| THE CHURCH | THE MARRIED |
| THE LAW | WHAT'S WHAT |

I haven't a clue.

The clock ticks too loud while I lie still, shrinking.

30 Please god make boulders crash through the roof. In three or four days when the Health Visitor comes she will find only mashed remains, marrowbone jelly oozing between the shards like bitumen. *Well*, she'll say, *We're not doing so well today, are we?* It's too cold. The hairs on my legs are stiff. I shiver and wish the phone would ring.

Needing people yet being afraid of them is wearing me out. I struggle with the paradox
35 all the time and can't resolve it. When people visit I am distraught trying to look as if I can cope. At work I never speak but I want to be spoken to. If anyone does I get anxious and stammer. I'm scared of the phone yet I want it to ring.

Questions

21. Look at lines 1—8.

    Analyse how Galloway makes the reader aware of Joy's efforts to cope with her situation.   **2**

22. Look at lines 9—23.

    By referring to at least two examples, analyse how the writer conveys Joy's desperation for Michael's presence.   **4**

23. Look at lines 29—37.

    By referring to at least two examples, analyse how Galloway conveys Joy's feelings of despair.   **4**

24. By referring to this extract and elsewhere in the novel, discuss how Galloway demonstrates Joy's fear and/or anxiety in relating to other people.   **10**

[Turn over

OR

Text 4 — Prose

If you choose this text you may not attempt a question on Prose in Section 2.

Read the extract below and then attempt the following questions.

Sunset Song **by Lewis Grassic Gibbon**

This extract is from the beginning of Part II (Drilling). In this extract Chris reflects on the death of her mother.

Lying down when her climb up the cambered brae was done, panting deep from the rate she'd come at — skirt flying and iron-resolute she'd turn back for nothing that cried or called in all Blawearie — no, not even that whistle of father's! — Chris felt the coarse grass crackle up beneath her into a fine quiet couch. Neck and shoulders and hips and
5 knees she relaxed, her long brown arms quivered by her side as the muscles slacked away, the day drowsed down an aureal light through the long brown lashes that drooped on her cheeks. As the gnomons of a giant dial the shadows of the Standing Stones crept into the east, snipe called and called —

Just as the last time she'd climbed to the loch: and when had that been? She opened her
10 eyes and thought, and tired from that and closed down her eyes again and gave a queer laugh. The June of last year it had been, the day when mother had poisoned herself and the twins.

So long as that and so near as that, you'd thought of the hours and days as a dark, cold pit you'd never escape. But you'd escaped, the black damp went out of the sunshine and
15 the world went on, the white faces and whispering ceased from the pit, you'd never be the same again, but the world went on and you went with it. It was not mother only that died with the twins, something died in your heart and went down with her to lie in Kinraddie kirkyard — the child in your heart died then, the bairn that believed the hills were made for its play, every road set fair with its warning posts, hands ready to snatch
20 you back from the brink of danger when the play grew over-rough. That died, and the Chris of the books and the dreams died with it, or you folded them up in their paper of tissue and laid them away by the dark, quiet corpse that was your childhood.

So Mistress Munro of the Cuddiestoun told her that awful night she came over the rain-soaked parks of Blawearie and laid out the body of mother, the bodies of the twins that
25 had died so quiet in their crib. She nipped round the rooms right quick and pert and uncaring, the black-eyed futret, snapping this order and that, it was her that terrified Dod and Alec from their crying, drove father and Will out tending the beasts. And quick and cool and cold-handed she worked, peeking over at Chris with her rat-like face. *You'll be leaving the College now, I'll warrant, education's dirt and you're better clear of it.*
30 *You'll find little time for dreaming and dirt when you're keeping house at Blawearie.*

And Chris in her pit, dazed and dull-eyed, said nothing, she minded later; and some other than herself went searching and seeking out cloths and clothes.   Then Mistress Munro washed down the body that was mother's and put it in a nightgown, her best, the one with blue ribbons on it that she hadn't worn for many a year; and fair she made her and
35 sweet to look at, the tears came at last when you saw her so, hot tears wrung from your eyes like drops of blood. But they ended quick, you would die if you wept like that for long, in place of tears a long wail clamoured endless, unanswered inside your head *Oh mother, mother, why did you do it?*

And not until days later did Chris hear why, for they tried to keep it from her and the
40 boys, but it all came out at the inquest, mother had poisoned herself, her and the twins,

Page eighteen

MARKS

because she was pregnant again and afraid with a fear dreadful and calm and clear-eyed. So she had killed herself while of unsound mind, had mother, kind-eyed and sweet, remembering those Springs of Kildrummie last of all things remembered, it may be, and the rooks that cried out across the upland parks of Don far down beyond the tunnels of
45 the years.

Questions

25. Look at lines 1—8.

    Explain fully how Chris feels in these lines.　　2

26. Look at lines 9—22.

    By referring to at least two examples, analyse how the writer conveys the impact her mother's death has had on Chris.　　4

27. Look at lines 23—45.

    By referring to at least two examples, analyse how the writer conveys the horror of Chris's memory of her mother's death.　　4

28. Discuss how Grassic Gibbon presents Chris's growing to maturity in this extract and elsewhere in the novel.　　10

[Turn over

OR

Text 5 — Prose

If you choose this text you may not attempt a question on Prose in Section 2.

Read the extract below and then attempt the following questions.

***The Cone-Gatherers* by Robin Jenkins**

This extract is taken from Chapter Four. Duror has gone to the Big House to see Lady Runcie-Campbell.

Lady Runcie-Campbell was in the office at the front of the house writing letters. When he knocked, she bade him enter in her clear courteous musical voice.

A stranger, hearing her, would have anticipated some kind of loveliness in so charming a speaker; he might not, however, have expected to find such outstanding beauty of face
5   and form married to such earnestness of spirit; and he would assuredly have been both startled and impressed.

Duror, who knew her well, had been afraid that in her presence he might be shamed or inspired into abandoning his scheme against the cone-gatherers. In spite of her clothes, expensive though simple, of her valuable adornments such as earrings, brooches, and
10 rings, and of her sometimes almost mystical sense of responsibility as a representative of the ruling class, she had an ability to exalt people out of their humdrum selves. Indeed, Duror often associated religion not with the smell of pinewood pews or of damp Bibles, but rather with her perfume, so elusive to describe. Her father the judge had bequeathed to her a passion for justice, profound and intelligent; and a determination to
15 see right done, even at the expense of rank or pride. Her husband Sir Colin was orthodox, instinctively preferring the way of a world that for many generations had allowed his family to enjoy position and wealth. Therefore he had grumbled at his wife's conscientiousness, and was fond of pointing out, with affection but without sympathy, the contradiction between her emulation of Christ and her eminence as a baronet's wife.

20 She would have given the cone-gatherers the use of the beach-hut, if Duror had not dissuaded her; and she had not forgotten to ask him afterwards what their hut was like. He had had to lie.

Now, when he was going to lie again, this time knowing it would implicate her in his chosen evil, he felt that he was about to commit before her eyes an obscene gesture,
25 such as he had falsely accused the dwarf of making. In the sunny scented room therefore, where the happy voices of the cricket players on the lawn could be heard, he suddenly saw himself standing up to the neck in a black filth, like a stags' wallowing pool deep in the wood. High above the trees shone the sun and everywhere birds sang; but this filth, as he watched, crept up until it entered his mouth, covered his ears, blinded
30 his eyes, and so annihilated him. So would he perish, he knew; and somewhere in the vision, as a presence, exciting him so that his heart beat fast, but never visible, was a hand outstretched to help him out of that mire, if he wished to be helped.

He saw her hand with its glittering rings held out to invite him to sit down.

"Good morning, Duror," she said, with a smile. "Isn't it just splendid?"

35 "Yes, my lady."

She looked at him frankly and sympathetically: it was obvious she attributed his subdued tone to sorrow over his wife. If at the same time she noticed with surprise that he hadn't shaved, it did not diminish her sympathy, as it would have her husband's.

MARKS

"How is Mrs. Duror?" she asked gently.

40 "Not too well, I'm sorry to say, my lady. This spell of fine weather has upset her. She asked me to thank you for the flowers."

She was so slim, golden-haired, and vital, that her solicitude for Peggy gripped him like a fierce cramp in his belly.

She noticed how pale he had turned, how ill he looked.

45 "I often think of your poor wife, Duror," she said.

She glanced at her husband's portrait in uniform on the desk in front of her.

Duror could not see the photograph from where he sat, but he could see clearly enough in his imagination the original, as gawky as she was beautiful, as glum as she was gay, and as matter-of-fact as she was compassionate.

50 "This war," she went on quickly, "with its dreadful separations has shown me at least what she has missed all these years. Something has come between us and the things we love, the things on which our faith depends: flowers and dogs and trees and friends. She's been cut off so much longer."

Questions

29. Look at lines 1—19.

By referring to at least two examples, analyse how Jenkins's use of language creates a positive impression of Lady Runcie-Campbell.

4

30. Look at lines 23—43.

By referring to two examples, analyse how the writer uses language to convey the contrast between Duror and Lady Runcie-Campbell.

4

31. Look at lines 50—53.

Explain why Lady Runcie-Campbell now feels more able to identify with Peggy's situation.

2

32. In the novel, Duror is presented not just as an evil character, but one who might be worthy of some sympathy.

With reference to this extract and elsewhere in the novel, explain how both aspects of Duror's character are portrayed.

10

[Turn over

SECTION 1 — SCOTTISH TEXT — 20 marks

Choose ONE text from Drama, Prose or Poetry.

Read the text extract carefully and then attempt ALL the questions for your chosen text.

You should spend about 45 minutes on this Section.

PART C — SCOTTISH TEXT — POETRY

Text 1 — Poetry

If you choose this text you may not attempt a question on Poetry in Section 2

Read the poem below and then attempt the following questions.

To a Mouse, On turning her up in her Nest, with the Plough, November 1785 by Robert Burns

Wee, sleekit, cowrin, tim'rous beastie,
O, what a panic's in thy breastie!
Thou need na start awa sae hasty,
       Wi' bickering brattle!
5 I wad be laith to rin an' chase thee,
       Wi' murd'ring pattle!

I'm truly sorry Man's dominion
Has broken Nature's social union,
An' justifies that ill opinion,
10   Which makes thee startle,
At me, thy poor, earth-born companion,
       An' fellow-mortal!

I doubt na, whyles, but thou may thieve;
What then? poor beastie, thou maun live!
15 A daimen icker in a thrave
       'S a sma' request:
I'll get a blessin wi' the lave,
       And never miss't!

Thy wee bit housie, too, in ruin!
20 It's silly wa's the win's are strewin!
An' naething, now, to big a new ane,
       O' foggage green!
An' bleak December's winds ensuin,
       Baith snell and keen!

25 Thou saw the fields laid bare an' waste,
An' weary Winter comin fast,
An' cozie here, beneath the blast,
       Thou thought to dwell,
Till crash! the cruel coulter past
30   Out thro' thy cell.

That wee bit heap o' leaves an' stibble,
Has cost thee monie a weary nibble!
Now thou's turn'd out, for a' thy trouble,
        But house or hald,
35 To thole the Winter's sleety dribble,
        An' cranreuch cauld!

But Mousie, thou art no thy lane,
In proving foresight may be vain:
The best-laid schemes o' Mice an' Men
40   Gang aft agley,
An' lea'e us nought but grief an' pain,
        For promis'd joy!

Still thou are blest, compar'd wi' me!
The present only toucheth thee:
45 But, Och! I backward cast my e'e,
        On prospects drear!
An' forward, tho' I canna see,
        I guess an' fear!

Questions

33. Look at lines 1—18.

    Analyse how Burns establishes at least two aspects of the speaker's personality in these lines.   4

34. Look at lines 19—36.

    By referring to at least two examples, analyse how Burns creates pity for the mouse and its predicament.   4

35. Look at lines 37—48.

    Explain how the final two verses highlight the contrast between the speaker and the mouse.   2

36. Discuss how Burns uses a distinctive narrative voice to convey the central concerns of this poem and at least one of his other poems.   10

[Turn over

OR

Text 2 — Poetry

If you choose this text you may not attempt a question on Poetry in Section 2.

Read the poem below and then attempt the following questions.

War Photographer **by Carol Ann Duffy**

In his dark room he is finally alone
with spools of suffering set out in ordered rows.
The only light is red and softly glows,
as though this were a church and he
5   a priest preparing to intone a Mass.
Belfast. Beirut. Phnom Penh. All flesh is grass.

He has a job to do. Solutions slop in trays
beneath his hands, which did not tremble then
though seem to now. Rural England. Home again
10 to ordinary pain which simple weather can dispel,
to fields which don't explode beneath the feet
of running children in a nightmare heat.

Something is happening. A stranger's features
faintly start to twist before his eyes,
15 a half-formed ghost. He remembers the cries
of this man's wife, how he sought approval
without words to do what someone must
and how the blood stained into foreign dust.

A hundred agonies in black and white
20 from which his editor will pick out five or six
for Sunday's supplement. The reader's eyeballs prick
with tears between the bath and pre-lunch beers.
From the aeroplane he stares impassively at where
he earns his living and they do not care.

Questions

37. Look at lines 1—6.

   Analyse how imagery is used to create a serious atmosphere.   2

38. Look at lines 7—12.

   Analyse how Duffy conveys the photographer's perception of the difference between
   life in Britain and life in the war zones abroad.   4

39. Look at lines 13—18.

   Analyse the use of poetic technique to convey the distressing nature of the
   photographer's memories.   2

40. Look at lines 19—24.

   Analyse how the use of poetic technique highlights the British public's indifference
   to the suffering shown in the newspapers they read.   2

41. Referring closely to this poem and to at least one other poem by Duffy, discuss how
   she explores the link between the past and the present.   10

[Turn over

OR

Text 3 — Poetry

If you choose this text you may not attempt a question on Poetry in Section 2.

Read the poem below and then attempt the following questions.

My Rival's House by Liz Lochhead

is peopled with many surfaces.
Ormolu and gilt, slipper satin,
lush velvet couches,
cushions so stiff you can't sink in.
5 Tables polished clear enough to see distortions in.

We take our shoes off at her door,
shuffle stocking-soled, tiptoe — the parquet floor
is beautiful and its surface must
be protected. Dust-
10 cover, drawn shade,
won't let the surface colour fade.

Silver sugar-tongs and silver salver,
my rival serves us tea.
She glosses over him and me.
15 I am all edges, a surface, a shell
and yet my rival thinks she means me well.
But what squirms beneath her surface I can tell.
Soon, my rival
capped tooth, polished nail
20 will fight, fight foul for her survival.
Deferential, daughterly, I sip
and thank her nicely for each bitter cup.

And I have much to thank her for.
This son she bore —
25 first blood to her —
never, never can escape scot free
the sour potluck of family.
And oh how close
this family that furnishes my rival's place.

30 Lady of the house.
Queen bee.
She is far more unconscious,
far more dangerous than me.
Listen, I was always my own worst enemy.
35 She has taken even this from me.

She dishes up her dreams for breakfast.
Dinner, and her salt tears pepper our soup.
She won't
give up.

MARKS

Questions

42. Look at lines 1—11.

    Explain why the speaker feels uncomfortable in her rival's house.   **2**

43. Look at lines 12—22.

    By referring to at least two examples, analyse how the poet creates a tense atmosphere in these lines.   **4**

44. Look at lines 23—39.

    By referring to at least two examples, discuss how the speaker's resentment of her rival is made clear.   **4**

45. Discuss how Lochhead uses descriptive detail to explore personality in this and at least one other poem.   **10**

[Turn over

OR

Text 4 — Poetry

If you choose this text you may not attempt a question on Poetry in Section 2.

Read the poem below and then attempt the following questions.

Visiting Hour **by Norman MacCaig**

The hospital smell
combs my nostrils
as they go bobbing along
green and yellow corridors.

5   What seems a corpse
is trundled into a lift and vanishes
heavenward.

I will not feel, I will not
feel, until
10 I have to.

Nurses walk lightly, swiftly,
here and up and down and there,
their slender waists miraculously
carrying their burden
15 of so much pain, so
many deaths, their eyes
still clear after
so many farewells.

Ward 7. She lies
20 in a white cave of forgetfulness.
A withered hand
trembles on its stalk. Eyes move
behind eyelids too heavy
to raise. Into an arm wasted
25 of colour a glass fang is fixed,
not guzzling but giving.
And between her and me
distance shrinks till there is none left
but the distance of pain that neither she nor I
30 can cross.

She smiles a little at this
black figure in her white cave
who clumsily rises
in the round swimming waves of a bell
35 and dizzily goes off, growing fainter,
not smaller, leaving behind only
books that will not be read
and fruitless fruits.

MARKS

Questions

46. Look at lines 1—7.

Analyse how the poet's use of language conveys his response to his surroundings.

2

47. Look at lines 8—18.

Analyse how MacCaig uses language to highlight his own sense of inadequacy.

4

48. Look at lines 19—38.

Analyse how the poet's use of language emphasises the painful nature of the situation for both patient and visitor.

4

49. By referring to this poem, and at least one other by MacCaig, discuss how he explores the theme of loss in his work.

10

[Turn over

OR

Text 5 — Poetry

If you choose this text you may not attempt a question on Poetry in Section 2.

Read the poem below and then attempt the following questions.

An Autumn Day by Sorley MacLean

On that slope
on an autumn day,
the shells soughing about my ears
and six dead men at my shoulder,
5 dead and stiff — and frozen were it not for the heat —
as if they were waiting for a message.

When the screech came
out of the sun,
out of an invisible throbbing,
10 the flame leaped and the smoke climbed
and surged every way:
blinding of eyes, splitting of hearing.

And after it, the six men dead
the whole day:
15 among the shells snoring
in the morning,
and again at midday
and in the evening.

In the sun, which was so indifferent,
20 so white and painful;
on the sand which was so comfortable,
easy and kindly;
and under the stars of Africa,
jewelled and beautiful.

25 One Election took them
and did not take me,
without asking us
which was better or worse:
it seemed as devilishly indifferent
30 as the shells.

Six men dead at my shoulder
on an Autumn day.

MARKS

Questions

50. Look at lines 1—12.

    By referring to at least two examples, analyse how the poet's use of language emphasises the impact of this experience.

    4

51. Look at lines 13—24.

    By referring to at least two examples, analyse how the poet uses language to highlight how meaningless the men's deaths were.

    4

52. Look at lines 25—32.

    Explain what the speaker finds puzzling when he reflects on the men's deaths.

    2

53. Nature is a significant aspect in MacLean's poetry. Discuss how he uses nature to convey the central concern(s) of this poem and those of at least one other poem.

    10

[Turn over

OR

Text 6 — Poetry

If you choose this text you may not attempt a question on Poetry in Section 2.

Read the poem below and then attempt the following questions.

Two Trees **by Don Paterson**

One morning, Don Miguel got out of bed
with one idea rooted in his head:
to graft his orange to his lemon tree.
It took him the whole day to work them free,
5   lay open their sides, and lash them tight.
For twelve months, from the shame or from the fright
they put forth nothing; but one day there appeared
two lights in the dark leaves. Over the years
the limbs would get themselves so tangled up
10 each bough looked like it gave a double crop,
and not one kid in the village didn't know
the magic tree in Miguel's patio.

The man who bought the house had had no dream
so who can say what dark malicious whim
15 led him to take his axe and split the bole
along its fused seam, and then dig two holes.
And no, they did not die from solitude;
nor did their branches bear a sterile fruit;
nor did their unhealed flanks weep every spring
20 for those four yards that lost them everything
as each strained on its shackled root to face
the other's empty, intricate embrace.
They were trees, and trees don't weep or ache or shout.
And trees are all this poem is about.

MARKS

Questions

54. Look at lines 1—12.

By referring to at least two examples, analyse how the poet's use of poetic technique emphasises the importance of the story of the trees.   4

55. Look at lines 13—16.

By referring to at least two examples, analyse how the poet's use of language creates an impression of "the man".   4

56. Explain the irony of the final two lines.   2

57. Discuss how Paterson develops the theme of relationships in this and at least one other poem.   10

[END OF SECTION 1]

[Turn over

SECTION 2 — CRITICAL ESSAY — 20 marks

Attempt ONE question from the following genres — Drama, Prose Fiction, Prose Non-fiction, Poetry, Film and Television Drama, or Language.

Your answer must be on a different genre from that chosen in Section 1.

You should spend approximately 45 minutes on this Section.

PART A — DRAMA

> *Answers to questions on Drama should refer to the text and to such relevant features as characterisation, key scene(s), structure, climax, theme, plot, conflict, setting . . .*

1. Choose a play in which a major character's actions influence the emotions of others.

   Briefly explain how the dramatist presents these emotions and actions and discuss how this contributes to your understanding of the play as a whole.

2. Choose a play in which there is a scene involving a moment of conflict or of resolution to conflict.

   By referring to details of the scene, explain how the dramatist presents this moment and discuss how this contributes to your appreciation of the play as a whole.

3. Choose a play which explores an important issue or issues within society.

   Briefly explain the nature of the issue(s) and discuss how the dramatist's presentation of the issue(s) contributed to your appreciation of the play as a whole.

PART B — PROSE FICTION

Answers to questions on Prose Fiction should refer to the text and to such relevant features as characterisation, setting, language, key incident(s), climax, turning point, plot, structure, narrative technique, theme, ideas, description . . .

4. Choose a novel **or** short story in which the method of narration is important.

   Outline briefly the writer's method of narration and explain why you feel this method makes such a major contribution to your understanding of the text as a whole.

5. Choose a novel **or** short story in which there is a moment of significance for one of the characters.

   Explain briefly what the significant moment is and discuss, with reference to appropriate techniques, its significance to the text as a whole.

6. Choose a novel **or** short story which has a satisfying ending.

   Discuss to what extent the ending provides a successful conclusion to the text as a whole.

PART C — PROSE NON-FICTION

Answers to questions on Prose Non-fiction should refer to the text and to such relevant features as ideas, use of evidence, stance, style, selection of material, narrative voice . . .

Non fiction texts can include travel writing, journalism, autobiography, biography, essays . . .

7. Choose a non-fiction text which recreates a moment in time.

   Discuss how the description effectively recreates this moment and show how important this is to your appreciation of the text as a whole.

8. Choose a non-fiction text which is structured in a particularly effective way.

   Explain how the structure enhances the impact of the writer's message.

9. Choose a non-fiction text which made you consider your views about a social or political or ethical issue.

   Explain what the issue is and how the writer uses language effectively to engage you.

[Turn over

PART D — POETRY

Answers to questions on Poetry should refer to the text and to such relevant features as word choice, tone, imagery, structure, content, rhythm, rhyme, theme, sounds, ideas . . .

10. Choose a poem which takes as its starting point a memorable experience.

Discuss how the poet's presentation of the experience helps you to appreciate its significance.

11. Choose a poem which encourages you to think differently or to understand something in a new way.

Discuss how the poet's ideas and techniques led you to change your thinking or understanding.

12. Choose a poem which is written in a particular poetic form or which has a particularly effective structure.

Discuss how the poet's use of form or structure contributes to the impact of the poem's central concern(s).

PART E — FILM AND TELEVISION DRAMA

Answers to questions on Film and Television Drama* should refer to the text and to such relevant features as use of camera, key sequence, characterisation, mise-en-scène, editing, music/sound, special effects, plot, dialogue . . .

13. Choose a film **or** television drama in which the setting in time or place is important.

Explain how the film or programme makers use media techniques effectively to create this setting.

14   Choose a film **or** television drama where the hero is not completely good and/or the villain is not completely bad.

Explain how the film or programme makers use media techniques to develop the hero and/or villain.

15. Choose a film **or** television drama in which lighting and/or sound makes an important contribution to the impact of a particular sequence.

Explain how the film or programme makers use lighting and/or sound to enhance your appreciation of the sequence.

* "television drama" includes a single play, a series or a serial.

PART F — LANGUAGE

Answers to questions on Language should refer to the text and to such relevant features as register, accent, dialect, slang, jargon, vocabulary, tone, abbreviation . . .

16. Choose the language associated with a particular vocational or interest group.

    Identify some examples of the language used within the group and discuss to what extent this shared language contributes to the effectiveness of the group's activities.

17. Choose the language of radio or television reporting on a topic such as sport, films, nature, science . . .

    Identify some of the features of this language and discuss to what extent they are effective in communicating with the target audience.

18. Choose a commercial advertising campaign which makes use of persuasive language.

    By examining specific examples, evaluate their effectiveness in achieving the purpose of the campaign.

[END OF SECTION 2]

[END OF QUESTION PAPER]

[BLANK PAGE]

DO NOT WRITE ON THIS PAGE

[BLANK PAGE]

DO NOT WRITE ON THIS PAGE

[BLANK PAGE]

DO NOT WRITE ON THIS PAGE

HIGHER FOR CfE | ANSWER SECTION

SQA AND HODDER GIBSON HIGHER FOR CfE ENGLISH 2015

HIGHER FOR CfE ENGLISH
MODEL PAPER 1

PAPER 1 — READING FOR UNDERSTANDING, ANALYSIS AND EVALUATION

Marking Instructions for each question

Passage 1

Question		Expected Response	Max Mark	Additional Guidance
1.	(a)	Candidates should analyse how the writer conveys the destructive nature of the First World War. Marks will depend on the quality of comment on appropriate language feature(s). 2 marks may be awarded for reference plus detailed/insightful comment; 1 mark for reference plus more basic comment; 0 marks for reference alone. *Possible answers are shown in the "Additional Guidance" column.*	4	Possible answers include: *Word choice* • any of "boomed … screamed … rattled … cracked … cries … echoed" with appropriate comment on connotation of chosen word(s), such as violent, aggressive, disturbing, discordant • "desolate" suggests barren land, no life, isolation • "reduced" suggests deterioration, a negative process of erosion • "piles" suggests random and unsightly nature of the ruins • "smoking rubble" highlights total devastation, nothing remained but debris • "acre upon acre" suggests the vast, endless area affected, all reduced to similar state of devastation • "splintered" suggests broken into small, unrecognisable pieces; the woodland was beyond hope of repair or regeneration • "blackened stumps" suggests trees are broken, fire-damaged remains of what they once were *Onomatopoeia* • any of "boomed … screamed … rattled … cracked" emphasises incessant, debilitating noise on the battlefield; conveys the varying pitches of sound (from low and threatening to high and frightening) *Sentence Structure* • list ("howitzers … dying") suggests never-ending/frantic activity, the variety of sensory assault • in the first sentence of paragraph one there is a lengthy build up of noise/drama followed the sudden simplicity of "suddenly fell quiet" to contrast the horror of war with the suddenness of peace or any other acceptable answer
	(b)	Candidates should explain what effects the war had on "those left behind"? Candidates must use their own words. No marks are awarded for verbatim quotations from the passage. *1 mark for each point from the "Additional Guidance" column.*	3	Possible answers include: • some could not celebrate the fact, could not feel happy that the war was finally over (explanation of "little cause for rejoicing") • they were exhausted/weakened (explanation of "enervated") • some thought deeply about their experience (explanation of "some were able to remember and reflect on what they had been through") • some soldiers were confused, adrift, numb (explanation of "Others simply felt lost") • their lives were dominated by the experience of war (explanation of "The war had swallowed them up …"/"occupied their every waking moment")

Question		Expected Response	Max Mark	Additional Guidance
	(b)	*(continued)*		• they would never be free from the nightmare/ could not escape from memories (explanation of "… just as it was to haunt their dreams in the future")
				or any other acceptable answer
2.		Candidates should explain what the writer suggests is surprising about the way people in Britain view the First World War? Candidates must use their own words. No marks are awarded for verbatim quotations from the passage. *1 or 2 marks (depending on the quality of the explanation) for each point from the "Additional Guidance" column.*	3	Possible answers include: • despite Britain's involvement in more recent/ equally terrible conflicts, we still view the First World War as having a greater significance (explanation of "There have been other wars since 1918 … collective imagination.") • despite the losses suffered by many countries involved in the First World War, Britain still considers itself to have suffered more than these other nations (explanation of "The international catastrophe that was the First World War has been adopted as a peculiarly national trauma.") or any other acceptable answer
3.		Candidates should identify three important ways the First World War affected Britain. Candidates must use their own words. No marks are awarded for verbatim quotations from the passage. *1 mark for each point from the "Additional Guidance" column.*	3	Possible answers include: • enormous numbers of (young) men were killed (as per statistics) • the talents and/or potential of a generation were destroyed (explanation of "flower of British youth") • a society which seemed ideal and had no evils or imperfections ceased to exist (explanation of "Eden"and/or "prelapsarian") • an imagined idyllic world was gone forever (explanation of "somehow always perfect summer weather") • the loss of hope/optimism (explanation of "yearningly back rather than expectantly forward") or any other acceptable answer
4.		Candidates should analyse how the writer's use of language conveys how important the First World War has become to us. Marks will depend on the quality of comment on appropriate language feature(s). 2 marks may be awarded for reference plus detailed/insightful comment; 1 mark for reference plus more basic comment; 0 marks for reference alone. *Possible answers are shown in the "Additional Guidance" column.*	4	Possible answers include: • "tremendously large place" suggests the war occupies an overwhelming space, is of great importance in our thoughts • "the world and its history" a somewhat grandiose concept of the War's all-encompassing influence • "seemingly endless resource" suggests the war is a continuous source of inspiration, has unlimited potential • list of professions ("novelists … composers") emphasises the vast range of literature and media which is inspired by the history of the First World War • "engraved" just as "engraved" is to have been permanently marked by cutting into a surface so the images from the First World War are permanently lodged in our minds • "the national consciousness" suggests the awareness is deeply ingrained in what it means to be British • "(recognise them) instantly" suggests that images of the war have become like old friends; we are deeply familiar with these images • list of the "images" emphasises the number/ range of images we have stored in our consciousness

Question		Expected Response	Max Mark	Additional Guidance
4.		*(continued)*	4	• sequence/order of list in final sentence: it could be argued that the final list acts rather like a condensed chronology/a series of snapshots of the war, thus reminding us that we are so familiar with these events that they can be summarized in a few powerful phrases • repetitive structure used to describe each image of war ("the foreign place ... the lines ... the rows ... the scarlet poppies.") repetition builds to a climax which reminds us of the power contained within the inevitable image of poppies/shell-holes or any other acceptable answer
5.		Candidates should explain in their own words the two opposing views of the First World War. Candidates must use their own words. No marks are awarded for verbatim quotations from the passage. *1 mark for each point from the "Additional Guidance" column.*	4	Possible answers include: *Traditional view:* • the leaders did not know what they were doing/made serious mistakes (explanation of "incompetent High Command") • the loss of life was a continual, relentless process (explanation of "repeatedly") • the High Command deliberately, callously sent soldiers to their deaths (explanation of "sacrificed") • the death toll was staggeringly high (explanation of "thousands of men") • there was so little gain (explanation of "a few yards of churned earth") • the conditions were especially squalid (explanation of "mud, blood") • it seemed a pointless waste of life (explanation of "futility") *Alternative view:* • the leaders were not all cold-hearted bunglers (explanation of "callous incompetents") • the front line soldiers were not all ill-fated conscripts (explanation of "hapless and unwilling") • some of the battles were extremely well executed (explanation of "brilliantly planned and fought") • we must remember that we did actually emerge victorious (explanation of "we did, after all, win the war") or any other acceptable answer
6.		Candidates should evaluate the effectiveness of the last two paragraphs as a thought-provoking and emotional conclusion to the passage as a whole. Marks will depend on the quality of evaluative comment. 2 marks may be awarded for reference plus detailed/insightful comment; 1 mark for reference plus more basic comment; 0 marks for reference alone. For full marks there must be reference to ideas and language, but there is no requirement for a balanced treatment of these elements. There must also be some comment on the effectiveness of these lines as "a thought-provoking and emotional conclusion to the passage". *Possible answers are shown in the "Additional Guidance" column.*	4	Possible answers include: *Ideas:* • the overall poignancy of referring to the very last survivor of the War, the last living link to this momentous event • the opening sentence of the penultimate paragraph stresses our interest in first-hand testimony, "what it was like" — Harry Patch is able to provide this • Harry Patch's experiences give us a view of war which is very different from that of military historians • Harry's lack of knowledge about military strategies reminds us of the writer's earlier point about the difference between ordinary soldiers and High Command

Question	Expected Response	Max Mark	Additional Guidance
6.	*(continued)*		• the writer has already mentioned the terrible conditions endured by combatants — Harry Patch's memories of "filth … discomfort … exhaustion …" remind us of these conditions • the writer chooses to conclude using direct quotation to highlight the authentic voice of someone directly involved • Harry Patch's comment on the "expendable" nature of ordinary soldiers harks back to the popular view that the war was "conducted by an incompetent High Command"/war was nothing but "mud, blood and futility" • Harry Patch's comment that the war was "a terrible waste" reinforces the writer's earlier point about the terrible losses sustained during the First World War *Language:* • italicization of "like" reminds reader of importance of eyewitness accounts and allows writer to introduce Harry Patch/links to "he knew what a battlefield was like." • "diminished band" — links back to writer's earlier points about loss • "wading around in the filth" — brings us back to the opening view of devastation on the battlefields of France and reminds us that Harry experienced this • "lice-ridden … discomfort … exhaustion … fear" — list of difficult conditions reinforces the writer's earlier point about the nature of warfare • "blown to pieces" — quotation reminds us of devastating nature of First World War • "millions of men" — enormous/indeterminate number is used to remind us of the immense scale of the conflict and the terrible human cost of the war • "expendable" — reminds us of the sacrifices made by Harry and his comrades • "waste … terrible waste" — repetition is used to highlight the futility of casualties in the First World War or any other acceptable answer

Passage 2

Question		Expected Response	Max Mark	Additional Guidance
7.		Candidates should identify key areas of agreement in the two passages by referring in detail to both. There may be some overlap among the areas of agreement. Markers will have to judge the extent to which a candidate has covered two points or one. Candidates can use bullet points in this final question, or write a number of linked statements. Evidence from the passage may include quotations, but these should be supported by explanations. *Approach to marking is shown in the "Additional Guidance" column.* *Key areas of agreement are shown in the grid below. Other answers are possible.*	5	The mark for this question should reflect the quality of response in two areas: • identification of the key areas of agreement in attitude/ideas • level of detail given in support The following guidelines should be used: **Five marks** — comprehensive identification of three or more key areas of agreement with full use of supporting evidence **Four marks** — clear identification of three or more key areas of agreement with relevant use of supporting evidence **Three marks** — identification of three or more key areas of agreement with supporting evidence **Two marks** — identification of two key areas of agreement with supporting evidence **One mark** — identification of one key area of agreement with supporting evidence **Zero marks** — failure to identify any key area of agreement and/or total misunderstanding of task

	Area of Agreement	Peter Parker	William Boyd
1.	it has had a profound effect on the British psyche	it still has strong hold on the national consciousness, more so than in any other country involved	a century later, WWI continues to loom large in the nation's consciousness and media
2.	it was a conflict which changed attitudes to war	the scale of the slaughter changed the British mind-set — we tend to look back to a Golden Age before 1914 rather than to the future	casualties were so high that they changed attitudes — no army or nation would accept them today
3.	the scale of casualties — never experienced before or since	British casualties were far greater than in any other war at any time in history	the unprecedented British and Empire casualty figures cannot be forgotten
4.	the horrific nature of warfare — trenches and weapons of mass destruction	the scale of the slaughter meant Britain lost a "generation" — "the flower of British youth"	in the minds of British people it is the mass slaughter of the Western front which dominates
5.	many people believe the conflict was futile (because of the leaders' incompetence)	conventional view that leadership was inept	the 500-mile line of trenches, the war of attrition; the outdated tactics in the face of modern weapons
6.	the enduring impact of war literature, iconography, music, films	the war features in a large body of work — history textbooks, novels, poems, plays, films and musical compositions	in Britain our literature, films and documentaries have kept memories alive
7.	the impact of combatants" personal narratives, memories, recollections	memoirs/memories such as those of Harry Patch inspire deep interest	his family connections with WW1 have ignited/sustained his interest

HIGHER FOR CfE ENGLISH
MODEL PAPER 1

PAPER 2 — CRITICAL READING

SECTION 1 — Scottish Text

For all Scottish Texts, marking of the final question, for 10 marks, should be guided by the following generic instruction in conjunction with the specific advice given for the question on each Scottish Text:

Candidates can answer in bullet points in this final question, or write a number of linked statements.

0 marks for reference/quotation alone.

Up to 2 marks can be achieved for identifying elements of commonality as identified in the question.
A further 2 marks can be achieved for reference to the extract given.
6 additional marks can be awarded for discussion of similar references to at least one other part of the text (or other story or poem) by the writer.

In practise this means:

Identification of commonality (2) (e.g.: theme, characterisation, use of imagery, settng, or any other key element ...)

from the extract:

1 × relevant reference to technique/idea/feature (1)
1 × appropriate comment (1)
(maximum of 2 marks only for discussion of extract)

from at least one other text/part of the text:

2 marks for detailed/insightful comment plus quotation/reference

1 mark for more basic comment plus quotation/reference

0 marks for quotation/reference alone

(Up to 6 marks).

SCOTTISH TEXT (DRAMA)

Text 1 — Drama — *The Slab Boys* **by John Byrne**

Question	Expected Response	Max Mark	Additional Guidance
1.	Candidates should identify an aspect of Lucille's character and support this with reference to the text. 1 mark for an aspect of character; 1 for reference and explanation. 0 marks for reference/quotation alone.	2	Possible answers include: *Character:* • brash, self-confident, menacing/bullying/ aggressive/threatening *Reference to and explanation of:* • "Burton's Corner ... quarter to ... okay?" — laying down the law • "put some cream on that pimple ... I swear it's twice the size it was this morning" — less than diplomatic • "look at him ... he's a skelf" — open insult • "Aw, go to hell" — rudely dismissive • "He eats smouts like you for his breakfast" — relishing possibility of Phil's suffering • "If you're not there on the dot ..." — she's the boss • "so be warned!" — threatening

Question	Expected Response	Max Mark	Additional Guidance
2.	Candidates should explain how Hector's words and actions reveal his new-found confidence. 1 mark for each appropriate reference with comment. 0 marks for reference/quotation alone.	4	Possible answers include: • speaks "Bravely" suggesting he is prepared to stand up for himself • not interested in apology/explanation from Alan • confidence shown in "Well, you guys …" • not ashamed/shy to say getting a lift from the boss • dismissive "keep that fitch" — he's moved on to better things • keeps the money — doesn't give in to Spanky's demand • has the confidence to come back in • issues orders to Spanky — puts him in his place • uses Spanky's surname to sound controlling, dominant • cheeky to Phil about his laziness • restores pen to rightful owner
3.	Candidates should analyse Alan's speech to explain his attitude to Phil and Spanky. 1 mark for the general tone of superiority, talking down to them, sneering … 1 mark for each appropriate reference and comment. 0 marks for reference/quotation alone.	4	Possible answers include: • sneers at Phil's self-pity ("doing a pretty good job of that on your own") • mock geniality of "buy you a small beer perhaps" • "Sparky" — pay-back for all the wrong names he's been called • reference to stepping on fingers portrays him as Neanderthal • "cabinet's an embarrassment" — repeating Curry's earlier words aligns Alan with bosses
4.	Candidates should discuss the role of Lucille or Hector in the play as a whole and should refer to appropriate textual evidence to support their discussion. 0 marks for reference/quotation alone.	10	The generic marking guide, covering aspects of commonality, can be found on page 193. In comments on the rest of the play, possible references include: *Lucille* • the complications over who is her date at the Staffie • her sharp-tongued ability to stand up to Phil • her being terrified by appearance of Hector at window *Hector* • the hapless butt of Phil and Spanky's mockery • the farcical nature of his make-over • his changed status by the end of the play — gets a desk Many other references are possible.

Text 2 — Drama — *The Cheviot, the Stag and the Black, Black Oil* by John McGrath

Question		Expected Response	Max Mark	Additional Guidance
5.	(i)	Candidates should identify an aspect of Andy's character and support this with reference to the text. 1 mark for an aspect of character; 1 for reference and explanation. 0 marks for reference/quotation alone.	2	Possible answers include: • spiv, on the make, self-seeking — the seemingly endless list of tacky money-making schemes he can reel off • cynical, corrupt ("these are the best men money can buy") • obsessed with modernity ("the thing of the future", "to cater for the younger set") • no sense of traditional beauty, values ("formerly there was hee-haw but scenery") • slovenly of speech: ("yous … wes've … and that … hee-haw")
	(ii)	Candidates should identify **four** specific details of Andy's plan and analyse how each one is made to sound comical. 1 mark for each acceptable explanation. 0 marks for simply identifying an aspect of the plan.	4	Possible answers include: • "Crammem Inn": "Inn" suggests something welcoming, traditional, but this has idea of cramming in as many as possible • "High Rise Motorcroft": "croft" suggests traditional, homely, but Motorcroft sounds industrial, lots of cars, etc.; also anything high rise would look hideously out of place • "Frying Scotsman" is a pun on Flying Scotsman (an object of pride, beauty); changing to "Frying" is a dig at Scots' penchant for fried food • "All Night Chipperama" — unhealthy food; "Chipperama" suggests on a lavish, garish scale; "all night" would be noisy, disruptive • "Fingal's Caff" — pun on Fingal's Cave; "caff" (as opposed to "café") has overtones of cheap and nasty • "seaweed-suppers-in-the-basket" — "supper" idea is joke from "fish supper" etc.; "in-the-basket" is a dig at the then current fashion for meals such as chicken-in-the-basket • "draught Drambuie" — having a powerful liqueur on draught is ludicrous, suggests Andy either doesn't know what it is or sees no problem in drinking spirits by the pint • "Grouse-a-go-go" — some kind of discotheque, coined with the "a-go-go" tag from current fashion with something/anything remotely Highland • "a drive-in clachan on every hill-top" — "clachan" suggests something old, established, with a sense of community; "drive-in" is the ultimate in modern convenience
6.		Candidates should explain how Lord Vat is made to be a figure of fun to the audience. 1 mark for each acceptable reference and comment. 0 marks for reference/quotation alone.	4	Possible answers include: • his very name: Vat of Glenlivet — meant to sound like a traditional Highland title, but in fact is a joke about whisky and overindulgence • "these are my mountains" ridiculous claim, as if he glibly believes he owns the landscape (+ humorous hint of song of same title) • "ancient Scotch family" — use of "Scotch" ironically shows he is anglified, out of touch • "I represent the spirit of the Highlands" — vain, pompous (perhaps, in an ironic way, true) • "hordes of common people" — shows his unquestioning contempt for "common people", comically condemned out of his own mouth • "No amount of money could" — we rather suspect this won't be true

Question		Expected Response	Max Mark	Additional Guidance
6.		*(continued)*		• "the couthie way of life" — cringe-making reference to imaginary lifestyle • confusion of Bantu and Highlander, Sherpa and stalker shows he doesn't even know which continent he's in • approves of Highlanders only because they're good servants • "ghillie-wallah" — again confusing Indian servant with Highland one • unconscious double entendre in "doing up your flies" • "wouldn't part [for] half a million" — yet quickly begins a bartering session which is soon settled • "Cash"/"Done": comic conclusion, like a rehearsed routine
7.		Candidates should discuss McGrath's use of caricatures and/or stereotypes (there will be an element of overlap, which should be allowed) and should refer to appropriate textual evidence to support their discussion. 0 marks for reference/quotation alone.	10	The generic marking guide, covering aspects of commonality, can be found on page 193. In comments on the rest of the play, possible references include: • the compliant Minister who connives with the landlord • Texas Jim with his square dance and love of his "home" • the characters represented by the two Singers (Dr Green of Surrey, Herr Heinrich Harr, etc.) Many other references are possible.

Text 3 — Drama — *Men Should Weep* by Ena Lamont Stewart

Question		Expected Response	Max Mark	Additional Guidance
8.		Candidates should explain what impressions are created of Jenny's character. 1 mark for each impression supported by reference. 0 marks for reference/quotation alone.	3	Possible answers include: • her appearance (make-up, clothing, hair) suggests someone rather brazen, "loose", unconcerned with appearances • "Leave me go" — suggests defiance, aggression, no fear of father • "shakes herself free" — suggests independence, lack of respect for father • "glaring at each other" — suggests she is strong-willed, not intimidated by her father • "... in front o ma friend!" — suggests concern for status, lack of concern for father's point of view, perhaps taunting him with unknown "friend" • " I'm grown up noo" — suggests she is assertive, tired of being treated like a child • "An I tellt ye!" — suggests anger in her voice, standing up for herself • "Nane o your damned interferin business" — suggests prepared to insult, defy her father, use provocative language

Question	Expected Response	Max Mark	Additional Guidance
9.	Candidates should explain how the playwright creates a dramatic conflict between John and Jenny. 1 mark for each relevant point supported by reference. 0 marks for reference/quotation alone.	4	Possible answers include: • the fact that all the speeches in these lines are short and aggressive, frequently indicated by use of exclamation marks • John grabs her — physical hostility • the aggression in "Where wis ye? Answer me!" — harsh question and command • Jenny's sullen, minimal response "At the pickshers." • John's relentless demand for more information (to begin with he wanted to know where she was, now it's where she was after that) • her behaviour when he lets her go — "flops" suggesting lack of respect; "glaring sullenly" showing her antagonism; "rubbing her shoulder" to remind John (and the audience) of his manhandling of her • John, with both questions answered, presses on with dismissive comment about her friend — "yon" sounds contemptuous • Jenny's provocative response "That's a peety. I dae." • John resorts to insulting language: "Ye impudent little bitch" • the open threat of more violence: "Tak ma belt tae ye." • Jenny's dismissive, sneering, challenging, defiant "Jist you try it!"
10.	Candidates should explain how John's anger is conveyed to the audience. 1 mark for each reference and comment. 0 marks for reference/quotation alone.	3	Possible answers include: • "paint smeared" — he belittles her appearance; "paint" instead of "make-up", "smeared" suggesting something messy, unattractive • "a ower yer face" — as if she has applied it randomly, made herself look hideous • "Look at yersel!" — antagonistic exclamation, implying she looks a mess • "drags … propels … holding … scrubs" — violent, aggressive actions suggesting his temper • "There!" — a sort of triumphant declaration of his victory • "the colour God meant it tae be" — self-righteous, pompous moralising
11.	Candidates should discuss the role of Jenny in the play and should refer to appropriate textual evidence to support their discussion. 0 marks for reference/quotation alone.	10	The generic marking guide, covering aspects of commonality, can be found on page 193. In comments on the rest of the play, possible references include: • Jenny as rebel, independent spirit • prepared to do anything to escape her family and its poverty • the showdown with her father at the end Many other references are possible.

Text 1 — Prose — *The Crater* by Iain Crichton Smith

Question	Expected Response	Max Mark	Additional Guidance
12.	Candidates should analyse how the writer uses sound to intensify the atmosphere. 2 marks for an insightful comment and reference. 1 mark for a basic comment and reference. 0 marks for reference/quotation alone.	4	Possible answers include: • "screamed" suggests uncontrolled, panicky, high-pitched, in pain • "bubbling" suggests feeble, dislocated, connotations of something vaguely supernatural, unworldly • "splashing" suggests frantic activity • "breathing, frantic breathing" suggests someone struggling to stay alive • "splashings came closer" suggests something menacing getting nearer • "voice was like an animal's" suggests inhuman, lack of control • "a mixture of curses and prayers" a surreal, confused combination of anger and invocation
13.	Candidates should explain how the writer creates a nightmarish atmosphere. 2 marks for an insightful comment and reference. 1 mark for a basic comment and reference. 0 marks for reference/quotation alone.	4	Possible answers include: • "as if there was a great fish at the end of a line" suggests that he's struggling with some mythical creature • "He felt it moving." — short sentence creates feeling of shock, threat • "moon shone suddenly out" — abrupt, dramatic change in light • "in that moment he saw it" — sudden revelation; use of unspecific "it" reinforces dreamlike effect • "covered with greenish slime" sickening, disgusting • "an obscene mermaid" — something usually considered attractive, glamorous is distorted • "two eyes, white in the green face" — disembodied, unsettling • "the mouth, gritted, tried not to let the blood through" — suggests the effort, the pain, the suffering • "monster of the deep" — frightening, threatening, aggressive being from another world • "he said to the monster below" — idea of dialogue with a "monster" is disturbing • "emerging from the deep" — suggestion of approaching threat, some sort of prehistoric monster rising from a swamp • "all green, all mottled, like a disease" — horrific description of a slimy, blotchy creature, which is likened to a sickness/virus • "stench" — emphasises the overwhelming unpleasantness and horror of the scene • "It hung there ..." — creates picture of something supernatural, defying gravity
14.	Candidates should discuss what the sentence "And over it poured the merciless moonlight." contributes to the conclusion of the extract. 2 marks for an insightful comment and reference. 1 mark for a basic comment and reference. 0 marks for reference/quotation alone.	2	Possible answers include: • it creates sense of the cruelty of nature, the moon as observer of the macabre proceedings below • it is as if, while Robert frantically (and heroically) seeks to rescue his comrade, a greater power knows the futility of it • it prepares the reader for the shattering of Robert's elation at his "rescue"

Question	Expected Response	Max Mark	Additional Guidance
15.	Candidates should discuss how Crichton Smith creates tension in *The Crater* and at least one other story and should refer to appropriate textual evidence to support their discussion. 0 marks for reference/quotation alone.	10	The generic marking guide, covering aspects of commonality, can be found on page 193. In comments on other stories, possible references include: • the elder's approach in *The Telegram* • the ending of *Mother and Son* • the dying man in *The Crater* Many other references are possible.

Text 2 — Prose — *The Bright Spade* by George Mackay Brown

Question	Expected Response	Max Mark	Additional Guidance
16.	Candidates should identify the narrator's tone and explain how it is created. 1 mark for an appropriate identification of tone + 2 marks for a single insightful explanation; 1 mark for a basic explanation. 0 marks for reference/quotation alone.	3	Possible answers include: Tone: unemotional, detached, purely factual References: • preponderance of simple, flat, sentences, no elaboration • as if simple reportage, statement of fact • absence of comment, reflection — even at a detail as gruesome as the dog gnawing the corpse or a detail as bizarre as Jacob's acceptance of the fiddle • even the imagery ("shell … chrysalis") sounds more factual than evocative
17.	Candidates should explain what impressions the narrator creates of Harald Ness as a person. 1 mark for each reference and comment. 0 marks for reference/quotation alone.	2	Possible answers include: • seems to be looked up to, respected — speaks uninterrupted, his plan is accepted without demur • unemotional, absence of self-pity when he describes what he has eaten • realistic, practical, pragmatic plan • includes himself in risky venture — brave, prepared to accept risks on behalf of others, sacrifice for the community
18.	Candidates should discuss the effect achieved by naming each one of the men who set off on the journey. 2 marks for a single insightful comment. 1 mark for a basic point. 0 marks for reference/quotation alone.	2	Possible answers include: • it humanises them, hence adds to the tragedy of their death • the length of the list emphasises the extent of the loss • it develops the idea that they were all known to everyone, sense of a small, close-knit community • it sustains the "chronicle" style, recording of basic facts (nothing said about their personalities, for instance)
19.	Candidates should explain what is revealed about Jacob as a person. 2 marks for a single insightful comment. 1 mark for a basic point. 0 marks for reference/quotation alone.	3	Possible answers include: • aware that he is benefitting from others' suffering ("I have done better this winter than anyone") • makes (minor) concession by not accepting payment for the seven men … • … but reverts to usual collection of something/anything ("set of Nantucket harpoons") • perhaps some sense of guilt ("God grant …") … • … but more likely a simple acceptance • deeply rooted in cycle of the seasons, knows that winter and death will come round again • accepts his role in the community with a sense of resignation

Question	Expected Response	Max Mark	Additional Guidance
20.	Candidates should discuss George Mackay Brown's use of symbolism in *The Bright Spade* and at least one other story and should refer to appropriate textual evidence to support their discussion. 0 marks for reference/quotation alone.	10	The generic marking guide, covering aspects of commonality, can be found on page 193. In comments on other stories, possible references include: • the money in *The Whaler's Return* • the wireless in *The Wireless Set* • the wreck of the Danish ship in *The Eye of the Hurricane* Many other references are possible.

Text 3 — Prose — *The Trick is to Keep Breathing* by Janice Galloway

Question	Expected Response	Max Mark	Additional Guidance
21.	Candidates should explain how Tony is portrayed as an unpleasant character. 2 marks for a single insightful comment and reference. 1 mark for a basic point and reference. 0 marks for reference/quotation alone.	4	Possible answers include: • his arrival is announced by "gravel and the crunch of brakes" suggesting something noisy, grating, impatient; he is de-personalised • "stare harder" suggests the thought of his arrival causes her to tense up • his approach is described menacingly in terms of feet getting closer • "thudding" is a harsh, pounding sound, intimidating • his flaunting of the bottle suggests someone rather brash, showy • the "clumsy orchid" description associates him with a distortion of beauty • "Always take it for granted I'm going to win" reeks of over-confidence (and possible double entendre) • the "lips … beard … teeth" references suggest something vaguely animal-like, rather unsettling • the clichéd compliments ("a real picture") are repeated ad nauseam
22.	Candidates should explain how the writer creates an uneasy atmosphere in the car. 2 marks for a single insightful comment and reference. 1 mark for a basic point and reference. 0 marks for reference/quotation alone.	2	Possible answers include: • the fact that it is an entirely one-sided conversation; Joy says nothing • "It plays Country and Western Music" — surreal idea of car as animate object • "The seat creaks with his weight" suggests he is overweight, oppressive • Tony's remarks are laden with innuendo, cheap come-ons ("Nearly as good as you", "Expect a treat tonight") • "He pats my leg" suggests making unwelcome advances • his overtly suggestive pausing at "it's hard …" waiting for a response • his leering way of looking at her, which is repeated after every sentence

Question	Expected Response	Max Mark	Additional Guidance
23.	Candidates should analyse how aspects of Tony's character are revealed. 2 marks for a single insightful comment and reference. 1 mark for a basic point and reference. 0 marks for reference/quotation alone.	4	Possible answers include: • short, clipped sentences suggest not much of a conversationalist, sees everything in simple terms • all one-way — suggests he's not interested in what Joy might have to say, single-mindedly pursuing his simple goal of seducing her • references to her weight, to her illness suggest high level of insensitivity • references to her appearance and potential for being a "stunner" reveal him as sexist, old-fashioned • "Just relax and listen to the music" sounds deeply insincere • "This one's my favourite" suggests he can't avoid self-centredness • "You don't mind if I run it again" is a statement rather than a question, he's going to do it regardless of any opinion Joy might have • "Hiding your best assets" — a lewd comment, which he pretends is a mistake • perhaps genuine shock, concern when he asks about her hands
24.	Candidates should discuss Joy's relationships with men and should refer to appropriate textual evidence to support their discussion 0 marks for reference/quotation alone.	10	The generic marking guide, covering aspects of commonality, can be found on page 193. In comments on the rest of the novel, possible references include: • her affair with Michael • her teenage romance with Paul • her relationship with David Many other references are possible.

Text 4 — Prose — *Sunset Song* by Lewis Grassic Gibbon

Question	Expected Response	Max Mark	Additional Guidance
25.	Candidates should explain how the writer conveys the strength of Rob's feelings about language. 2 marks for an insightful comment and reference. 1 mark for a basic comment and reference. 0 marks for reference/quotation alone.	4	Possible answers include: • "shame"/"shamed" suggests that non-users of Scots/Scotch are a source of dishonour, humiliation • "the split-tongued sourocks!" suggests a contemptuous attitude, accusation of hypocrisy • "Every damned little narrow dowped rat" is an all-inclusive condemnation of English-speakers ("Every"); contemptible ("damned"); insubstantial, lacking substance ("little, narrow dowped"); loathsome, to be looked down on ("rat") • "put on the English" suggests use of English forced, affected, pretentious • "thin bit scraichs" suggests he thinks of English as weak, anaemic, shrill, strident • *"You can tell me, man …"* Rob's tone is quite belligerent, challenging Gordon to dare to disagree • the list of words which Rob claims have no English equivalent suggests how extensive he thinks such a category is

Question	Expected Response	Max Mark	Additional Guidance
26.	Candidates should explain how the writer conveys the harshness of life working the land. 1 mark for each appropriate reference + comment. 0 marks for reference/quotation alone.	2	Possible answers include: • repetition ("coarse, coarse", "work, work, work, and chave, chave, chave") stresses the amount of effort required, echoes the repetitive nature of the work • "from the blink of day till the fall of night" conveys the extreme length of the working day • "soss and sotter" the alliteration/onomatopoeia emphasises the filth, unpleasantness of the work
27.	Candidates should explain how the writer's use of language conveys the conflicting views about "scientific" farming methods. For full marks there should be reference to and comment on at least two features of language. 2 marks for an insightful comment and reference. 1 mark for a basic comment and reference. 0 marks for reference/quotation alone.	4	Possible answers include: • there are four different (reported) speakers involved: Cuddieston, Banker's son, Chae, Long Rob; shows range of views being put forward • sentence openers ("Syne ... So ... But ... And") indicate different points of view being proposed • "childe" suggests contempt for banker's son, suggests naïve, inexperienced • "clutter of machines" presents machinery as untidy, chaotic, not effective • "the best friend of man" suggests human quality, of extreme usefulness • Chae's forceful tone: "*Damn't, no ...*" • Rob's mocking, humorous tone: "damned machine that would muck you a pigsty even though they all turned socialist to-morrow"
28.	Candidates should discuss to what extent *Sunset Song* is a celebration of a traditional way of life or an illustration of the inevitability of change and should refer to appropriate textual evidence to support their discussion. 0 marks for reference/quotation alone.	10	The generic marking guide, covering aspects of commonality, can be found on page 193. In comments on the rest of the novel, possible references include: • the closeness of the community, e.g. the fire at Peesie's Knapp, the wedding • Chris's decision to stay on the farm • the impact of the War • technological developments in farming Many other references are possible.

Text 5 — Prose — *The Cone-Gatherers* by Robin Jenkins

Question	Expected Response	Max Mark	Additional Guidance
29.	Candidates should analyse how word choice conveys Duror's loathing for Calum. 2 marks for an insightful comment and reference. 1 mark for a basic comment and reference. 0 marks for reference/quotation alone.	2	Possible answers include: • "feebleminded" suggests he sees him as stupid, sub-normal • "hunchback" a very belittling, offensive word, suggests he focuses on the deformity • "grovelling" distorts Calum's attempts at mercy into something demeaning, as if he's begging, bowing and scraping • "obscene" suggests any sound from Calum would be seen as something disgusting, lascivious

Question	Expected Response	Max Mark	Additional Guidance

30.	Candidates should explain how the writer makes the reader aware of Duror's disturbed state of mind.
	
	2 marks for an insightful comment and reference.
	1 mark for a basic comment and reference.
	0 marks for reference/quotation alone.
		4	Possible answers include:
			
			• that he had "waited over an hour" just to see them suggests it is an obsession
			• "purgatory of humiliation" is an exaggerated way to describe his feelings, suggests how deeply affected he is
			• "as if … forced to wait upon them as upon his masters" — a reversal of the norm, suggests how distorted his view is
			• his apparent desire to see the cone-gatherers come to harm, a sense of relish in "come crashing down" and "lie dead on the ground"
			• the extended metaphor in which he imagines himself standing on a sea floor and sees features around him as if they were underwater — bizarre, dreamlike, surreal:
			  • "standing on the floor of a fantastic sea" — acknowledges that it's dreamlike, fanciful
			  • "with an owl and a herd of roe-deer flitting by quiet as fish" — terrestrial creatures transformed in his mind into aquatic ones
			  • "ferns and bronzen bracken … gleamed like seaweed" — terrestrial flora transformed into aquatic, ironically described in terms of great beauty
			  • "spruce trees … like submarine monsters" — distorted view of trees as dangerous/threatening underwater beasts

31.	Candidates should analyse how the imagery gives insight into Duror's feelings. 2 marks for an insightful comment and reference. 1 mark for a basic comment and reference. 0 marks for reference/quotation alone.	4	Possible answers include: • "the overspreading tree of revulsion in him" sees, recognises the hatred within him as organic, taking him over totally • "his stronghold and sanctuary" gives the idea of him being at war, needing to defend himself, being isolated • "fortify his sanity and hope" shows awareness that he is mentally unstable and wishes to fight against this • "invaded and defiled" depicts the cone-gatherers as an enemy, a threat, corrupting, dirty • "its cleansing and reviving virtues" depicts the wood as a place of healing, suggests he views nature as more powerful perhaps than human agency • "like the whining prostrations of a heathen in front of an idol" sees Calum as something alien, primitive, submissive, lacking dignity, entirely different • "diabolical joke" as if dreamed up by the devil, intended to cause him (Duror) suffering; "joke" because of the incongruity of the ugly features and the beautiful face
32.	Candidates should discuss the importance of the conflict between Duror and Calum and should refer to appropriate textual evidence to support their discussion. 0 marks for reference/quotation alone.	10	The generic marking guide, covering aspects of commonality, can be found on page 193. In comments on the rest of the novel, possible references include: • Duror's lying about Calum exposing himself • the deer drive • the ending Many other references are possible.

Text 1 — Poetry — *To a Mouse* by Robert Burns

Question	Expected Response	Max Mark	Additional Guidance
33.	Candidates should analyse the use of poetic technique to create sympathy for the mouse's situation. 1 mark for reference and comment. 0 marks for reference/quotation alone.	2	Possible answers include: • word choice of "wee-bit housie" suggests something modest, basic, unelaborate • the minor sentence/exclamation suggests the poet feels shocked at the loss • word choice of "silly" suggests something very simple, basic • word choice of "strewin" suggests the relentless destruction caused by the wind • alliteration of "naethin, now" slightly emphasises the mouse's plight • word choice of "bleak December" suggests the depressing, austere situation at the height of winter • word choice of "Baith snell an' keen!" suggests the unpleasantness and suffering the mouse will face

34.	Candidates should identify two themes of the poem and explain how each is clarified by the poet's technique.
	
	2 marks for a clear statement of theme, supported by reference and comment. 1 mark for a less clear statement or for weak support. 0 marks for reference/quotation alone.
		4	Possible answers include:
			
			• mouse's foresight, preparation, supported by:
			  • "thou saw … thou thought" suggesting planning
			  • contrast of "bare an' waste" and "cozie" to suggest what mouse was trying to guard against
			  • "dwell" suggests the safety, protection the mouse had hoped for
			  • "cost thee mony a weary nibble" — emphasises the effort that has been expended on the nest
			• man's destruction of his plans, supported by:
			  • "crash!" — onomatopoeic representation of the sudden destruction
			  • "thou's turn'd out" — idea of him being rejected
			  • "cruel coulter" — alliteration emphasises the harshness of the plough
			  • "cranreuch cauld" — alliteration emphasises the harshness of the weather he will face as a result of man's interference

Question	Expected Response	Max Mark	Additional Guidance
35.	Candidates should discuss the mood created in the last two verses. They should show understanding of the key ideas and analyse the use of poetic technique to create mood. One or more than one mood could be discussed. For full marks there should be clear understanding of the key ideas and thoughtful analysis of how the mood is created. Reference and a basic comment will be worth 1 mark. Reference and an insightful comment may be worth 2 marks. 0 marks for reference/quotation alone.	4	Possible answers include: Mood(s): • contemplative, wistful, melancholy, regretful, sympathetic, pessimistic, maudlin References: • "But Mousie" — the "but" suggests moving on from the bleak picture painted in preceding lines • "thou art no thy lane" — offers some sympathy, fellow feeling that others suffer as well • "the best-laid schemes" — no matter how well planned things are • "o' mice an' men" — links man and beast, shows this happens to all • "aft" — it is a frequent occurrence • "grief an' pain" — very pessimistic picture of suffering • "For promis'd joy!" — reminds us of the hopes, the expectations we once had • "Still" — concedes that mouse has one advantage • "thou art blest compar'd wi' me" — self-pity? • "But och!" — tone of frustration perhaps • "I guess an' fear!" finishes on an enigmatic note, but pessimism seems to dominate
36.	Candidates should discuss Burns' use of verse form in To a Mouse and at least one other poem and should refer to appropriate textual evidence to support their discussion. 0 marks for reference/quotation alone.	10	The generic marking guide, covering aspects of commonality, can be found on page 193. In comments on other poems, possible references include: • aspects of the Standard Habbie (*Holy Willie's Prayer*, *Address to the Deil*, *A Poet's Welcome* …) • song and chorus in *A Man's A Man* • rhyming couplet in *Tam o' Shanter* Many other references are possible.

Text 2 — Poetry — *Mrs Midas* by Carol Ann Duffy

Question	Expected Response	Max Mark	Additional Guidance
37.	Candidates should analyse the use of poetic techniques to create an ordinary, everyday atmosphere. 2 marks for an insightful comment and reference. 1 mark for a basic comment and reference. 0 marks for reference/quotation alone.	4	Possible answers include: • the use of simple statement "It was late September", as if recounting a simple recollection • the use of informal contraction "I'd just poured" suggests relaxed tone • the absence of "and" between "wine and begun" is informal, sounds comfortable • everyday detail "a glass of wine" suggests relaxation, contentment • word choice of "unwind" suggests calmness, composure • imagery/personification "The kitchen/filled with the smell of itself" suggests warmth, pleasant smells, promise of good food • "steamy breath/gently blanching the windows" — personification of kitchen as something alive, warm, tender • conversational tone of "So I opened one" as if continuing a simple story

Question	Expected Response	Max Mark	Additional Guidance
37.	*(continued)*		• "wiped the other's glass like a brow" — affectionate, caring, unthreatening gesture • simple description of what husband is doing "standing under a pear tree ..." • "snapping a twig" suggests a small, unthreatening action
38.	Candidates should analyse the use of poetic techniques to convey the confusion beginning to arise in the speaker's mind. 2 marks for an insightful comment and reference. 1 mark for a basic comment and reference. 0 marks for reference/quotation alone.	2	Possible answers include: • tone of "Now the garden was long and the visibility poor" — as if offering an excuse for possibly not seeing correctly • the imagery of "the dark of the ground seems to drink the light of the sky" suggests something mysterious, dark, deprived of light, uncertain • the delayed assertion "but that twig in his hand was gold" as if unwilling to state what she is seeing • the parenthetical "- we grew Fondante d'Automne -" seems an unnecessary detail as if trying to hold onto reality by including it • the minor sentence "On" conveys a sense of stupefaction, unable to say anything more than a single syllable • question "Is he putting fairy lights in the tree?" suggests doubt, almost an attempt to rationalise
39.	Candidates should explain how the poet conveys the strangeness of the husband's behaviour in these two stanzas. 2 marks for an insightful comment and reference. 1 mark for a basic comment and reference. 0 marks for reference/quotation alone.	4	Possible answers include: • the juxtaposition of the ordinary ("He came into the house") with the extraordinary ("The doorknobs gleamed") • the way his behaviour causes her mind to jump to a schoolroom memory • the simile "like a king on a burnished throne" presents him as a regal figure amid great splendour • "strange, wild, vain" — use of three monosyllables to convey a wide range of emotions • "He started to laugh" suggests an almost irrational response to the situation • "spitting out the teeth of the rich" — a grotesque image combining pain/discomfort with reference to wealth • structure of "toyed with his spoon, then mine, then with the knives, the forks" suggests random actions, as if he is confused • "glass, goblet, golden chalice" shows the progression from simple drinking vessel to exotic "chalice"; emphasised by the alliteration • structure of "picked up the glass, goblet, golden chalice, drank" — suggests staccato movement, unusual behaviour
40.	Candidates should discuss how Duffy creates and develops unusual or surprising ideas and/or situations and should refer to appropriate textual evidence to support their discussion. 0 marks for reference/quotation alone.	10	The generic marking guide, covering aspects of commonality, can be found on page 193. In comments on other poems, possible references include: • the rejection of the conventional in *Valentine* • the prose/poetry types of love in *Anne Hathaway* • the outspoken ideas/language of Miss Havisham Many other references are possible.

Text 3 — Poetry — *Last Supper* by Liz Lochhead

Question	Expected Response	Max Mark	Additional Guidance
41.	Candidates should explain how the poet develops the metaphor of "this feast". 1 mark for each relevant reference and comment. 0 marks for reference/quotation alone.	2	Possible answers include: • "leftover hash" — the idea of making something from the remaining scraps (of the relationship) • "soup … render from the bones" — the idea of squeezing the last possible scrap of nutrition, also the idea of totally destroying the relationship, of grinding it to dust • "something substantial … tasty" — idea of being able to provide an ample meal (i.e. worthwhile topic of conversation about the relationship)
42.	Candidates should analyse the use of sound to create a negative impression of "The Girls". 2 marks for an insightful comment and reference. 1 mark for a basic comment and reference. 0 marks for reference/quotation alone.	4	Possible answers include: • alliteration in "cackling around the cauldron" suggests harsh, aggressive sound of their (witchlike) voices • onomatopoeic effect from "spitting" — suggestion of contempt, disgust • alliteration/series of plosive consonants in "spitting out the gristlier bits/of his giblets" suggests harshness, contempt, element of comedy also • echoic nature of "bits of his giblets" — comic element, imitating their relish at the dismemberment • alliteration in "gnawing on the knucklebone" — emphasised "n" almost imitates gnawing sound • the rhythmical similarity of "intricate irony" echoes/mocks the faux-sophisticated conversation • alliteration in "getting grave … — gout" suggests harsh, gritty nature of their voices
43.	Candidates should analyse the use of poetic techniques to describe the people at the Supper. 2 marks for an insightful comment and reference. 1 mark for a basic comment and reference. 0 marks for reference/quotation alone.	4	Possible answers include: • irony/double meaning in "That's rich!" suggests self-consciously clever or unaware of what they're saying • word choice of "splutter" suggests inelegant, lacking poise • imagery of "munching the lies" suggests the enjoyment with which they accept/digest untruths about the man • simile of "fat and sizzling as sausages" describes the "lies" as unhealthy but appealing • word choice of "sink back" suggests a smug self-satisfaction • metaphor "gorged on truth" suggests bloated, self-satisfied; also ironic since they've been consuming lies • paradox in "savage integrity" suggests their hypocrisy • word choice of "sleek" suggests glossy, superficial, slightly smug • simile "preening/like corbies" suggests they are predatory
44.	Candidates should discuss, by referring to this poem and at least one other by Liz Lochhead, her ability to describe characters in a precise way and should refer to appropriate textual evidence to support their discussion. 0 marks for reference/quotation alone.	10	The generic marking guide, covering aspects of commonality, can be found on page 193. In comments on other poems, possible references include: • the mother in *View of Scotland/Love Poem* • the grandmother (and other family members) in *For My Grandmother Knitting* • the mother in *My Rival's House* Many other references are possible.

Text 4 — Poetry — *Assisi* by Norman MacCaig

Question	Expected Response	Max Mark	Additional Guidance
45.	Candidates should analyse how the use of sound enhances the description of the dwarf. 2 marks for an insightful comment and reference. 1 mark for a basic comment and reference. 0 marks for reference/quotation alone.	2	Possible answers include: • sibilance in "sat, slumped" suggests lethargy, discomfort • long vowel sounds in "sat, slumped" suggest heaviness, tiredness • onomatopoeic effect in "slumped" to suggest heaviness, defeat, echoes of "lump", "dumped" • alliteration in "tiny twisted" draws attention to the unpleasantness, ugliness • line break between "which" and "sawdust" creates a small dramatic pause before the horrors of the description
46.	Candidates should explain how the poet creates an ironic tone. 2 marks for an insightful comment and reference. 1 mark for a basic comment and reference. 0 marks for reference/quotation alone.	2	Possible answers include: • juxtaposition of grand church ("three tiers") with St Francis' reputation ("brother/of the poor") and/or his simple lifestyle ("talker with birds") • sardonic observation that dwarf has an "advantage" over St Francis, but only that he is "not dead yet"
47.	Candidates should discuss what the speaker's statement suggests about his feelings at that moment. 2 marks for an insightful comment (reference is likely to be implicit). 1 mark for a basic comment. 0 marks for reference/quotation alone.	2	Possible answers include: • presenting himself as the detached observer • mock admiration for the "cleverness" • hint of superiority (especially if read with emphasis on "I") • a line of thought could be developed around the idea of a poet as user of words contemplating visual art communicating with the illiterate

48.	Candidates should explain what the poet means by describing the dwarf as a "ruined temple".
	
	For full marks, candidates should develop the implications of both words.
	
	2 marks for an insightful comment and reference.
	1 mark for a basic comment and reference.
	0 marks for reference/quotation alone.
	
	General statements comparing the dwarf to the church as described earlier in the poem will be worth 2 marks at most.
		4	Possible answers include:
			
			• "ruined" in the sense that he is physically deformed, a distortion of a "normal" human being:
			  • "eyes wept pus" — not shedding tears in conventional way, but leaking infected fluid
			  • ugly sound of word "pus"
			  • heavy sound of three stressed syllables
			  • "back ... higher/than his head" — distortion of the normal
			• a "temple" in the sense of something with deep religious significance, often of immense beauty:
			  • despite all the unpleasant surface appearances, the dwarf is polite "Grazie")
			  • his voice is compared with that of a child (innocent) speaking to its mother (Madonna and child idea)
			  • compared with a bird (nature, innocence) speaking to St Francis (icon of compassion, humility)

49.	Candidates should discuss MacCaig's use of wry humour in *Assisi* and at least one other poem and should refer to appropriate textual evidence to support their discussion. 0 marks for reference/quotation alone.	10	The generic marking guide, covering aspects of commonality, can be found on page 193. In comments on other poems, possible references include: • the description of the drip in *Visiting Hour* • the description of the shark in *Basking Shark* • some of the imagery in *Aunt Julia* Many other references are possible.

Text 5 — Poetry — *Hallaig* by Sorley MacLean

Question		Expected Response	Max Mark	Additional Guidance
50.	(i)	Candidates should identify two central concerns of the poem.	2	Possible answers include: • the influence of past • landscape of Hallaig/Raasay • poet's sense of connection to the history of the community • celebration of tradition and heritage
	(ii)	Candidates should analyse how the poet's use of symbolism develops either or both of the concerns identified in 50(i). 2 marks for an insightful comment and reference. 1 mark for a basic comment and reference. 0 marks for reference/quotation alone.	4	Possible answers include: • "their daughters and their sons are a wood" — connects generations to natural growth, organic development, continuity • dislike/criticism of non-native species ("pine") seen as "proud", "crowing" • "birch wood" as the natural, preferred species — poet is prepared to wait for it, sees it as something that will eventually provide comfort ("shade" for the whole area)
51.		Candidates should explain how the poet creates a fusion of past and present. 2 marks for an insightful comment and reference. 1 mark for a basic comment and reference. 0 marks for reference/quotation alone.	4	Possible answers include: • "Sabbath of the dead" — suggests an ongoing, present day celebration of the dead • "people are frequenting" — suggests current presence, movement, community; use of present tense makes it appear to be happening now • "every single generation gone" — emphasises extent of past destruction • "They are still in Hallaig" — unambiguous assertion of presence • "MacLeans and MacLeods" — use of local names in the plural suggests continuity, many generations • "all who were there" — past tense draws attention to what is gone • "the dead have been seen alive" — direct reference to the past in the present; clear contrast of "dead" and "alive" • absence of verb in final stanza creates ambiguity • "men lying" suggests death • "girls a wood of birches" suggests no longer alive as people, but alive in nature • "straight their backs" suggests alive, proud • "bent their heads" suggests mourning
52.		Candidates should discuss how MacLean explores ideas of tradition and heritage in *Hallaig* and at least one other poem and should refer to appropriate textual evidence to support their discussion. 0 marks for reference/quotation alone.	10	The generic marking guide, covering aspects of commonality, can be found on page 193. In comments on other poems, possible references include: • various descriptions in *Screapadal*, e.g. the effects of the Clearances, and of the warships • the love of landscape in *Shores* • the references to bygone heroes and warriors in *Heroes* Many other references are possible.

Text 6 — Poetry — The Thread by Don Paterson

Question	Expected Response	Max Mark	Additional Guidance
53.	Candidates should analyse the poet's use of imagery to describe his feelings about Jamie at the time of his birth. 2 marks for an insightful comment and reference. 1 mark for a basic comment and reference. 0 marks for reference/quotation alone.	2	Possible answers include: • "made his landing" — compares baby with something arriving, descending from the sky, depicting his birth as something exciting, mystical • "ploughed straight back into earth" — compares baby with something disastrous, hinting at death, burial • "the thread of his one breath" compares his life to a single, fragile strand by which "they" held on to him and rescued him, expresses his wonder, his gratitude
54.	Candidates should explain how the poet expresses his feelings now. 2 marks for an insightful comment and reference. 1 mark for a basic comment and reference. 0 marks for reference/quotation alone.	4	Possible answers include: • "I thank what higher will/brought us" — gratitude to a higher power (expressed in a rather vague way: "what" seems to imply "whatever — I don't really know or care") • "the great twin-engined swaying wingspan" — metaphor used to describe the appearance of him and his children's arms out and linked (him as fuselage, children as wings/engines), suggests a feeling of joy, power within the family unit • "roaring down" — noisy, enjoying themselves thoroughly • "out-revving/every engine in the universe" — exaggeration to convey his pride, relief, delight that the boy's lungs are healthy
55.	Candidates should show understanding of the term "conclusion" and show how the content of the last sentence continues — or contrasts with — ideas and/or language from the rest of the poem. 4 marks can be awarded for four appropriate, basic comments. A detailed, insightful comment on one example may be awarded 2 marks. 0 marks for reference/quotation alone.	4	Possible answers include: • continues image of the "thread" (from title and line 3) as what holds life together, but now applied to whole family not just Jamie • "all of us" emphasises the unity within the family • "tiny house" conveys the distance they are at the moment from home, but even so, the thread unifies them, holds them together • very personal "us ... our ... son ... your" continues personal nature of the whole poem • image of the mother waving, despite her being only a "white dot", is welcoming, warm, a very optimistic, uplifting way to conclude the poem
56.	Candidates should discuss Paterson's use of verse form to explore important themes in *The Thread* and at least one other poem and should refer to appropriate textual evidence to support their discussion. 0 marks for reference/quotation alone.	10	The generic marking guide, covering aspects of commonality, can be found on page 193. In comments on other poems, possible references include: • sonnet form in *Waking with Russell* • rhyming couplets in *Two Trees* • use of half rhyme/pararhyme in *11.00 Baldovan* Many other references are possible.

SECTION 2 — Critical Essay

Please see the assessment criteria for the Critical Essay on page 245.

HIGHER FOR CfE ENGLISH
MODEL PAPER 2

PAPER 1 — READING FOR UNDERSTANDING, ANALYSIS AND EVALUATION

Marking Instructions for each question

Passage 1

Question		Expected Response	Max Mark	Additional Guidance
1.	(a)	Candidates should identify two ways the mall seems to encourage consumerism. Candidates must use their own words. No marks are awarded for verbatim quotations from the passage. *1 mark for each point from the "Additional Guidance" column.*	2	Possible answers include: • retailers do not want consumers to sit down and take a break from shopping (explanation of "wooden bench purposely designed to be uncomfortable") • deliberate/careful positioning of bench to maximise marketing opportunities (explanation of "placed alongside a digital screen") • energetic use of technology to market products and tempt consumers (explanation of "screen pulsing ever-changing adverts") • the mall offers diverse/seemingly endless methods for consumers to dispose of their income (explanation of "other outlets, other products, other ways") or any other acceptable answer
	(b)	Candidates should analyse how the writer's use of language emphasises the intensity of consumerism in the mall. Marks will depend on the quality of comment on appropriate language feature(s). 2 marks may be awarded for reference plus detailed/insightful comment; 1 mark for reference plus more basic comment; 0 marks for reference alone. *Possible answers are shown in the "Additional Guidance" column.*	2	Possible answers include: *Word choice* • "purposely designed" suggests drive and focus on the part of retailers • "pulsing" suggests screen is full of life, constantly moving; a heartbeat which empowers consumers • "ever-changing" suggests incessant activity on screen, vast amount of items on offer • "shoals" suggests the vast number of people who are in the mall/suggests that the consumers move in a darting, frantic manner similar to that of a shoal of fish • "hurrying (in and out)" suggests pressurised, frenetic, single-minded activity • "honouring" suggests that consumers view shopping as a duty to be carried out with devotion • "creed" just as a creed is a set of religious beliefs or principles so the consumers in the mall place great faith in shopping • "turbo-consumer" suggests the activity of the shoppers is super-charged • "live to shop" suggests a fundamental importance, as if a motto of the "creed"; climactic, summative statement *Sentence structure* • list ("other … ways") emphasises the many options available to consumers • repetition of "other" highlights the many ways in which consumers can spend/vast range of shopping choices • repetition of "spend" mimics the furious exhortations of retailers/the fast pace of consumer transactions

Question		Expected Response	Max Mark	Additional Guidance
	(b)	*(continued)*		• juxtaposition of repeated options ("other … other …") and repetition of a single course of action ("spend") it could be argued that the juxtaposition of choice and single activity highlights the narrowing focus/determination of consumers as they shop in the mallcolon followed by "live to shop" creates a climactic, summative statement or any other acceptable answer
2.	(a)	Candidates should explain why, according to the writer, consumerism might be considered harmless but also unable to make us happy. Candidates must use their own words. No marks are awarded for verbatim quotations from the passage. *1 mark for each point from the "Additional Guidance" column. For full marks there must be at least one point from each list.*	4	Possible answers include: *Harmless* • it is not detrimental to one's health (explanation of "doesn't kill anyone") • it contributes to the national wealth (explanation of "keeps the economy going") • many people are employed in the retail industry (explanation of "it … provides one in six jobs") • it creates contentment/pleasure (explanation of "it makes people happy") *Unable to make us happy* • there will always be new products which we crave (explanation of "Every time … better than the one you have.") • consumerism acts like an addictive drug (explanation of "the heroin of human happiness") • consumerism can never fulfil our wishes (explanation of "our needs are never satisfied.") • the happiness offered by consumerism is only temporary (explanation of "The brief high we feel … just enough to keep us going") • consumerism distracts us from what is really important (explanation of "… compensation for not having a richer, fuller life.") • acceptable reference could be made to aspects of lines 6–10, e.g. the implications of "treadmill" or any other acceptable answer
	(b)	Candidates should analyse how the writer's use of imagery emphasises her criticism of consumerism. Marks will depend on the quality of comment on imagery. When dealing with imagery, answers must show recognition of the literal root of the image and then explore how the writer is extending it figuratively. A detailed/insightful comment will be worth 2 marks; a more basic comment will be worth 1 mark. Mere identification of an image will be 0 marks. *Possible answers are shown in the "Additional Guidance" column.*	3	Possible answers include: • "Turbo-(consumerism)": just as a "turbo" is a supercharger which gives an engine or mechanical system much more power so the writer suggests that consumerism has become overpowering, having the potential to overwhelm other more meaningful aspects of life • "voracious appetite": just as a voracious appetite describes an insatiable desire to consume food greedily/ravenously, so consumerism encourages an over-indulgent approach to shopping • "seduced": to seduce is to tempt an individual, possibly into a sexual liaison or an unwise deed, so the writer suggests that the temptations of consumerism are hard to resist and may corrupt us • "heroin": just as heroin is a highly addictive narcotic, so the writer suggests that we can become dependent on consumerism • "(brief) high": just as a "high" is a temporary feeling of extreme happiness, so the writer suggests that consumerism offers only temporary happiness or any other acceptable answer

Question		Expected Response	Max Mark	Additional Guidance
3.		Candidates should analyse how the writer's use of language conveys her disapproval of the large amount of space that is now devoted to shopping. Marks will depend on the quality of comment on appropriate language feature(s). 2 marks may be awarded for reference plus detailed/insightful comment; 1 mark for reference plus more basic comment; 0 marks for reference alone. *Possible answers are shown in the "Additional Guidance" column.*	4	Possible answers include: *Word Choice* • "giant" suggests that malls are an overwhelming or frightening presence • "taking over" has connotations of conquest/ invasion, suggests retail space is a hostile force winning a war • "worldwide" suggests there is no escape from this takeover/global domination • "mainstream" associates the vast amount of retail space with the humdrum/mediocre • "footfall" suggests that so much retail space depersonalises us/shoppers become mere statistics • "grazing time" suggests that exposure to more retail space has lessened our ability to think for ourselves: we become like animals, following the herd/latest trend • "(retail) creep" to creep is to move forward stealthily, possibly with the intention of causing harm, suggesting that the growth of shopping space has been insidious and may be harmful to society • "increasingly" suggests an on-going, almost unstoppable process • "diminished" suggests reductive properties of increasing retail space *Imagery* • "monoculture": just as a monoculture is a crop of a single species, often grown in vast fields, so the enormous amount of shopping space lacks variety and restricts the growth of other activities which we could pursue • "Kings as consumers, pawns as citizens": allows the writer to express the key idea that increased retail opportunities may lead us to believe we have power and control ("kings"), but the opposite is true: consumerism removes our ability to control our lives and, like "pawns" on a chessboard, we are manipulated by others and have very little power in the game as a whole/ society *Sentence structure* • list of different types of retail space ("shops … malls") emphasises relentless expansion of shopping areas • escalating nature of retail outlets within list ("shops, retail centres, giant malls") suggests an evolutionary process/growth which is difficult to stop or inevitable • balanced structure/contrast of "The more … the less …" allows the writer to highlight the spiralling negative consequences of increasing retail space • "Kings as consumers, pawns as citizens" the very basic parallel structure of this final sentence emphasises the dismissive tone of "pawns as citizens", thereby allowing the writer to highlight her view that we are deluded into thinking we are important when in fact basic rights of citizenship are denied us

Question	Expected Response	Max Mark	Additional Guidance
3.	*(continued)*		*Tone* • "… there's not much else to do but shop." creates a despairing/frustrated tone by using basic vocabulary in a matter-of-fact statement • "citizens … make decisions … equally and collectively … world …" rather overblown language suggests that increased shopping space removes our higher values, leaving us intellectually poorer and deprived of our basic rights • balanced structure of "It may be … but we simply have …" creates a dismissive/sceptical tone which allows the writer to highlight that more space devoted to shopping will ultimately deprive us of our liberty or any other acceptable answer
4.	Candidates should discuss to what extent the writer's description of the shoppers suggests she is "over-catastrophising the consumer phenomenon". They may argue for either side or for both sides. Marks will depend on the quality of evaluative comment. 2 marks may be awarded for reference plus detailed/insightful comment; 1 mark for reference plus more basic comment; 0 marks for reference alone. *Possible answers are shown in the "Additional Guidance" column.*	3	Possible answers include: • "teeming with shoppers despite the credit crunch" suggests it's not a problem, because so many are still shopping and benefiting the economy (even in financially straitened times) • "people don't look … disempowered" suggests it's not a problem, because these shoppers still have the right to exercise control • "people don't look … depressed" suggests it's not a problem, because the shoppers do not appear to be unhappy • "purposeful" suggests it's not a problem, because the shoppers are clear-sighted in their aims • "teeming with shoppers despite the credit crunch" suggests it is a problem, because large numbers are shopping even though they can ill afford to • use of qualifying adverb "particularly" before "disempowered or depressed" suggests that the writer cannot be whole-heartedly positive in her description of the shoppers • "I suppose" suggests a reluctance on the writer's part to see consumers in a positive light • "strangely distracted … magnetic shop signs" suggests it is a problem, because the shoppers are not in control of their own actions, are in an almost hypnotic state or any other acceptable answer
5.	Candidates should explain how "evolutionary psychology" can explain our need for material goods, but why "much of this is simply not true". Candidates must use their own words. No marks are awarded for verbatim quotations from the passage. *1 mark for each point from the "Additional Guidance" column, but at least one from each side.*	4	Possible answers include: *"Can explain"* • we think our outward appearance, as represented by a display of material goods (explanation of "self-marketing") … • … has become the means by which we can indicate our suitability as a mate to the opposite sex (explanation of "practical tool for reproduction and survival")

Question		Expected Response	Max Mark	Additional Guidance
5.		*(continued)*		*"Not true"* • most people are not aware of or concerned with what we wear (explanation of "the vast majority of people … wearing" and/or "The fundamental consumerist delusion …") • it is people's ability to express themselves, to display lively intelligence and to express love which matters more than superficial adornments (explanation of "their conversation, their wit, or their affection") or any other acceptable answer
6.		Candidates should evaluate the final paragraph's effectiveness as a conclusion to the ideas of the passage as a whole. Marks will depend on the quality of comment. For full marks there must be appropriate attention to the idea of a conclusion. A sophisticated intelligent answer may be awarded 3 marks; a sensible but not fully developed answer may be awarded 2 marks; a basic comment may be awarded 1 mark. *Possible answers are shown in the "Additional Guidance" column.*	3	Possible answers include: • the attitude and behaviour of the "two young shoppers" are the embodiment of "modern consumerism" as mentioned in the opening sentence; they follow the creed of "live to shop", illustrating the idea behind the title • the "two young shoppers", as a device, allow the writer to return to the physical setting of the mall which is used at the beginning, in the middle and at the end, illustrating the scale of the shopping phenomenon • the persistence of the "two young shoppers", as illustrated by the frivolous nature of their words, allows the writer to end the passage on a light-hearted note, perhaps suggesting she realises she is, to an extent, "over-catastrophising" or any other acceptable answer

Passage 2

Question		Expected Response	Max Mark	Additional Guidance
7.		Candidates should identify key areas of disagreement in the two passages. There may be some overlap among the areas of disagreement. Markers will have to judge the extent to which a candidate has covered two points or one. Candidates can use bullet points in this final question, or write a number of linked statements. Evidence from the passage may include quotations, but these should be supported by explanations. *Approach to marking is shown in the "Additional Guidance" column.* *Key areas of disagreement are shown in the grid below. Other answers are possible.*	5	The mark for this question should reflect the quality of response in two areas: • identification of the key areas of disagreement in attitude/ideas • level of detail given in support The following guidelines should be used: **Five marks** — comprehensive identification of three or more key areas of disagreement with full use of supporting evidence **Four marks** — clear identification of three or more key areas of disagreement with relevant use of supporting evidence **Three marks** — identification of three or more key areas of disagreement with supporting evidence **Two marks** — identification of two key areas of disagreement with supporting evidence **One mark** — identification of one key area of disagreement with supporting evidence **Zero marks** — failure to identify any key area of disagreement and/or total misunderstanding of task

	Area of Disagreement	Carol Midgley	Will Hutton
1.	general	damages individuals and society — an addiction	actually benefits individuals and society (a problem only in the minds of the minority)
2.	happiness	gives short-term pleasure but longer-term unhappiness as consumers can never be satisfied	is fun and gives continuous pleasure through seeing and/or acquiring new "things"
3.	architecture	makes town and city centres look the same	can (at its best) create attractive buildings
4.	public space	restricts public space where people can meet to participate in the democratic process	creates public space where people do something imaginatively and economically important
5.	motivation	is motivated by people's need to attract a mate (but is not effective in that respect)	is motivated by people's need to express themselves through what they buy/own
6.	values	makes people superficial, obsessed with appearance rather than things that really matter	provides people with the opportunity to do something important for themselves as individuals and for society as a whole
7.	manipulation	the market is all-powerful, manipulative, degrading to shoppers	consumer as individual has free will, retains autonomy

HIGHER FOR CfE ENGLISH
MODEL PAPER 2

PAPER 2 — CRITICAL READING

SECTION 1 — Scottish Text

SCOTTISH TEXT (DRAMA)

Text 1 — Drama — *The Slab Boys* by John Byrne

Question	Expected Response	Max Mark	Additional Guidance
1.	Candidates should explain how the audience is made to feel sorry for Hector. 2 marks for an insightful comment and appropriate reference(s). 1 mark for a basic comment and reference(s). 0 marks for reference/quotation alone.	4	Possible answers include: • the general idea that Hector is facing humiliation in his new clothing • the fact that the attempt by Alan to warn him is thwarted by Phil's threat with the pen … • … such that (even) Alan is obliged to lie to him • Hector's pathetic enthusiasm: "Will I go now and ask her? Will I?" • Phil's and Spanky's apparent determination that he face humiliation at the hands not just of Lucille, but Willie Curry also • Hector's enthusiasm for "swanking" and his belief that his clothes are "up to date" • the way he is forced into putting on the coat and the balaclava, showing him as at the mercy of others • Phil's justification for the balaclava ("it's draughty in Willie's room") verges on the insulting • the stage direction "*Slightly bamboozled*" paints him as a sad, put-upon figure • the glibness of Phil's invented story for him shows how much contempt he has for Hector, how much he enjoys manipulating him • the "Triple pneumonia … Double rupture …" knockabout might amuse Phil and Spanky, but it is further evidence of their having fun at someone else's expense • Hector's "I'll away along then" is pathetic in its simplicity and naivety • the insincerity of Phil and Spanky's good wishes • their bursting into uncontrollable laughter the moment he leaves
2.	Candidates should explain how the language of lines 30—32 allows Phil and Spanky to make fun of Alan. 2 marks for an insightful comment and appropriate reference(s). 1 mark for a basic comment and reference(s). 0 marks for reference/quotation alone.	2	Possible answers include: • they take the rather "public school" turn of phrase "a lousy trick" … • … and echo it sneeringly in similar terms: "by jove" and "you cad" • they mock Alan's (to them) posh way of speaking by pretending to speak in the same way

Question	Expected Response	Max Mark	Additional Guidance
3.	Candidates should explain how the playwright emphasises the animosity between Alan and Phil. 2 marks for an insightful comment and appropriate reference(s). 1 mark for a basic comment and reference(s). 0 marks for reference/quotation alone.	4	Possible answers include: • Alan's quite aggressive, forceful "Hey, watch it! Chuckit!" • knows he's "speaking out of turn", but is prepared this time to stand up to Phil • (for Alan) the use of "poor little bastard" shows how angry he is, trying to make Phil see how awful things are going to be for Hector • he reels off what is going to happen to Hector ("thinking … he really does cut a dash … he'll probably stop off … doff the coat and hat") to paint a full scenario of Hector's humiliation as a result of Phil behaviour • the rather extreme "she'll wet herself" shows just how amoral he think's Phil's behaviour is • contempt in "you and your crummy friend" • Phil's response is couched in mock public school language, implying that the ethics of the public school don't operate here • refers to Alan as Steerforth Minor, reducing to a public school stereotype (with the added barb of "Minor") • throws Alan's words "poor little bastard" back at him, as if to say "don't you dare call him that" • claims he and Spanky have some sort of right to humiliate Hector • as if there are situations Alan could never understand • Alan has the staying power to come back with "More than a bit" showing he doesn't accept Phil's argument.
4.	Candidates should discuss the importance of the conflict between Phil and Alan in exploring at least one theme in the play, and should refer to appropriate textual evidence to support their discussion. 0 marks for reference/quotation alone.	10	The generic marking guide, covering aspects of commonality, can be found on page 193. In comments on the rest of the play, possible references include: • Alan is the butt of many of Phil's jokes and sarcasm • Alan represents the successful, privileged middle class whom Phil despises • Alan is the antithesis of Phil in terms of work ethic, conventional manners, respect for "superiors" Many other references are possible.

Text 2 — Drama — *The Cheviot, the Stag and the Black, Black Oil* by John McGrath

Question	Expected Response	Max Mark	Additional Guidance
5.	Candidates should explain how the playwright creates a relaxed mood. 1 mark for each acceptable explanation. 0 marks for simply identifying an aspect of the plan.	4	Possible answers include: • the "quiet" song will be peaceful, calm • "It begins, I suppose" sounds like a natural speaking voice, not assertive, almost diffident • "and all that" is very colloquial • "in a bit of a mess" is very understated, not being dramatic • light humour in the response of the singer to information about Gaelic and the plaid • "So ..." is very conversational • the visually amusing appearance of the cottage • two girls singing in Gaelic — unthreatening, pleasing • "making it all seem fine" suggests there was no panic, no unrest • "invented ... introduced" underplaying the severe impact of the Cheviot • "not too pleased about it" is something of an understatement in the light of what actually happened
6.	Candidates should explain how the playwright conveys the difference in outlook between the Young Highlander and the Two Women. 2 marks for an insightful comment and reference. 1 mark for a basic comment and reference. 0 marks for reference/quotation alone.	4	Possible answers include: the Women are unconcerned, don't complain, shown by: • the dismissive "blethers" which suggests idle talk, not to be taken seriously • defence of the Countess as having been "kind" to them • sees no problem with the Countess living the high life ("Why wouldn't she be?") • invalidates the Y.H.'s criticism of misuse of rent by claiming he never pays any • not interested in Y.H.'s news about 150 soldiers; ignore its and tell him (or the other woman?) to get on with the work the Young Highlander criticises the Duchess, is full of complaints, is agitated about idea of soldiers, shown by: • sneering remark about the Countess an absentee ("away in England") • obvious antipathy at "fancy palaces and feasts for Kings and fine French wines" — sees her as living in luxury (while they have to scrape a living) • accuses her of doing so at their expense ("it's our rent she's spending") • sense of accumulating grievance in structure of ("If it's not bad weather ... it's mildew ... and last year it was both together ... And now they're talking about ...")
7.	Candidates should explain how the extract ends on a humorous note. 2 marks for a clear explanation. 1 mark for a basic explanation. 0 marks for reference/quotation alone.	2	Possible answers include: • the apparently innocuous "You might find a good use for this" when he hands her the bucket, is actually inviting her to throw the urine at Sellar and Loch, the approaching representative of authority • the tongue-in-cheek use (and repetition) of "gentlemen" to describe two notoriously cruel and heartless characters

Question		Expected Response	Max Mark	Additional Guidance
8.		Candidates should discuss how effective they find the unconventional staging of the play in exploring at least one key idea in the play and should refer to appropriate textual evidence to support their discussion. 0 marks for reference/quotation alone.	10	The generic marking guide, covering aspects of commonality, can be found on page 193. In comments on the rest of the play, possible references include: • audience participation (e.g. in the "Walla Walla Wooskie" section) • reciting/quoting detailed statistics (e.g. about population decline) • musical extravaganzas such as Texas Jim's square dance Many other references are possible.

Text 3 — Drama — *Men Should Weep* by Ena Lamont Stewart

Question		Expected Response	Max Mark	Additional Guidance
9.	(i)	Candidates should explain what important aspects of Maggie's character are revealed in these lines. 2 marks for an insightful comment and reference. 1 mark for a basic comment and reference. 0 marks for reference/quotation alone.	4	Possible answers include: • defensive of her role: "Ye canna help …", "I dae the best I can" • defensive of her family: "You leave John alane", "He does his best for us" • sentimental: "I still love John. And whit's more, he loves me" • self-deluding: "Aye! I'm happy!", "I'm sorry for you, Lily"
	(ii)	Candidates should explain one important aspect of Lily's character which is revealed in these lines. 2 marks for an insightful comment and reference. 1 mark for a basic comment and reference. 0 marks for reference/quotation alone.	2	Possible answers include: • she speaks her mind, not afraid to be negative: "midden", "No much o a best", "nae" repeated • quick to placate, conciliate: "OK. OK. …" • sense of humour: "photies to the Sunday papers … Is this a record?"

10.		Candidates should analyse how lines 16–28 are structured in such a way as to provide a lively dramatic exchange between Maggie and Lily.
		
		 2 marks for an insightful comment and reference.
		 1 mark for a basic comment and reference.
		 0 marks for reference/quotation alone.
			4	Possible answers include:
				
				 • the key ideas are (i) the back and forth, "tennis match", balanced nature of the exchanges, and (ii) the way each pair of lines is linked to the next by a word or an idea:
				   • balance: "Servin …" — "Livin …"; "in a Coocaddens pub" — "in a slum"; "brutes o men" — "a useless man"
				   • link: "weans"
				   • balance: "his greetin weans" — "They're *my* weans!"
				   • link: "workin … work"
				   • balance: "*paid* for my work" — "paid wi love"
				   • link: "airms roon ye/me"
				   • balance "a man's …" — "*Men*!"
				   • link: "They're a dirty beasts" — "a lumped thegither"
				   • balance: "Ye're daft!" — "You're *saft*!

11.		Candidates should discuss to what extent men in the play are presented as weak and should refer to appropriate textual evidence to support their discussion. 0 marks for reference/quotation alone.	10	The generic marking guide, covering aspects of commonality, can be found on page 193. In comments on the rest of the play, possible references include: • John's less than convincing efforts to support his family • John's inability to cope with Jenny • Alec's submissiveness to Isa Many other references are possible.

Text 1 — Prose — *The Painter* by Iain Crichton Smith

Question	Expected Response	Max Mark	Additional Guidance

12.	Candidates should explain how the narrator's account creates an ambiguous impression of how serious the fight is.
	
	For full marks there must be acknowledgement of both sides. 2 marks for an insightful comment and reference. 1 mark for a basic comment and reference. 0 marks for reference/quotation alone.
		4	Possible answers include:
			
			• suggestions that it is serious:
			  • the ferocity suggested by word choice of "kill … enraged … frustrated … tortured"
			  • metaphor in "gradually grew more demoniac" suggests father-in-law as almost possessed
			  • detail of actual injury in "cutting his son-in-law's left leg so that he fell to the ground"
			
			• suggestions that it may not be serious:
			  • inclusion of "perhaps", "to a certain extent" suggest narrator's uncertainty
			  • "however" (used twice) shows a willingness to contradict himself, lessen the seriousness of what has just been said
			  • "ponderously" suggests rather lethargic movement
			  • "looked as if …" suggests speculation, lack of certainty
			  • "odd … as if each was trying to cut corn" — they're merely "odd", not frightening, and appear as if engaged on everyday activity
			  • description of wife is essentially comic

13.	Candidates should analyse how the writer makes clear the contrast between William and the two fighters. For full marks there must be reference to both William and the fighters. 2 marks for an insightful comment and reference. 1 mark for a basic comment and reference. 0 marks for reference/ quotation alone.	4	Possible answers include: *William* • "sitting comfortably" suggests he is relaxed, at ease • "no expression on his face at all" suggests he is emotionless • "a cold clear intensity" suggests a deep, almost disturbing concentration • "as if he were asleep" suggests he is detached • "he sat there" suggests he is passive • "nor … did he make any attempt to pull his chair back" suggests he is unaware of (or not bothered by) any danger *the fighters* • "the scythes swung to and fro" suggests repeated intense and dangerous activity • "faces … contorted" suggests the effort is twisting the shape of their faces • "in the fury of battle" suggests a sense of ferocious engagement • "suffused with blood and rage" suggests a sense of all-consuming anger • "teeth were drawn back in a snarl" suggests an animal-like savagery
14.	Candidates should describe in their own words why the narrator is so incensed at William. 1 mark for each acceptable point. 0 marks for quotation alone.	2	Possible answers include: • revulsion at his coldness, callousness • thinks he is as unfeeling as a natural predator • compares his response with a rat, i.e. aggressive when challenged • resents his apparent assumption that events had been organised for his benefit • his attitude reduces human participants to inanimate objects ("house … wall") • [possibly] recognises in William the urge to capture the moment, which he, as a writer, shares

Question	Expected Response	Max Mark	Additional Guidance
15.	Candidates should discuss the impressions Crichton Smith creates of life in a small community in *The Painter* and at least one other story and should refer to appropriate textual evidence to support their discussion. 0 marks for reference/quotation alone.	10	The generic marking guide, covering aspects of commonality, can be found on page 193. In comments on other stories, possible references include: • the tensions between the two women in *The Telegram* • the son's sense of isolation in *Mother and Son* • the pressure to conform in *The Red Door* Many other references are possible.

Text 2 — Prose — *The Eye of the Hurricane* by George Mackay Brown

Question	Expected Response	Max Mark	Additional Guidance
16.	Candidates should explain the various methods the Captain uses to convince the narrator to buy him alcohol. 2 marks for an insightful comment and reference. 1 mark for a basic comment and reference. 0 marks for reference/quotation alone.	4	Possible answers include: • very matter of fact opening ("Now, Barclay, about this cold of mine.") as if the whole conversation will be business-like, not admitting of any disagreement. • disparages Miriam early on, an attempt to neutralise her influence on the narrator, to get him "on-side" • tells narrator that his drinking is not something he can control, claims it's a natural phenomenon which has to be faced up to • addresses him like teacher/pupil: "Do you understand that, Barclay?" • flatters the narrator with a reference to his writing • ingratiates himself to the narrator ("I like you. I'm very glad you're living in this house.") • uses an elaborate sea-going metaphor to justify asking narrator to help • asserts his dominant role as "skipper" • tries to make it simple: "And the first thing I want you to do ..." • completely ignores the narrator's repeated refusals • resorts to open threat of raising rent, evicting him
17.	Candidates should analyse how the narrator uses imagery to explain his views on charity. 2 marks for an insightful comment and reference. 1 mark for a basic comment and reference. 0 marks for reference/quotation alone.	4	Possible answers include: • "Charity is no hard-minted currency ... a shilling here and a sovereign there": it is not a simple matter of tangible coinage, cash to be handed out as and when you wish • "it is the oil and wine that drop uncertainly through the fingers": it is like liquid, not easily defined, not easily controlled • "the wounds of the world": the idea that suffering can happen at any time in any place • "wherever the roads of pity and suffering cross": compares pain and the compassion to alleviate it to roads which, when they intersect, allow "charity" to be delivered
18.	Candidates should explain what the last three lines suggest about the narrator's feelings for the Captain. 2 marks for an insightful comment and reference. 1 mark for a basic comment and reference. 0 marks for reference/quotation alone.	2	Possible answers include: • pity — sees him as a lonely, lost figure, caught up in his own fantasies • concern — the constant pacing must be indicative of mental struggle

Question	Expected Response	Max Mark	Additional Guidance
19.	Candidates should discuss how George Mackay Brown creates confrontations between characters in *The Eye of the Hurricane* and at least one other story and should refer to appropriate textual evidence to support their discussion. 0 marks for reference/quotation alone.	10	The generic marking guide, covering aspects of commonality, can be found on page 193. In comments on other stories, possible references include: • Bill and Sinclair in *A Time to Keep* • Flaws and the minister in *The Whaler's Return* • the Vikings and the villagers in *Tartan* Many other references are possible.

Text 3 — Prose — *The Trick is to Keep Breathing* by Janice Galloway

Question	Expected Response	Max Mark	Additional Guidance
20.	Candidates should explain how the writer establishes an unwelcoming atmosphere at the start of the extract. 2 marks for an insightful comment and reference. 1 mark for a basic comment and reference. 0 marks for reference/quotation alone.	3	Possible answers include: • the doctor's lateness suggests a lack of care • "sea-coloured corridor" — the sea has unpleasant associations for Joy • "no pictures and all the curtains closed" suggests cold, dark, claustrophobic, inhospitable • "smells like dog in the rain" suggests pungent, non-human, sickening • the absence of any preliminary chat suggests a very functional, bureaucratic approach • "Well?" suggests a very abrupt, uncaring tone • "horrible jacket" suggests even his clothing is off-putting • "gloom" reinforces the darkness in the room • "his eyes are all iris" suggests something unnatural, creepy, threatening
21.	Candidates should analyse how the exchange between the Patient and Dr Three highlights the lack of communication between them. 2 marks for an insightful comment and reference. 1 mark for a basic comment and reference. 0 marks for reference/quotation alone.	4	Possible answers include: reference to general points such as: • the profusion of short questions • the "stage directions" about Patient being "Mesmerised", "Confused", not able to speak, tears welling reference to specific points in the dialogue such as: • "Well what" — her response to Dr's opening shows she doesn't understand • "I thought you would start" — shows she doesn't know what's going on • "Start what?" — Dr is (deliberately?) showing he doesn't want to engage • "Yes. So what …" — a very perfunctory response to Patient's statement • "I want to know …" — "I don't know …" — total breakdown of communication • "So." — as if it's all been explained, nothing further to say • "Any other questions?" — with a hint that they will be dismissed as quickly as the first • "How long have you been here did you say?" — she's already told him

Question	Expected Response	Max Mark	Additional Guidance
22.	Candidates should explain how the Doctor's uncaring approach is made clear. 2 marks for an insightful comment and reference. 1 mark for a basic comment and reference. 0 marks for reference/quotation alone.	3	Possible answers include: • "Sighing" suggests impatience, as if dealing with a stupid child • "I suppose" as if he's having to do the thinking for her • "To go home for the weekend?" questioning intonation as if explaining something very simple to someone not very bright • "… all right?" — patronising tone • "I don't know what that's supposed to mean" — unhelpful reply to someone obviously distressed • "Take your time. [Silence] Right then" — invites her to take her time and then doesn't give her any • "… taps the bundle of papers … folds his arms" — making his impatience obvious • "The interview is over." — very abrupt
23.	Candidates should discuss how *The Trick Is To Keep Breathing* explores the way the individual is treated within the Mental Health system and should refer to appropriate textual evidence to support their discussion. 0 marks for reference/quotation alone.	10	The generic marking guide, covering aspects of commonality, can be found on page 193. In comments on the rest of the novel, possible references include: • the Health Visitor • Joy's experiences in the hospital • Doctor Two and the *Courage and Bereavement* pamphlet Many other references are possible.

Text 4 — Prose — *Sunset Song* by Lewis Grassic Gibbon

Question	Expected Response	Max Mark	Additional Guidance
24.	Candidates should analyse how the writer's use of language emphasises the offensiveness of Ewan's behaviour. 2 marks for an insightful comment and reference. 1 mark for a basic comment and reference. 0 marks for reference/quotation alone.	4	Possible answers include: • "sneered" suggests contempt in his voice • "*Hell, Chris, what a bloody place!*" the coarse language suggests a lack of respect • "flung his pack one way and his hat the other" suggests a lack of care, self-respect • "as though she were a tink" compares Chris to someone to be looked down on, of no value • "hot and questing and wise" suggests he is being sexually aggressive, selfish, that he is more experienced now than he was and isn't afraid to make Chris aware of it • "the hot smoulder fire in his eyes" suggests he is almost demonic, malevolent • "red with other things" suggests he is sexually aroused in a frightening way • "*Well, we'll hope so, eh Chris?*" crude, sexual innuendo • "*unless you're too bloody stand-offish*" open insult to his wife coarsened by use of offensive language • "picked the thing up and flung it …" — such lack of respect for his own child's picture book (emphasised by "thing" and "flung") is an especially upsetting detail • the commanding tone of "*Here, give us some tea.*" as if Chris were a servant to be bossed about

Question	Expected Response	Max Mark	Additional Guidance
25.	Candidates should analyse how the writer makes the reader aware of Chris's perception of Ewan. 2 marks for an insightful comment and reference. 1 mark for a basic comment and reference. 0 marks for reference/quotation alone	4	Possible answers include: • "like a beast at a trough" suggests she sees him as non-human, merely satisfying basic needs, no self-respect; the harsh, plosive consonants at "beast" and "trough" add a hint of disgust • "coarse hair that sprang like short bristles" suggests she sees him a rough, unrefined, compares him with an inanimate object • "red and angry circle about the collar" shows that she can sense his aggressiveness in the chafing left by his uniform • "a great half-healed scar … glinted putrescent blue" — a revolting description of something deeply unhealthy, unnatural, almost alive
26.	Candidates should identify the change in young Ewan's reaction to his father. 1 mark for identifying/explaining each reaction. 0 marks for reference/quotation alone.	2	Possible answers include: • at first, he is cautious, but acknowledges Ewan as his father • at the end he is scared/seeks Chris's protection, calling him "that soldier", i.e. denying any relationship
27.	Candidates should discuss the development of the relationship between Chris and Ewan and should refer to appropriate textual evidence to support their discussion. 0 marks for reference/quotation alone.	10	The generic marking guide, covering aspects of commonality, can be found on page 193. In comments on the rest of the novel, possible references include: • the nervousness of the initial wooing • early passion, happy domestic life with young Ewan • the disparity in intellect, e.g. attitude to history at Dunnottar Castle Many other references are possible.

Text 5 — Prose — *The Cone-Gatherers* by Robin Jenkins

Question	Expected Response	Max Mark	Additional Guidance
28.	Candidates should analyse how the sentence structure helps to convey how Calum is feeling. 2 marks for an insightful comment and reference. 1 mark for a basic comment and reference. 0 marks for reference/quotation alone.	2	Possible answers include: • the balancing around the semicolon helps to convey the idea that Calum has changed from being a beater to thinking of himself as a deer • the sentence beginning "He could not, however …" serves to introduce the contrast between the deer's agility and Calum's clumsiness • the structure of the sentence beginning "He fell and rose again …" imitates the frantic, headlong action it describes with a list of movements ("fell … rose avoided … collide"); it also lists all the things Calum feels are ignoring him and the deer, so many that he feels completely cut off from help or sympathy

Question	Expected Response	Max Mark	Additional Guidance
29.	Candidates should analyse how the writer's use of language creates a sense of "commotion". 2 marks for an insightful comment and reference. 1 mark for a basic comment and reference. 0 marks for reference/quotation alone.	4	Possible answers include: • some of the many references to sound (e.g. "barked … roared … shouts … bellowed … bawled" etc.) could be dealt with collectively with a comment suggesting the way they create a sense of confusion of cacophonous sound • "barked fiercely" suggests harsh, loud, aggressive noise • "rush into the danger" suggests a reckless dash • "roared to him" suggests an impassioned, panicked cry • "resounded with their exultant shouts" suggests an echoing effect, all the calls mixing together • "bellowed" suggests loud, deep, fanatical • "bawled" suggests frantic, hysterical • list of adjectives "silent, desperate, and heroic" suggests the extent of their plight • "guns banged" suggests loud, aggressive noise, associated with death/violence • "wails of lament" suggests high-pitched exclamations of mourning • "dashed on at a demented speed" suggests reckless speed, desperate, almost out of control • "shot out" suggests a sudden, dramatic appearance • "a deer screaming" suggests high-pitched, suffering, in pain • "scrabbling about" suggests agitated, distressed movement • "feverishly reloading" suggests excited, tense movement • the rather paradoxical "Screaming in sympathy" suggests the confusion at the scene • list of actions "flung … clasped … tried to comfort" suggests a rush of actions" • "flung" suggests acting with passion, no thought of consequences • "dragged him about with it in its mortal agony" suggests frantic movement back and forth at the moment of death

Question	Expected Response	Max Mark	Additional Guidance
30.	Candidates should explain how the reader is made aware of Duror's state of mind at this point. 2 marks for an insightful comment and reference. 1 mark for a basic comment and reference. 0 marks for reference/quotation alone.	4	Possible answers include: • the contrast between the immobility of Forgan, Roderick and Lady Runcie-Campbell, and Duror "leaping out of the wood" like something possessed emphasises Duror's disturbed state of mind • the paradoxical "berserk joy" depicts him as out of control, unaware of what his real emotions are • the blunt abruptness of the simple sentence "There was a knife in his hand" focuses attention on it and foreshadows the violence he is about to carry out • "he never heard her" suggests he is "switched off", so caught up in his emotions that he cannot process the sound of her words • "Rushing ... he threw ... with furious force, ... seizing ... cut its throat savagely" combine to depict someone in a uncontrolled, violent bloodlust, acting with tremendous strength and energy • the ambiguity of his pose after the kill, not proud, but apparently grieving suggests a confusion in his own mind • clinging onto the knife suggests he is in shock, doesn't know what to do
31.	Candidates should discuss how the writer explores the theme of death and should refer to appropriate textual evidence to support their discussion. 0 marks for reference/quotation alone.	10	The generic marking guide, covering aspects of commonality, can be found on page 193. In comments on the rest of the novel, possible references include: • the War — the death and suffering it is causing • the contrast between Duror's and Calum's attitude to the death of animals • the deaths of Duror and Calum at the end of the story Many other references are possible.

Text 1 — Poetry — *Tam o' Shanter* by Robert Burns

Question	Expected Response	Max Mark	Additional Guidance
32.	Candidates should analyse how the extended simile creates a vivid picture of what is happening. For full marks there must be reference to all three of the comparisons. 1 mark for a comment and reference. 0 marks for reference/quotation alone.	3	Possible answers include: • "As bees …" suggests a sense of outrage, a need to escape assault; idea of the small and vulnerable ("bees") being threatened by something larger ("herds") • "As open pussie's …" suggests a sudden ("pop") attack close at hand ("before their nose") which causes extreme alarm • "As eager …" suggests a concerted response to a rallying cry, one being chased by many
33.	Candidates should explain how Burns makes this part of the poem dramatic. 2 marks for an insightful comment and reference. 1 mark for a basic comment and reference. 0 marks for reference/quotation alone.	4	Possible answers include: • the pause to lecture Tam creates tension by delaying the continuation of the story • direct address to Meg ("do thy speedy utmost") reminds reader of the urgency involved • setting a sort of target for Meg/Tam ("There at them …") sets up the dramatic chase, creating uncertainty about their fate

Question	Expected Response	Max Mark	Additional Guidance
33.	*(continued)*		• idea of Nannie being way out in front of the other witches creates fear that she will catch Tam • referring to Maggie as "noble" increases the sense of good versus evil in the chase • the frantic efforts by Nannie ("flew at Tam wi' furious ettle") increase the tension • "But little wist she …" — a last minute turn of fortune, the hero has a trick up his sleeve • "Ae spring" — a single leap, one last final effort • "But left behind …" the sacrifice involved in saving her master
34.	Candidates should discuss to what extent they think lines 27—32 are meant as a serious warning to the reader. Marks will depend on the thoughtfulness of the discussion and the appropriateness of reference. 2 marks for an insightful comment 1 mark for a basic comment. 0 marks for reference/quotation alone.	3	Possible answers include: • Not serious: it's just a conventional conclusion, with the expected element of moralising and instruction ("take heed … Think … Remember"); it can't really be a "tale o' truth" so any reluctant moral isn't convincing; it's just a bit of fun, developing the idea of men as in need of guidance, playing on superstitions of witchcraft • Serious: it warns reasonably enough about over-indulgence (in drink or lascivious thoughts), of paying a high price for unwise behaviour; it is addressed only to men, the weaker sex as far as irresponsible behaviour is concerned
35.	Candidates should discuss the extent to which Burns passes judgements in *Tam o' Shanter* and at least one other of his poems, and should refer to appropriate textual evidence to support their discussion. 0 marks for reference/quotation alone.	10	The generic marking guide, covering aspects of commonality, can be found on page 193. In comments on other poems, possible references include: • judgement on Hamilton and on Holy Willie himself in *Holy Willie's Prayer* • on the upper classes and the pompous in *A Man's a Man for a' That* • on his detractors (and on himself) in *A Poet's Welcome to his Love-Begotten Daughter* Many other references are possible.

Text 2 — Poetry — *Anne Hathaway* by Carol Ann Duffy

Question	Expected Response	Max Mark	Additional Guidance

36.	Candidates should analyse how the first sentence establishes the speaker's passion.
	There must be reference to two techniques. 1 mark for an acceptable comment and reference. 0 marks for reference/quotation alone.
		2	Possible answers include:
			• metaphor/imagery comparing the bed to:
			  • "a spinning world …" suggests lively, exhilarating, breathless
			  • "forests, castles, torchlight, clifftops" (collectively or singly) suggests romantic, exotic, thrilling, dangerous
			  • "seas/where he would dive for pearls" suggests both depth and thrilling activities with potential for wealth
			• list structure:
			  • "forests, castles, torchlight, clifftops, seas" suggests a vast range of different things, as if she is reeling them off with pleasure

Question	Expected Response	Max Mark	Additional Guidance
37.	Candidates should explain how the poet uses references to writing to convey the speaker's feelings. 2 marks for an insightful comment and reference. 1 mark for a basic comment and reference. 0 marks for reference/quotation alone.	4	Possible answers include: • the general idea is about the blurring of the distinction between life and art, that Anne sees their love as being as vital, exciting, as fulfilling as her husband's work; this idea should be developed by specific references such as: • "words/were shooting stars" could possibly refer to written words, hence suggesting she sees them as exciting, romantic • "my body now a softer rhyme" creates a sense of their being joined together, of belonging together (Duffy is also touching on the idea of masculine and feminine rhyme) • "now echo, assonance" continues the idea of things being joined together in a pleasing way (imitated by the string of words linked by assonance: "on", "body", "softer", "to", "echo", "assonance", "touch" and "noun") • "a verb dancing in the centre of a noun" suggests joyous action, sexually suggestive; hints at Shakespeare's fondness for creating verbs from nouns and therefore suggests energy, freshness in their lovemaking • "I dreamed he'd written me" suggests how her love has sparked her imagination, she loves him so much that she dreams of being one of his creations • "the bed/a page" continues the conflation of his creativity and their lovemaking; almost punning on idea of sheets of paper/sheets on a bed; his creativity on paper is matched by his creativity in bed • "Romance/and drama played" elevates their love to a full theatrical production; as if they are acting out a dramatic (and poetic) script
38.	Candidates should evaluate the effectiveness of lines 11–14 as a conclusion to the poem. Candidates should show understanding of the term "conclusion" and show how the content of the last four lines continues – or contrasts with – ideas and/or language in lines 1–10. 4 marks can be awarded for four appropriate, basic comments. An insightful comment on one example may be awarded 2 marks. 0 marks for reference/quotation alone.	4	Possible answers include: • the contrast between the exuberant love of Anne and her lover and the dullness of the guests, seen in "dozed" which suggests they are inactive and in "dribbling their prose" a disdainful reference to the difference between the everyday nature of "prose" and the excitement, energy of poetry • the vitality suggested in "living, laughing love" – emphasised by the alliteration, the smooth, liquid sound of the repeated "l" (which contrasts with the harsher sounds of "dozed", "dribbling" and "prose") • the dash leads into the conclusion, a dramatic separation of the descriptions of her husband alive and the acknowledgement that he lives on in her imagination • the consonance in "hold" and "held" recalls that the lovers rhymed with each other • the imagery of "casket" suggests that like a strongbox for valuables her memories are precious • the final rhyming couplet (in imitation of the Shakespearean sonnet) brings the poem to an aural conclusion

Question	Expected Response	Max Mark	Additional Guidance
39.	Candidates should discuss how Duffy explores the theme of love in *Anne Hathaway* and at least one other poem, and should refer to appropriate textual evidence to support their discussion. 0 marks for reference/quotation alone.	10	The generic marking guide, covering aspects of commonality, can be found on page 193. In comments on other poems, possible references include: • the destructive power of love in *Havisham* • the unusual take on love in *Valentine* • the relationship between husband and wife in *Mrs Midas* Many other references are possible.

Text 3 – Poetry – Some Old Photographs by Liz Lochhead

Question	Expected Response	Max Mark	Additional Guidance
40.	Candidates should explain how the poet creates a dream-like atmosphere. For full marks there should be reference to more than one technique. 2 marks for an insightful comment and reference. 1 mark for a basic comment and reference. 0 marks for reference/quotation alone.	4	Possible answers include: • the lack of punctuation/the ungrammatical nature of each line creates a muddled, dreamlike impression; it's like one enormous list of impressions • the uneven, irregular lines give it a distorted, random feel • the synaesthesia in "weather evocative as scent" suggests a confusion, in which something inanimate can be described as strong, lingering • paradox in "romance of dark stormclouds" describes what is usually seen as threatening ("stormclouds") in terms of pleasure, passion • stress pattern in "low wide river", three consecutive long vowel sounds creates a heavy, slowed down effect • word play in "long … and longer" suggests confusion, uncertainty (+ hint of "long" = yearning) • the enjambment in "of light/of smoke" draws out the sound as if one image is piling up on another • "fabulous film-noir stills" conjures up images of stylish Hollywood movies; also suggests a hint of menace, anything can happen • slightly incongruous comparison of Central Station with Hollywood chic • the repeated "f" sound in "fabulous film … freezing fog" creates an echo effect • assonance and rhyme in "silvering the chilled, stilled" continues the echo effect • "the glamorous past" suggests a world/time where everything was stylish, no flaws or problems • metaphor in "drops on a rainmate are sequins" turn something prosaic ("rainmate") into something dazzling, sophisticated

Question	Expected Response	Max Mark	Additional Guidance
41.	Candidates should explain how the poet reminds the reader that these photographs are old. 1 mark for an acceptable comment and reference. 0 marks for reference/quotation alone.	2	Possible answers include: • "still-lovely mother" indicates the photograph shows the mother before she aged/lost her youthful beauty • "before you were born" as if the poet is talking to herself about a very distant time • reference to "all" dads being "in hats" must be a time (50s at the latest) when all adult males wore hats • "Central at five past five" suggests a bygone time when all offices and businesses closed at five o'clock • "belted dark overcoats" suggest, again, the 50s or earlier
42.	Candidates should explain what impression the poet creates of George Square. 2 marks for an insightful comment and reference. 1 mark for a basic comment and reference. 0 marks for reference/quotation alone.	2	Possible answers include: • a sense of movement/bustle in "starlings swarming" • a sense of urban grit in "noise and stink and smoky breath" • a sense of relentless activity in the list "all the passing now/and noise and stink and smoky breath" • a slightly surreal impression from "above what was/never really this photograph" — as if the photograph has vanished and she is/thinks she is actually in the Square
43.	Candidates should explain how the poet creates a sense of excitement in the last three lines of the poem.	2	Possible answers include: • the apparently random list "wee boays, a duchess, bunting" as if there's something out of the ordinary about to happen • using local speech in "wee boays" creates a lively, realistic picture of the scene • "a/big launch" — idea of something starting off fresh, new • "that boat is yet to sail" — slightly enigmatic, but hints at the future, good things to come
44.	Candidates should discuss whether criticism of Liz Lochhead for being overly nostalgic is fair, by referring to *Some Old Photographs* and at least one other poem, and should refer to appropriate textual evidence to support their discussion. 0 marks for reference/quotation alone.	10	The generic marking guide, covering aspects of commonality, can be found on page 193. In comments on other poems, possible references include: • the depiction of a past way of life in *For My Grandmother Knitting* • the description of the mother's preparations in *View of Scotland/Love Poem* • the recollections of Hogmanay traditions in *View of Scotland/Love Poem* Many other references are possible.

Text 4 — Poetry — *Memorial* by Norman MacCaig

Question	Expected Response	Max Mark	Additional Guidance

45.	Candidates should analyse how one of the images conveys how the speaker has been affected by the death.
	
	2 marks for an insightful comment. 1 mark for a basic comment. 0 marks for reference/quotation alone.
		3	Possible answers include:
			• "The silence of her dying sounds through/the carousel of language"
			  • compares silence with something that can make a sounds, suggesting confusion or heightened awareness of her absence; compares language to a carousel — something associated with joyful sound and happy experiences, suggesting she is felt/sensed at all times, albeit in an incongruous way [this image is not easy to pick apart — there is no "correct answer"; candidates should be rewarded for all plausible comment]
			• "It's a web/on which laughter stitches itself"
			  • compares the silence with an intricate pattern, and imagines laughter as capable of attaching itself to the web, suggesting her presence/absence is capable of causing happiness ("laughter"), an apparently contradictory emotion [this image is not easy to pick apart — there is no "correct answer"; candidates should be rewarded for all plausible comment]

46.	Candidates should explain how the poet uses contrast to reveal the persona's feelings. 2 marks for an insightful comment and reference. 1 mark for a basic comment and reference. 0 marks for reference/quotation alone.	4	Possible answers include: • various contrasts of living/dying suggest confusion, unwillingness to accept the death • contrast of the vivid and natural ("bird … sun … fish … crocus") with sense of death, emptiness ("black words … the sound/of soundlessness … nowhere") • contrast between what "she tells …" and what "I hear …" suggests he is living with both happiness and sadness • contrast between beauty of "No crocus is carved more gently" and the bleakness of "the nowhere/she is continuously going into" shows the persona feels the death in a contradictory way • contrast/contradiction in "sound/of soundlessness" suggests confusion, or a heightened awareness of the absence
47.	Candidates should explain how the persona makes clear the impact the death has had on him. 2 marks for an insightful comment and reference. 1 mark for a basic comment and reference. 0 marks for reference/quotation alone.	3	Possible answers include: • he says she "can't stop dying" — in his mind he relives her death all the time • she has the power to make him "her elegy" — he personifies everything he would want to say about her death • the extended "artistic" metaphor ("elegy … masterpiece … fiction … music") creates an elaborate sense of how her death/memory permeates every aspect of his life and his creativity • the apparently contradictory nature of "walking masterpiece" and "true fiction" suggests bewilderment, disorientation • the enigmatic last line suggests they have almost merged in personality

Question	Expected Response	Max Mark	Additional Guidance
48.	Candidates should discuss Norman MacCaig's exploration of deeply emotional situations in *Memorial* and at least one other poem, and should refer to appropriate textual evidence to support their discussion. 0 marks for reference/quotation alone.	10	The generic marking guide, covering aspects of commonality, can be found on page 193. In comments on other poems, possible references include: • the feelings experienced by the persona in *Visiting Hour* • the sense of loss in *Sounds of the Day* • the relationship between persona and the aunt in *Aunt Julia* Many other references are possible.

Text 5 — Poetry — *Shores* by Sorley MacLean

Question	Expected Response	Max Mark	Additional Guidance
49.	Candidates should analyse how the poet conveys the power of natural features. 2 marks for an insightful comment and reference. 1 mark for a basic comment and reference. 0 marks for reference/quotation alone.	3	Possible answers include: • imagery: "great white mouth … two hard jaws" personifies the bay as capable of devouring; the promontories as the powerful "jaws" ready to snap shut • "beside the sea/renewing love" suggests healing power of the sea, able to renew something as powerful as love • "the ocean was filling/Talisker bay forever" suggests eternal power of the ocean • "Prishal bowed his stallion head" compares landscape feature to a powerful, graceful animal
50.	Candidates should explain how the poet conveys his commitment to the person he is addressing. 2 marks for an insightful comment and reference. 1 mark for a basic comment and reference. 0 marks for reference/quotation alone.	3	Possible answers include: • "I would stay there till doom" — i.e. until the end of time, a strong, if conventional, promise of fidelity • "measuring sand, grain by grain" — an exaggerated notion of counting out an almost infinite number • "the sea draining drop by drop" — another infinite task
51.	Candidates should evaluate the last verse as a conclusion to the poem as a whole by referring to structural similarities and differences. Up to 2 marks for identification of similarities/differences. 2 marks for an insightful comment on the last verse as a conclusion. 1 mark for a basic point. 0 marks for reference/quotation alone.	4	Possible answers include: • Structural similarities: • "And if I were … I would … I would"; • use of "shore" in first line of each verse • Structural differences: • "And if we" (vv 1 and 2) but "And if I" (v 3) • "And if …" appears once in vv 1 and 2 but twice in v 3 • vv 1 and 2 are single sentences but v 3 is two sentences • "I would …" in vv 1 and 2 is followed by stasis ("stand … stay … wait") but by action in v 3 ("put up … build" • Comments: • brings together "I" and "we" — sense of resolution • continues idea of power of nature, but combines elements from previous verses ("ocean and the sand, drop and grain" • continues idea of commitment ("synthesis of love for you") • introduces a desire to protect ("I would build the rampart wall") • conclusion could be argued as pessimistic contrary to previous sense of hope, commitment

Question	Expected Response	Max Mark	Additional Guidance
52.	Candidates should discuss the importance of landscape in MacLean's poetry and should refer to appropriate textual evidence to support their discussion. 0 marks for reference/quotation alone.	10	The generic marking guide, covering aspects of commonality, can be found on page 193. In comments on other poems, possible references include: • Cnoc an Ra and Beinn na Lice in *Hallaig* • Carn Mor and Creag Mheircil in *Screapadal* • the effects of the Clearances in both *Hallaig* and *Screapdal* Many other references are possible.

Text 6 — Poetry — *Two Trees* by Don Paterson

Question	Expected Response	Max Mark	Additional Guidance
53.	Candidates should explain how the poet makes the first verse sound like the start of a simple folk tale or parable. 2 marks for an insightful comment and reference. 1 mark for a basic comment and reference. 0 marks for reference/quotation alone.	4	Possible answers include: • typical story opening "One morning …" • simplicity of "… got out of bed" • focuses on his "one idea" and states it simply "to graft …" • the hint that there is something potentially symbolic in what he is doing, i.e. attempting to bring together two different entities • keeps it focuses on one person and his activities: "work … lay open … lash" • "twelve months" pass — the story moves on quickly • "nothing" for a while, "but one day …", i.e. the next stage in the story has arrived • "Over the years …" — another long passage of time leading to … • … the wondrous outcome: "each bough looked like it gave a double crop" • Miguel becomes a figure famous for his "magic tree" i.e. he has (or appears to have) supernatural attributes
54.	Candidates should explain how lines 13–16 act as a link or turning point in the poem as a whole. 1 mark for establishing link with what goes before; 1 mark for establishing link with what follows.	2	Possible answers include: • the new purchaser's lack of a "dream" links back to Don Miguel's "one idea" and forward to the potentially destructive nature of his action • his splitting of the tree links back to Don Miguel's successful grafting and forward to the effect of the separation • the "fused seam" links back to Don Miguel's "lash[ing]" them together and forward to the "split[ting]" • "two holes" links forward to the separation of the two trees and recalls Don Miguel's enthusiasm to turn two into one

Question	Expected Response	Max Mark	Additional Guidance
55.	Candidates should explain how the poet subverts the idea that the poem is a parable or a tale with a message. 2 marks for an insightful comment and reference. 1 mark for a basic comment and reference. 0 marks for reference/quotation alone.	4	Possible answers include: • "And no ..." sounds almost as if addressed directly to readers who might be jumping ahead, warning them not to engage in fanciful interpretations • "they did not ... nor did ... nor did" provides a list of the kind of interpretations readers might be expecting, a is forcefully negative about each one • the possible interpretations are all a little romanticised, whimsical (all involve anthropomorphism of a sort) almost in mockery of what readers might be expecting • concludes with two one-line sentences (the only ones in the poem) as if making a very simple, direct point • repetition of "trees" emphasises that they are (he claims) the only topic of the poem • denies bluntly the possibility of tress having human qualities ("don't weep or ache or shout") • the assertiveness of the last two lines is emphasised by the straightforward, conclusive rhyme
56.	Candidates should discuss Paterson's use of symbolism to explore important themes and should refer to appropriate textual evidence to support their discussion. 0 marks for reference/quotation alone.	10	The generic marking guide, covering aspects of commonality, can be found on page 193. In comments on other poems, possible references include: • the stone in *Nil Nil* • the pool table or the ferry in *The Ferryman's Arms* • the bus journey in *Baldovan 11.00* Many other references are possible.

SECTION 2 — Critical Essay

Please see the assessment criteria for the Critical Essay on page 245.

HIGHER FOR CfE ENGLISH
MODEL PAPER 3

PAPER 1 — READING FOR UNDERSTANDING, ANALYSIS AND EVALUATION

Marking Instructions for each question

Passage 1

Question		Expected Response	Max Mark	Additional Guidance
1.	(a)	Candidates should analyse how the writer's word choice emphasises the "conventional wisdom" that reading books is better than playing video games. Marks will depend on the quality of comment on appropriate language feature(s). 2 marks may be awarded for reference plus detailed/insightful comment; 1 mark for reference plus more basic comment; 0 marks for reference alone. *Possible answers are shown in the "Additional Guidance" column.*	2	Possible answers include: • "enriches" suggests that reading adds to one's knowledge, awareness; is rewarding, beneficial; improves one • "the mind" suggests reading is influencing something greater than just the brain; it influences our consciousness: thought, perception, emotions and imagination • "deadens" suggests video games make kids less aware, less sensitive, less vigorous; they make kids think less; lifeless • "zoning out" suggests video games make kids detached from people and things around them, unresponsive, unstimulated or any other acceptable answer
	(b)	Candidates should explain "the question" the writer asks about "other forms of culture". Candidates must use their own words. No marks are awarded for verbatim quotations from the passage. *Depending on clarity of explanation, 1 mark or 2 marks for the suggested answer "Additional Guidance" column.*	2	Possible answers include: • the writer is asking if these other forms of culture involve discrete thinking skills/have qualities which benefit, stimulate, challenge, stretch our minds in ways which are different from – but just as important as – reading or any other acceptable answer
	(c)	Candidates should analyse how the writer uses at least two language features to emphasise the contrast between his positive view of "other forms of culture" and the negative view held by "most critics". Marks will depend on the quality of comment on appropriate language feature(s). 2 marks may be awarded for reference plus detailed/insightful comment; 1 mark for reference plus more basic comment; 0 marks for reference alone. *Possible answers are shown in the "Additional Guidance" column.*	4	Possible answers include: *Imagery* • "(progressive) story": just as a "story" is a developing, organised narrative, so the writer sees the positive influence of popular culture as gradual, logical, coherent, interesting … • "our brains sharper": just as sharpening involves giving cutting tools a better edge, this suggests making our brains keener, more accurate … • "we soak in": soaking in is a process of absorption, of taking in as much liquid as possible; this suggests we become immersed in popular culture, that its influence is natural, irresistible, all-consuming, profound, deep … • "(lowbrow) fluff": fluff is light, downy material (for example, small pieces of wool); its use suggests critics believe popular culture is light, trivial, worthless, superficial, irrelevant, trifling … • "honing": just as honing is a (refined) process of giving cutting tools a perfect edge, this suggests gradually making our brains as sharp as possible, more and more precise, accurate, productive … *Word choice* • "allege" suggest doubt, calls the critics' views into question • "dumbing down" suggests popular culture offers people a reduced intellectual challenge **or** is responsible for making people less educated, less intelligent, more lowbrow

Question		Expected Response	Max Mark	Additional Guidance
	(c)	*(continued)*		• "progressive" suggests developing, advancing, moving forward steadily, leading to improvement • "steadily" suggests reliable, consistent progress • "imperceptibly" suggests change is gradual, subtle • "sharper" suggests keener, more precise, more accurate • "soak in" suggests it's not a superficial process; influence is deep; we are fully engaged, absorbed • "dismissed" suggests brushed aside, considered beneath contempt, irrelevant, unimportant, trivial • "lowbrow" suggests vulgar, anti-intellectual, uncultured, plebeian • "fluff" suggests worthless, trivial, inconsequential, superficial • "honing" suggests sharpening, perfecting, refining *Sentence structure* • balanced structure/contrast of "Where … story" allows the writer to trump the critics' argument; this is heightened by the greater certainty of his "see" set against the dubious nature of what they "allege" • use of colon to introduce a full development of his "progressive story" argument • use of parenthesis "but … imperceptibly" to explain that this positive development is so gradual that it's easy for the less astute (like the critics) to miss it • positioning of "I hope to persuade you" at the start of the final sentence alerts the reader to the fact that the writer is about to make what he believes is his most important point • positioning of "increasingly" just before his key statement stresses that the point he is about to make is more and more relevant, true • balanced nature of final statement, hinging on the "just as important as" comparison stresses skills developed by popular culture are of a comparable standard to the skills developed by reading or any other acceptable answer
2.		Candidates should analyse how the writer conveys the difficulty of playing video games by his use of sentence structure and imagery. Marks will depend on the quality of comment on appropriate language feature(s). For full marks there must be reference to both features. 2 marks may be awarded for reference plus detailed/insightful comment; 1 mark for reference plus more basic comment; 0 marks for mere identification of a feature of sentence structure. *Possible answers are shown in the "Additional Guidance" column.*	4	Possible answers include: *Sentence structure* • the positioning of **and/or** rhythmic/repetitive nature of "And the first and last thing" conveys the definitive 'Alpha and omega' nature of this phrase, especially when placed at the start of the sentence, suggests the difficulty of video games is a fundamental point to the writer • use of parenthesis "the thing … hear" adds to the mystery, adds to the dramatic build-up to the final announcement of video games' difficulty • additional phrase "sometimes maddeningly" has two functions: again adds to the build-up **and/or** ramps up the notion of extreme difficulty that "fiendishly" has introduced

Question		Expected Response	Max Mark	Additional Guidance
2.		*(continued)*		• use of climax in the sentence "The dirty ... fun." — the somewhat awkward/unusual construction of this sentence is designed to stress the "not having fun" element of its conclusion • repetition of the "you may be" structure stresses — and this is heightened by the use of the inclusive direct address — the variety of problems playing video games may cause • repetition of adjectives ("frustrated", "confused", "disorientated", "stuck") — rat-a-tat run of adjectives suggests 'the sea of troubles' playing video games may involve • anticlimax of "you may be stuck" in its definitive downbeat simplicity, it is a stark summation of the seemingly insoluble challenge these games present • use of the continuous tense in final sentence — an argument might be made that this reflects the ongoing, nagging nature of the problems involved *Imagery* • "wrestling": just as wrestling involves close, physical combat with a single opponent, so it suggests a demanding, exhausting battle with an unforgiving enemy • "worrying a loose tooth": just as this involves the constant working away at a persistent physical annoyance, so it suggests that the difficulties presented by video games are nagging frustrations that constantly prey on one's mind • "stuck": just as to be stuck is to be fixed immovably, so it suggests being trapped in a situation which offers no escape • "dirty little secret": usually used in the realms of ethics or morality, a deliberate attempt to hide the truth, a cover-up of some sort, a hidden scandal; used in relation to the difficulty of video games, it heightens the potentially damaging nature of this feature, suggests it is a very negative feature that is deliberately glossed over or any other acceptable answer
3.		Candidates should identify three reasons why "reward" is so important to the learning process involved in playing video games. Candidates must use their own words. No marks are awarded for verbatim quotations from the passage. *1 mark for each point from the "Additional Guidance" column.*	3	Possible answers include: • people are hard-wired to respond strongly to rewards • people find rewards a great stimulus to action, learning etc. • video games are designed to be full of rewards • rewards in video games are precise, with clear outcomes (explanation of "clearly defined") • the rewards are attractive • the rewards are presented in a variety of forms • players are constantly reminded about the rewards • the rewards are vitally important to achieving success in the games • the rewards are more intense, striking, colourful than in real life • players aren't always aware that they are learning (explanation of "without realising ...") or any other acceptable answer

Question		Expected Response	Max Mark	Additional Guidance
4.		Candidates should identify two criticisms and two defences the writer makes of video games. Candidates must use their own words. No marks are awarded for verbatim quotations from the passage. *1 mark for each point from the "Additional Guidance" column; maximum of 2 marks for criticism and 2 marks for defence.*	4	Possible answers include: *Criticisms* • the games may seem attractive but the attractions flatter to deceive, are rather superficial, blind one to the truth (explanation of "dazzled") • the games are addictive (explanation of "hooked") • the subject matter is infantile, petty, puerile, trivial … (explanation of "actual content … childish") • unnecessarily threatening, unjustifiably scary (explanation of "gratuitously menacing" — but explanation of "menacing" alone: 0) • the subject matter is very limited **and/or** moves between the two extremes of violence and childish fantasy (explanation of "alternates … princess-rescuing") • the games are violent (explanation of "drive-by shooting") • the games are pure fantasy (explanation of "princess-rescuing") *Defences* • the activities involved are beneficial for mental training/development ("good for the brain") • the skills developed will be of use in other spheres ("come in handy elsewhere") • it resembles learning algebra, which might seem pointless and abstract but exercises the brain • like chess, games might seem very basic (and aggressive in concept), but they are every bit as cerebral and mind-developing as chess; they develop strategic, tactical thinking or any other acceptable answer
5.	(a)	Candidates should explain in their own words the key distinction the writer makes between reading a novel and playing a video game. Candidates must use their own words. No marks are awarded for verbatim quotations from the passage. *1 mark for each point from the "Additional Guidance" column.*	2	Possible answers include: *reading a novel* • can get us thinking in a creative way, transport us to in different situation (explanation of "activate our imagination") • can affect our feelings, arouse passions (explanation of "conjure up powerful emotions") *playing a game* • makes you explore, study carefully (explanation of "analyse") • makes you weigh up options (explanation of "choose") • makes you evaluate options (explanation of "priotitise") • makes you reach a conclusion (explanation of "decide") or any other acceptable answer

Question		Expected Response	Max Mark	Additional Guidance
	(b)	Candidates should analyse how the writer's use of language conveys the contrast between what a gamer looks like from "the outside" and what is happening "inside the gamer's mind". For full marks there must be reference to both "outside" and "inside"; 2 marks may be awarded for reference plus detailed/insightful comment; 1 mark for reference plus more basic comment; 0 marks for reference alone. *Possible answers are shown in the "Additional Guidance" column.*	4	Possible answers include: *the gamer from "the outside"* • "looks like" suggests this may be an unreliable perspective, a superficial, unquestioning way to approach an analysis of gamers • "fury" suggests the gamer is behaving in an impulsive, uncontrolled way; everything is being done at top speed, in a blur of unthinking activity • "clicking" suggests mindless, repetitive activity • "shooting" suggests destructive, homicidal activity • "clicking and shooting" automatic, unthinking, mechanical, robotic, repetitive ... • the general simplicity of the penultimate sentence (especially when compared to the much more complex final sentence) heightens the impression that this is a naïve, simplistic way to view gamers *the gamer on the inside* • "peer" suggests an active approach involving close examination • "turns out" suggests a sense of some kind of revelation, surprise, discovery • "another creature" suggests something mysterious, surprising, unexpected, interesting but hard to define, a new form of life we didn't know existed • use of colon introduces a detailed description of the full range of intellectual activities involved in gaming • balance/repetition of "some of them" stresses range of activities involved • contrast in "snap judgements ... long-term strategies" shows range of important decision-making skills involved from quick, smart thinking to overall planning • "judgements" suggests wise, fair thinking • "strategies" suggests considered, creative thinking or any other acceptable answer

Passage 2

Question	Expected Response	Max Mark	Additional Guidance
6.	Candidates should identify key areas of disagreement in the two passages. There may be some overlap among the areas of disagreement. Markers will have to judge the extent to which a candidate has covered two points or one. Candidates can use bullet points in this final question, or write a number of linked statements. Evidence from the passage may include quotations, but these should be supported by explanations. Approach to marking is shown in the "Additional Guidance column. Key areas of disagreement are shown in the grid below. Other answers are possible.	5	The mark for this question should reflect the quality of response in two areas: • identification of the key areas of disagreement in attitude/ideas • level of detail given in support The following guidelines should be used: **Five marks** — comprehensive identification of three or more key areas of disagreement with full use of supporting evidence **Four marks** — clear identification of three or more key areas of disagreement with relevant use of supporting evidence **Three marks** — identification of three or more key areas of disagreement with supporting evidence **Two marks** — identification of two key areas of disagreement with supporting evidence **One mark** — identification of one key area of disagreement with supporting evidence **Zero marks** — failure to identify any key area of disagreement and/or total misunderstanding of task

	Area of Disagreement	Steven Johnson	Boris Johnson
1	general status	they are viewed as pointless, but they are not	they are harmful, narcotically addictive
2	intellectual benefits	they develop the brain in a number of ways	they require no thought or effort
3	educational benefits	high level thinking skills are developed	they may pretend to be educational but are totally lacking in educational value; a threat to literacy
4	the challenge involved	they can appear simple but are often very complex the process is more important than the (often simplistic) content	they encourage slovenly behaviour and thinking
5	the reward(s) involved	they are at times extremely hard unlike other entertainment, pleasure is not immediate	they offer immediate and simple pleasures

HIGHER FOR CfE ENGLISH
MODEL PAPER 3

PAPER 2 — CRITICAL READING

SECTION 2 — Critical Essay

Please see the assessment criteria for the Critical Essay on page 245.

HIGHER FOR CfE ENGLISH
2015

PAPER 1 — READING FOR UNDERSTANDING ANALYSIS AND EVALUATION

Marking Instructions for each question

Question	Expected Answer(s)	Max Mark	Additional Guidance
1.	Candidates should identify two positive aspects of Central Valley, California, given in lines 1—5. Candidates must use their own words. No marks for straight lifts from the passage. *Any two of the points in the "Additional Guidance" column for 1 mark each.*	2	Possible answers: • idyllic/pastoral ("almond trees", "sweet air", "orchards", "fields of …") • perfect/attractive ("sweet air", "vision") • diverse ("pomegranates, pistachios, grapes and apricots") • bountiful/fertile/productive ("million almond trees", "Beyond the almond orchards … fields of …", "two million dairy cows … six billion dollars' worth …") • vast/expansive/scale ("a million almond trees", "Beyond … were fields of …", "Somewhere in the distance")
2.	Candidates should analyse how the writer's use of language creates a negative impression of Central Valley in lines 6—10. For full marks there should be comments on at least 2 examples. 2 marks may be awarded for reference plus detailed/insightful comment; 1 mark for more basic comment; 0 marks for reference alone. *Possible answers shown in the "Additional Guidance" column.*	4	Possible answers: • "deeply disturbing" suggests unsettling/ unnatural nature of agriculture in Central Valley • contrast e.g. "it may sound like … but it is …" — emphasises the unnatural qualities of Central Valley • repetition/list of "no birds, no butterflies, no beetles" — drives home the absence of nature/ lack of wildlife • "single blade of grass" suggests that the most basic elements of nature have been eradicated here/wild nature is not tolerated • "only bees" highlights the strange lack of insect life • "arrive by lorry"/"the bees are hired by the day" — highlights the artificiality of Central Valley • "multibillion-dollar"/"industry" suggests anonymity/mass-produced for profit
3.	Candidates should analyse how the writer makes clear her disapproval of dairy farming methods used in Central Valley. For full marks there must be comment on both word choice and sentence structure, but these do not need to be evenly divided. 2 marks may be awarded for reference plus detailed/insightful comment; 1 mark for more basic comment; 0 marks for reference alone. Possible answers shown in the "Additional Guidance" column.	4	Possible answers: Word Choice • "last" suggests farmers see the cows as disposable objects, to be dismissed like rubbish when no longer productive • "crammed" suggests stifling, dangerous conditions • "barren" suggests emptiness, sterility, discomfort of the pens • "tiny patches" suggests restrictive, cramped areas in which cows are housed • "listlessly" suggests lack of life, lethargy, conditions weaken cows • "artificial (diets)" — emphasises the unnatural, unhealthy treatment of these cows • "pushed" suggests forceful manipulation • "grotesquely" suggests this type of dairy farming is monstrous, hideous • "worn out" suggests this type of farming is destructive • "short lives" — poignant description emphasises the tragic and unnatural consequences

Question	Expected Answer(s)	Max Mark	Additional Guidance
3.	(continued)	4	Sentence Structure • positioning of "As for the cows," at the start of this paragraph creates a despairing tone and/or introduces the negative description of the cows' lives • inversion used in "Crammed … antibiotics." highlights the atrocious conditions in which the cows are kept • list "fed, milked or injected with antibiotics" emphasises the assembly line/uncaring manner of the farms, suggesting the cows are merely part of a repetitive industrial process • list of procedures ("selective breeding … hormones") highlights the seemingly scientific procedures involved, making this type of farming seem like a cold and uncaring experiment on animals • climactic final sentence ("In their short lives … grass.") emphatically/dramatically highlights the contrast between these cows and the environment with which we would normally associate them
4.	For full marks candidates should show understanding of the key point: the movement from farming methods in California to their application in the UK. 2 marks may be awarded for detailed/insightful comment supported by appropriate use of reference/quotation; 1 mark for more basic comment; 0 marks for reference alone. *Possible answers shown in the "Additional Guidance" column.*	2	Possible references include: • the writer's change of focus from the USA to UK is signalled by the question "Could the British … look like this?" • the writer's move to consider intensive farming in the UK is suggested by "Farming in Britain … intensification from America" • the writer goes on to suggest that some of the intensive farming methods used in the USA — "bees arrive by lorry"— may soon arrive in the UK — "Bees are disappearing" • the writer goes on to suggest that some intensive farming methods are already being adopted in the UK, "mega-dairies and mega-piggeries" • the writer highlights the impact of intensive farming already being witnessed in the UK "countryside too sterile … native birds"
5.	Candidates should summarise the differences between Government food policy and consumer wishes. For full marks, both sides must be dealt with but not necessarily equally divided. Candidates must attempt to use their own words. No marks for straight lifts from passage. *Any four points from the "Additional Guidance" column for 1 mark each.*	4	Possible answers include: Government food policy: • buy more British/regional produce ("urging families to buy British food") • buy less foreign food ("Choosing to buy fewer imports") • ease pressure on farmers ("churn out more for less") • be more environmentally aware ("more eco-friendly way of eating") • buy in-season/healthy food ("seasonal fruit and vegetables") Consumer wishes: • drawn to less expensive produce ("addicted to cheap meat … products") • not concerned about origins of food ("supply lines … globe") • previously exotic/expensive food now commonplace/inexpensive ("once delicacies … cheap as chips") • expectation of variety "supply lines … globe"

Question	Expected Answer(s)	Max Mark	Additional Guidance
6.	Candidates should analyse how imagery and sentence structure convey the writer's criticism of industrial farming. For full marks there should be comments on both imagery and sentence structure but these do not have to be evenly divided. 2 marks may be awarded for reference plus detailed/insightful comment; 1 mark for more basic comment; 0 marks for reference alone. *Possible answers shown in the "Additional Guidance" column.*	4	Possible answers: Imagery: • "dirty secret": suggests that the methods used in factory farming are so shocking that they cannot be revealed • "front line": suggests that industrial farming is a desperate struggle against competitors, with frequent business casualties • "treadmill": suggests that industrial farming is very hard work and consists of never-ending repetitive chores • "plummeting": suggests that proximity to an industrial farm causes a devastating drop in the value of local homes Sentence structure: • Parenthesis "to investigate … produced" makes clear the specific nature of the "truth" • List of countries "France … South America" indicates extent of intensive farming • Colon in line 38 introduces example of people directly affected • Dash in line 39 introduces example of people directly affected • Repetitive sentence openings "I talked … I also talked" emphasises the scale the problem, based on her evidence gathering/variety of people affected • List "their homes … pollution" emphasises range of stories by people affected
7.	Candidates should explain how the writer continues the idea that the Central Valley dairy farming is "nightmarish", by making 3 key points. Candidates must attempt to use their own words. No marks for straight lifts from passage. *Any three points from the "Additional Guidance" column for 1 mark each.*	3	Possible answers include: • visible contamination of air/pollution ("yellowish-grey smog") • waste products in the ground ("bovine population … people") • the animals are kept in terrible conditions ("mud, corrugated iron and concrete.") • the overpowering smell ("nauseating reek") • huge buildings are a blight on the landscape ("array of towering … muddy pens.") • (apocalyptic) sense of desolation ("human population is sparse")
8.	Candidates should evaluate the final paragraph's effectiveness as a conclusion to the writer's criticism of industrial farming. For full marks there must be appropriate attention to the idea of a conclusion but this does not have to be limited to points about structure. Candidates may make valid points about the emotive/rhetorical impact of the conclusion. 2 marks awarded for detailed/insightful comment plus reference. 1 mark awarded for a more basic comment. *Possible answers shown in the "Additional Guidance" column.*	2	Possible answers include: • by giving details of the proposed mega-dairy in Lincolnshire, the writer reminds us of her earlier point that the British countryside faces a similar fate to that of Central Valley • the writer reminds us of the ludicrous size of these factory farms by revealing the enormous number of cows planned for this mega-dairy • by including the ridiculous claim that "cows do not belong in fields" the writer forcefully reminds us that those who practise intensive farming have scant regard for nature or natural processes • the writer concludes the passage with a warning that factory farms are getting larger in a rather surreptitious way, suggesting that we are being duped by the unscrupulous owners of these farms • the writer's rather poignant final sentence reminds the readers of the unnatural nature of this transition from the outdoors to indoors

Question	Expected Answer(s)	Max Mark	Additional Guidance
9.	Candidates should identify three key areas of agreement in the two passages. Candidates can use bullet points in this final question, or write a number of linked statements. *Approach to marking shown in the "Additional Guidance" column.* *Key areas of agreement shown in grid below. Other answers are possible.*	5	The following guidelines should be used: Five marks — identification of three key areas of agreement with detailed/insightful use of supporting evidence Four marks — identification of three key areas of agreement with appropriate use of supporting evidence Three marks — identification of three key areas of agreement Two marks — identification of two key areas of agreement One mark — identification of one key area of agreement Zero marks — failure to identify any key area of agreement and/or misunderstanding of task

	Area of Agreement	Passage 1	Passage 2
1.	Intensive farming is a highly productive process.	• size and fertility of the farms in Central Valley • high yields from dairy cows in Central Valley • farmers "churn out m ore or less"	• increased productivity of farms following introduction of intensive methods after Second Word War • higher numbers of chickens raised in less space • shorter time taken for animals to reach "edible size"
2.	Intensive farming yields affordable food for everyone.	• meat, fish and dairy products from factory farms are much cheaper • whole chickens sell for ridiculously low prices • farmers are under pressure to produce cheaper food	• factory farming fulfilled post-war policy of "cheap meat, eggs and cheese for everyone" • intensive farming allowed poorer people to have a much richer diet
3.	Intensive farming has brought about a change in people's dietary habits.	• previously expensive foods are now within the reach of everyone • exotic foods are now widely available • cheap meats contain more fat	• we have switched from a diet which was based on cereals/vegetable to one which is high in animal fats
4.	Intensive farming damages the environment and wildlife.	• nature is almost absent in Central Valley • bee populations are in decline • bird populations are in decline • natural habitats are disappearing • the UK countryside is increasingly barren • "desecration" of countryside • Central Valley is heavily polluted	• traditional, attractive farms are disappearing • hedgerows and wildlife are being lost • rivers and streams are being polluted
5.	Intensive farming causes undue stress and suffering to farm animals.	• factory farm animals are treated like machines rather than living creatures • these farm animals have shorter lifespans • conditions are very poor for these animals	• too many animals crammed into small spaces • unnatural for animals to be indoors all of the time • animal growth rates are unnatural • our misguided view that farm animals and pets have different needs causes suffering
6.	People who live beside or work in factory farms are adversely affected.	• property values are affected by industrial farms • people become ill because of pollution from these farms • air quality in Central Valley is worse than that of a big city • ruined aesthetics of Central Valley • farmers are under constant pressure to produce "more with less"	• introduction of intensive farming in the UK caused thousands of job losses in rural areas • the livelihoods of many traditional farmers have been badly affected

	Area of Agreement	Passage 1	Passage 2
7.	We need to restrict/oppose this development of intensive farming in the UK.	• the writer argues that factory farming is not the only way to produce affordable food • Central Valley is presented as a warning about what could happen in the UK • the writer notes that the movement of farm animals indoors is insidious and unnatural	• in the final paragraph, the writer provides us with a set of guidelines on what "we need to" do in order to return to the "environmentally friendly, humane and healthy" farming methods of the past
8.	Intensive farming may have a negative impact on human health	• cheap meats contain more fat • meat contaminated with drugs • quality of produce is low • health problems linked to pollution produced by intensive farms	• contaminated meat enters the human food chain • degenerative diseases connected to a high fat diet
9.	The unnatural nature of intensive farming	• limited lifespan of animals • animals prevented from living naturally outdoors • natural processes subject to human intervention	• animals denied natural living conditions • farm animals' lives considerably shortened in recent years • detrimental effects of unnatural animal diets

HIGHER FOR CfE ENGLISH
2015

PAPER 2 – CRITCAL READING

SECTION 1 – Scottish Text

SCOTTISH TEXT (DRAMA)

Text 1 – Drama – *The Slab Boys* **by John Byrne**

Question	Expected Answer(s)	Max Mark	Additional Guidance
1.	Candidates should explain the contrast between the attitudes of Jack and Phil to Alan. For full marks both sides of contrast must be covered.	2	Possible answers include: • Jack: helpful, friendly, deferential, due to Alan's social position/family connections/youth • Phil: aggressive/hostile as he does not want to be patronised after being dismissed
2.	Candidates should analyse how the tension between Spanky and Phil is made clear in lines 16–31. 2 marks awarded for detailed/insightful comment plus quotation/reference. 1 mark for more basic comment plus quotation/reference. 0 marks for quotation/reference alone.	4	Possible answers include: • Spanky's use of questions/exclamations show his irritation with Phil eg 'How should I know? I've got all these dishes to wash! Can you not give us a hand?' • Spanky's wounding retaliation about Phil losing his job: 'At least I still am one (a Slab Boy)' • Phil's sarcastic response to Spanky's comment identifying himself with Alan: 'Aw, it's 'me and the boy' now, is it?' • Phil's disgust at Spanky's abandonment of him/conforming to the conventional work ethic 'I think I'm going to be sick'

Question	Expected Answer(s)	Max Mark	Additional Guidance
3.	Candidates should analyse how language is used to convey the feelings of Phil and/or Curry. 2 marks awarded for detailed/insightful comment plus quotation/reference 1 mark for more basic comment plus quotation/reference. 0 marks for quotation/reference alone.	4	Possible answers include: **Curry:** • Dismissive towards Phil/gloating about his dismissal, shown in mock-helpful tone of 'Still here … any time' • Unsympathetic initially towards Phil/rules are rules attitude: formal language of 'Only urgent personal calls allowed' • Sympathetic (later) when discussing the plight of Phil's mother: 'She must've been badly injured' **Phil:** • Repeated questions demonstrating his incredulity and growing indignation that Curry is intruding into his personal life 'What … about it?' • Defiance/refusal to be an object of pity: use of blunt language/description emphasising the ludicrous visual effect rather than real pain of his mother's 'accident': 'What she done … simple'
4.	Candidates should discuss how humour is used to develop Phil's character. Candidates may choose to answer in bullet points in this final question or write a number of linked statements.	10	Up to 2 marks can be achieved for identifying elements of commonality as identified in the question, ie how humour is used to develop Phil's character. A further 2 marks can be achieved for reference to the extract given. 6 additional marks can be awarded for discussion of similar references from at least one other part of the text. In practice this means: Identification of commonality eg: Phil uses sarcasm/mockery/irony as a defence mechanism to help him cope with work or home problems From the extract: 2 marks for detailed/insightful comment plus quotation/reference; 1 mark for more basic comment plus quotation/reference; 0 marks for quotation/reference alone. eg "Nope … a Ford Prefect" use of bathos/name of car to 'correct' Curry's comment about the miracle shows his refusal to acknowledge the pain or seriousness of his mother's situation in front of Curry/humour used to protect/defend his own pride (2 marks) From at least one other text/part of the text: 2 marks for detailed/insightful comment plus quotation/reference; 1 mark for more basic comment plus quotation/reference; 0 marks for quotation/reference alone (Up to 6 marks). Possible answers include: • Phil and Spanky's witty banter and teasing of other characters/"Oh … what trade was that, Mr. Curry?" shows how he copes with his mundane life (2) • The farcical nature of Hector's "makeover"/reference to Phil forcing Hector into the clothes/the balaclava … shows Phil's cruelty towards others (2) • The use of black humour in the descriptions of Phil's mother/"The old dear's impromptu dip" — euphemism describes his mother's suicidal tendencies (2) • The attempts to get Lucille to accompany Hector to the Staffie shows that, underneath, Phil is a compassionate character (2) • Uses humour to show off/appear to be 'top dog'/put people down … — eg "You can't even get the tin trunks off a chocolate soldier, Jack" (2) Many other answers are possible.

Text 2 — Drama — *The Cheviot, the Stag and the Black, Black Oil* by John McGrath

Question	Expected Answer(s)	Max Mark	Additional Guidance
5.	Candidates should analyse how language is used to create different tones in the Duke's speeches, by referring to at least two examples. For full marks candidates must make reference to at least two distinct tones, but not necessarily in equal measure. 2 marks are awarded for detailed/insightful comment plus quotation/reference. 1 mark for more basic comment plus quotation/reference. 0 marks for quotation/reference alone	4	Possible answers include: Lines 1—4 • persuasive, evoking national pride and loyalty through "the Queen"/use of precedent and tradition through "as always" • business-like/authoritarian in evoking "My Commissioner informs me …" Lines 8—10 • patronising in the assumption that they can be bought off for personal gain: "6 golden sovereigns" • arrogant/presumptuous: "step up in an orderly manner" Lines 12—18 • angry in the demands for "an explanation" and swearing "damn it" because of Highland defiance • frustration that his argument has failed: "Have you no pride …?" • scaremongering tone in the use of hyperbole/threats: "the cruel Tsar of Russia installed in Dunrobin Castle" • accusatory/hectoring tone in the series of questions
6.	Candidates should analyse how both the stage directions and dialogue in lines 17—27 convey the local people's defiance of the Duke. For full marks candidates must cover both stage directions and dialogue, but not necessarily in equal measure 2 marks are awarded for detailed/insightful comment plus quotation/reference. 1 mark for more basic comment plus quotation/reference. 0 marks for quotation/reference alone.	4	Possible answers include: Stage Directions • *'Silence.'* Creates an unsettling atmosphere, showing the tension between the Highlanders and the Duke • *'Nobody moves.'* The inaction of the Highlanders shows a passive resistance • *'OLD MAN stands'* shows the shift from passive resistance to active resistance • *'in the audience'* makes the audience identify with the man as a representative of the people/puts the audience in the position of the tenants Dialogue • The old man's respectful, reasonable response adds weight to his argument: "I am sorry …"/"your Grace" • The old man takes the Duke's threat as the basis of his counter-argument: "we could not expect worse treatment" • Use of personal pronouns "We … you" emphasises the lack of identification that the Highlanders have with the Duke's cause • Climactically mocking the Duke by suggesting that the Duke conscripts the sheep • The humorous solidarity shown by the collective "Baa-aa"
7.	Candidates should explain how the MC's speech brings this section of the play to an ironic conclusion. 2 marks are awarded for detailed/insightful comment. 1 mark for more basic comment. 0 marks for quotation/reference alone.	2	Possible answers include: • Description of the fate of the one man who did enlist whose family was treated badly, in contrast to the promise of financial reward • Duke's expectations/efforts in contrast to the lack of response • The futility of the Highlanders' defiance: after they were cleared off the land they had to enlist anyway • Use of the phrase 'The old tradition of loyal soldiering' when it was based on desperation rather than duty

Question	Expected Answer(s)	Max Mark	Additional Guidance
8.	Candidates should discuss how McGrath develops the theme of change/resistance to change in this and at least one other extract from the play. Candidates may choose to answer in bullet points in this final question, or write a number of linked statements.	10	Up to 2 marks can be achieved for identifying elements of commonality as identified in the question, ie the development of the theme of change/resistance to change in the play. A further 2 marks can be achieved for reference to the extract given. 6 additional marks can be awarded for discussion of similar references to at least one other part of the text. In practice this means: Identification of commonality (theme, characterisation, use of imagery, setting, or any other key element …) eg Cultural/economical and social changes that have affected Scotland (1 mark) Variety of responses from the population to these changes (1 mark) From the extract: 2 marks for detailed/insightful comment plus quotation/reference; 1 mark for more basic comment plus quotation/reference; 0 marks for quotation/reference alone. eg Change in the attitude of the common people to authority from unquestioning obedience to resistance (2 marks) From elsewhere in the play: 2 marks for detailed/insightful comment plus quotation/reference; 1 mark for more basic comment plus quotation/reference; 0 marks for quotation/reference alone (Up to 6 marks). Possible answers include: Role of women as defenders of the community in resisting the introduction of Cheviot sheep to the Highlands for example, female members' direct appeal to the audience when recounting Patrick Sellar's evictions in their community (2) The erosion of Gaelic culture through the banning of language, music etc for example, the role of the MC in disseminating historical information (2) Forced emigration to the colonies to maximise profit at the behest of figures of authority for example, the Duke of Selkirk's movement of his Lowland tenants to Canada (2) The continued eviction of tenants to free up land for hunting for example, Lady Phosphate's preference for gaming estates at the expense of the tenants in the area (2) The continued exploitation of the Highlands by entrepreneurial outsiders for example, Andy McChuckemup plans to exploit the landscape through commercialisation (2) Many other answers are possible.

Text 3 — Drama — *Men Should Weep* **by Ena Lamont Stewart**

Question	Expected Answer(s)	Max Mark	Additional Guidance
9.	Candidates should explain two of Jenny's reasons for visiting the family home.	2	Possible answers: • Jenny wants to correct her mother's misunderstanding of Bertie's situation: the hospital will not let him come back to Maggie's very unhealthy slum tenement • Jenny wants to make sure her parents actively pursue the Corporation about getting a Council house, using Bertie's ill-health as a lever • When Jenny was considering suicide by drowning, she thought of her father and all the love and kindness he had shown her when she was a child • Jenny regrets her ill-treatment, partly influenced by Isa, of her parents; she has come back to admit her guilt and regret
10.	Candidates should analyse how Lily and Jenny's differing attitudes are shown in lines 22–42. For full marks, both Lily and Jenny's attitudes must be covered, although equal coverage is not necessary. 2 marks awarded for detailed/insightful comment plus quotation/reference. 1 mark for more basic comment plus quotation/reference. 0 marks for quotation/reference alone.	4	Possible answers: Lily: • does not believe in couples living together unless they're married — "livin in sin" • is contemptuous, highly critical of the money or gifts Jenny has received; she implies that what Jenny is doing is little better than prostitution — "We've had an eye-fu o yer wages o sin"; "she'll hae earned it, Maggie. On her back." • suggests strongly that Jenny has damned herself in exchange for material possessions "The wages o sin's nae deith, it's fancy hairdos an a swanky coat an pur silk stockins" • assumes that a woman who lives with a man outwith marriage will inevitably be punished, disappointed, discarded — "till yer tired business man gets tired o you an ye're oot on yer ear" • is unswervingly conventional, is determined not to behave in a way society might find unacceptable — "I've kept ma self-respect" Jenny: • sees nothing wrong with couples living together outside marriage — "Aye, if ye want tae ca it sin! I don't." • is dismissive of conventional morality — "You seem tae ken yer Bible … I never pretended tae." • favours happiness over convention — "kind", "generous", "I'm happy, an I'm makin him happy" • sees no point in sacrificing all hope of happiness, love or companionship just to follow the norms of society — "Aye. An that's aboot a ye've got."

Question	Expected Answer(s)	Max Mark	Additional Guidance
11.	Candidates should analyse the dramatic impact of at least two of the stage directions in lines 43–62. 2 marks awarded for detailed/insightful comment plus quotation/reference. 1 mark for more basic comment plus quotation/reference. 0 marks for quotation/reference alone.	4	Possible answers: (Her hands to her head): • conveys the depth of Maggie's distress and unhappiness. The argument between Lily and Jenny, which she has just brought to an end, has pushed her to her wits' end • creates a dramatic pause before Maggie goes on to reflect that the happiness she had felt on seeing Jenny return has gone • emphasises Maggie prefers to avoid confrontation and often ignores the reality of her problems (She draws a couple of chairs together … watching): • conveys Jenny's desire to discuss important matters with Maggie • Jenny only draws up two chairs, not three, clearly signaling she is excluding Lily from the discussion • Lily feels she is an important enough figure in the family and has the right to listen, so she withdraws but only a little (She doesn't even look at Lily): • conveys Jenny's determination to get somewhere with Maggie (Maggie nods): • shows the start of Maggie's acceptance that she must listen to Jenny and perhaps act on her advice. (She opens her handbag … She gasps) • given the Morrisons' poverty, producing the "roll of notes" has a powerful physical impact on Maggie (John comes in … lips tighten) • conveys his conflicting emotions about his daughter: initial pleasure at seeing her followed by his anger at her current situation

Question	Expected Answer(s)	Max Mark	Additional Guidance
12.	Candidates should discuss how Jenny's growing maturity is made clear and should refer to appropriate textual evidence to support their discussion. Candidates may choose to answer in bullet points in this final question, or write a number of linked statements.	10	Up to 2 marks can be achieved for identifying elements of commonality as identified in the question, ie how Jenny's growing maturity is made clear. A further 2 marks can be achieved for reference to the extract given. 6 additional marks can be awarded for discussion of similar references from at least one other part of the text. In practice this means: Identification of commonality eg: Jenny's concern for her family shows a sense of responsibility (1 mark) her earlier behaviour was self-centred and immature (1 mark) From the extract: 2 marks for detailed/insightful comment plus quotation/ reference; 1 mark for more basic comment plus quotation/ reference; 0 marks for quotation/reference alone. eg Jenny's admission of her previous lack of respect towards her mother shows her willingness to accept responsibility for her actions (2 marks) OR "Listen, Mammy. We canna wait for a hoose … So while ye're waitin, ye're goin tae flit tae a rented hoose." shows that Jenny is now capable of taking control where her mother has been unable to do so (2 marks) From at least one other part of the play: 2 marks for detailed/insightful comment plus quotation/ reference; 1 mark for more basic comment plus quotation/ reference; 0 marks for quotation/reference alone (Up to 6 marks). Possible answers include: Jenny shows little sympathy for her parents' financial plight "I'm chuckin the shop"/she does not want to be disgraced by bringing home the "chipped apples and bashed tomaties" to help eke out the family budget (2) Jenny's late arrival home from the "pickshers" and her impudent response to John's concern shows that she is selfish and often irresponsible (2) Jenny's desperate attempts to carve her own identity often result in cruel, unloving behaviour towards her parents – "Ye needna worry! When I leave this rotten pig-stye I'm no comin back. There's ither things in life … " (2) Jenny's guilt over abandoning her home and family becomes apparent through her attempts to reassure Maggie/"Ma, ye've got Dad and Alec and the weans. Ye'll no miss me oot of the hoose." (2) Mrs Bone and Mrs Harris' description of Jenny as "a right mess" reveals the difficult circumstances Jenny has managed to overcome before returning to the family home (2) Many other answers are possible.

SCOTTISH TEXT (PROSE)

Text 1 — Prose — *Mother and Son* by Iain Crichton Smith

Question	Expected Answer(s)	Max Mark	Additional Guidance
13.	Candidates should analyse the writer's use of language in lines 1—22 to reveal the nature of the relationship between mother and son. 2 marks awarded for detailed/insightful comment plus quotation/reference. 1 mark for more basic comment plus quotation/reference. 0 marks for quotation/reference alone.	4	Possible answers include: • pattern of relationship has been set/it had happened before/likely to happen again — "beginning again …" • Their conflict followed a regular pattern — "always …"/emphasis on repeated pattern of sentence structure — "You know well enough" • He is tired of the inevitable, repetitive conflicts — "spoke wearily" • She dominates him by hurtful comments — "same brutal pain stabbed him" • little chance of success in being understood/ making his point — "retired defeated" • mother appears to give the son the chance to change/take responsibility but doesn't really mean it — "if you'll only say"
14.	Candidates should identify the tone of the mother's words in lines 27—28 and analyse how this tone is created. 1 mark awarded for identification of appropriate tone. Analysis: 2 marks awarded for detailed/insightful comment plus quotation/reference; 1 mark for more basic comment plus quotation/reference. 0 marks for quotation/reference alone.	3	Possible answers include: **Tone:** • cruel/vicious/dismissive/critical … • dismissive put-down — "Lessons aren't everything." • repetition of accusatory "you" — "You aren't a mechanic." • Repeated use of negatives — "aren't"/"can't" … • short, quick-fire list of complaints/criticisms — "You … Why don't you hurry up with that tea?" • accusatory question — "Why don't you hurry up with that tea?" • escalating list of her perception of his inadequacies — "You aren't a mechanic … Fat good you'd be at a job."
15.	Candidates should analyse how the language of lines 29—38 conveys the son's reaction to his mother's words. 2 marks awarded for detailed/insightful comment plus quotation/reference. 1 mark for more basic comment plus quotation/reference. 0 marks for quotation/reference alone.		Possible answers include: • defeated in the face of mother's constant criticism — "despairingly leaning"; "head on his hands" • acceptance of inadequacies — "wasn't a mechanic"; "never could understand" • deepening lack of self-esteem/self-doubt — "something had gone wrong" • unhappy/despairing — "sad look on his face"

Question	Expected Answer(s)	Max Mark	Additional Guidance
16.	Candidates should discuss how Iain Crichton Smith uses contrasting characters to explore theme. Candidates may choose to answer in bullet points in this final question, or write a number of linked statements.	10	Up to 2 marks can be achieved for identifying elements of commonality as identified in the question, ie contrast used to explore character and/or theme. A further 2 marks can be achieved for reference to the extract given. 6 additional marks can be awarded for discussion of similar references from at least one other short story. In practice this means: Identification of commonality eg: Iain Crichton Smith will often create contrast between characters from different backgrounds (1 mark) with differing personalities (1 mark) **OR** the sense of an outsider in a closed community or alien environment (1 mark) such as restricted island setting or war-time situation (1 mark) From the extract: 1 × relevant reference to technique/idea/feature 1 × appropriate comment (2 marks) (maximum of 2 marks only for discussion of extract) eg The domineering mother contrasts with the submissive son — "her spiteful, bitter face"/"his head in his hands" (2 marks) The mother's directness contrasts with the son's tentative responses — "you'd be no good in a job"/"I'll take a job tomorrow ... if you'll only say" (2 marks) From at least one other text: 2 marks for detailed/insightful comment plus quotation/reference; 1 mark for more basic comment plus quotation/reference; 0 marks for quotation/reference alone (Up to 6 marks). Possible answers include: • *The Telegram* — the fat woman and thin woman contrast as the thin woman is an incomer whereas the fat woman has always lived in this village — highlights small-mindedness of village "she was an incomer from another village and had only been in this one for thirty years or so" (2) • *The Telegram* — contrasting attitudes towards education/aspiration — "thin woman was ambitious: she had sent her son to university ..." whereas the fat woman has lived there all her life/is more conventional/her son was only an ordinary seaman but both are equally affected by the war (2) • *The Red Door*: Murdo contrasts with the rest of the islanders through his ultimate willingness to be different when he accepts the red door instead of re-painting it (2) • *The Painter*: painter sees the fight as an artistic opportunity whereas the other villagers are horrified by his apparent lack of concern for the violence — "... a gaze that had gone beyond the human and was as indifferent to the outcome as a hawk's might be." (2) • *The Crater*: contrast in attitude between Lt Robert Mackinnon and Sergeant Smith to the war. Mackinnon is sensitive/horrified by the brutality of war whereas Sergeant Smith is stolidly accepting — happy to be back (2) Many other answers are possible.

Text 2 — Prose — *The Wireless Set* by George Mackay Brown

Question		Expected Answer(s)	Max Mark	Additional Guidance
17.		For full marks, candidates should explain how Mackay Brown creates a sense of both community life and the role of the wireless set within it. Marks are awarded (1) + (1). 0 marks for reference/quotation alone.	2	Possible answers include: • "passed the shop and the manse and the schoolhouse" — postman's journey encapsulates the centres of community life • "the island postman" — suggests he is a central part of the community/small community requiring only one postman • "Joe Loss and his orchestra" — alien (from London) music intruding into island life via wireless set • Contrast traditional island life ("croft"/"track") with new, modern music (from outside/London)
18.	(a)	Candidates should analyse how Mackay Brown reveals the postman's attitude to Betsy in lines 6—15. 2 marks may be awarded for detailed/insightful comment plus quotation/reference. 1 mark for more basic comment plus quotation/reference. 0 marks for reference/quotation alone.	2	Possible answers include: • Repetition/parallel expressions in "Is there anybody with you?" and "There should be somebody with you" — reveals his insistence that she have support before he gives her the bad news — sympathetic/concerned • "miser parting with a twenty pound note" — image reveals his extreme reluctance to tell her the news/telling her the news is compared with parting with a thing that is precious : protective towards her/relishing power the knowledge gives him • "disappearing on his bike round the corner"- already left (by the time she has read the telegram) suggests he doesn't know how to deal with her/his concern is not deep/he has now moved on and left her to someone else to care for her (the missionary)
	(b)	Candidates should analyse how Mackay Brown uses language to convey the differing reactions of the missionary and Betsy to the news in lines 16—22. Marks are awarded (1) + (1). 0 marks for reference/quotation alone.	2	Possible answers include: Missionary: • "He died for his country"/"He made the great sacrifice" — platitudes/conventional clichés suggest insincerity/no real sympathy Betsy: • "It's time the peats were carted" suggests that Betsy is taken up with the work on the land rather than facing her personal tragedy/a coping strategy • "That isn't it at all" suggests Betsy's simple dismissal of the missionary's cliché/reveals her honesty in the face of his platitudes • "Howie's sunk with torpedoes. That's all I know" — blunt statement of the fact shows that she is forced to face up to the brutal reality of what has happened
19.		Candidates should refer to both sides of the contrast: the couple's real feelings and the missionary's perception of their feelings. 2 marks awarded for detailed/insightful comment plus quotation/reference. 1 mark for more basic comment plus quotation/reference. 0 marks for quotation/reference alone.	4	Possible answers include: The couple: • "How many lobsters … I got two lobsters … I got six crabs" determined focus on practicalities/modest numbers which define their frugal life/getting on with normalities of life as coping mechanism • "The wireless stood, a tangled wreck, on the dresser" — utter destruction of the object which 'brought the war' shows Hugh's agony The missionary's view: • "I'll break the news to him" — slightly officious/patronising attempt to take charge of the situation — he does not realise that Hugh already knows • "awed by such callousness" — complete failure to understand their stoical way of dealing with extreme grief • "slowly shaking his head" — demonstrates that the missionary doesn't understand their coping strategy/thinks they don't care • "My poor man" — tries to impose what he thinks their reaction should be

Question		Expected Answer(s)	Max Mark	Additional Guidance
20.		Candidates should discuss how the writer deals with the relationship between the island community and the outside world. Candidates may choose to answer in bullet points in this final question, or write a number of linked statements.	10	Up to 2 marks can be achieved for identifying elements of commonality as identified in the question, ie the relationship between the island community and the outside world. A further 2 marks can be achieved for reference to the extract given. 6 additional marks can be awarded for discussion of similar references from at least one other short story. In practice this means: Identification of commonality eg George Mackay Brown often reveals the intrusion of the modern or violent outside world (1 mark) into the traditional/safe/secure world of an island community (1 mark). From the extract: 2 marks for detailed/insightful comment plus quotation/reference; 1 mark for more basic comment plus quotation/reference; 0 marks for quotation/reference alone. eg The music belongs to another world outside the island "The wireless was playing music inside, Joe Loss and his orchestra." (2 marks) **OR** The news of the Howie's death, arriving by telegram, shows the destructive intrusion of the war on the local community (2 marks) From at least one other text: 2 marks for detailed/insightful comment plus quotation/reference; 1 mark for more basic comment plus quotation/reference; 0 marks for quotation/reference alone (Up to 6 marks). Possible answers include: *Tartan* — the Vikings' journey through the village — apparently aggressive/predatory but villagers' silent, brooding presence follows them to shore — they leave hastily/gaining little from the raid (2) *Tartan* — the Vikings are searching for anything valuable to plunder but, ironically, give a silver coin to a child because of his wit (the only money to change hands in the raid) (2) *Tartan* — Vikings threaten violence/pillaging/attacking dark-haired woman but the only death is Kol, murdered by the villagers while he lies drunk (2) *The Eye of the Hurricane* — the narrator, Barclay's, slightly patronising attempt to relate to the island people shown in his description of them: "I had come to live ... among simple, uncomplicated people" (2) *A Time to Keep* — the "missionary" (title suggests patronising attempt to bring enlightened religion to the community) offers comfort on death of Ingi but his words are hollow and meaningless and are rejected by Bill: "She's in the earth"/"The ground isn't a particularly happy place to be." (2) Many other answers are possible.

Text 3 — Prose — *The Trick is to Keep Breathing* by Janice Galloway

Question	Expected Answer(s)	Max Mark	Additional Guidance
21.	Candidates should analyse how Galloway makes the reader aware of Joy's efforts to cope. 2 marks may be awarded for detailed/insightful comment plus quotation/reference. 1 mark for more basic comment + quotation/reference. 0 marks for quotation/reference alone.	2	Possible answers include: • Repetition of "I" eg "I wanted"; "I made"; "I kept going" emphasises all the things she was trying to do/creates a listing effect • Comparison to Bunyan's Pilgrim and Dorothy emphasises her determination • Reference to "endurance test" demonstrates the effort needed just to keep going • "all I had to do was last out" emphasises that she is trying to convince herself that she can cope
22.	Candidates should analyse how the writer uses language to convey Joy's desperation for Michael's presence. 2 marks awarded for detailed/insightful comment plus quotation/reference. 1 mark for more basic comment plus quotation/reference. 0 marks for quotation/reference alone.	4	Possible answers include: • Repetitive sentence structure in lines 9—14 emphasises her obsession with Michael • Use of list in sentence beginning "I saw him in cars" emphasises the number and variety of places she imagines seeing him • Use of question "How could he be …?" emphasises that she wants to believe/is trying to convince herself that he is still alive • Use of the senses eg smell ("I started smelling …") and sight ("I saw him …") emphasises that she can imagine his presence/wants his presence • "roaring past"; "drifting by"; "hovering in a cloud" emphasises that he is always just out of reach • "sunk my face into his clothes" emphasises how she totally immerses herself; wants to feel his presence • "howled" emphasises how much despair she feels at his absence • "invisible presence" emphasises her emptiness; imagines he is there but cannot see him
23.	Candidates should analyse how the writer conveys Joy's feelings of despair. For full marks at least two different examples must be commented on. 2 marks awarded for detailed/insightful comment plus quotation/reference. 1 mark for more basic comment plus quotation/reference. 0 marks for quotation/reference alone.	4	Possible answers include: • Sentence structure "Please god …" — plea/prayer emphasises her desire to die • "mashed remains"; "marrowbone jelly oozing" — word choice creates vivid visual image of the aftermath of boulders crashing through the roof; emphasises her desire to be wiped out completely • Use of humour in the Health Visitor's words emphasises her sarcasm/bitterness towards the medical professionals who are supposed to be helping her • "shrinking" emphasises that she feels as if she is disappearing • "shiver" emphasises her coldness/fear • Use of contrast in the final paragraph helps us to understand her despair at her situation

Question	Expected Answer(s)	Max Mark	Additional Guidance
24.	Candidates should discuss how the writer conveys Joy's fear/anxiety about relating to other people and should refer to appropriate textual evidence to support their discussion. Candidates may choose to answer in bullet points in this final question, or write a number of linked statements.	10	Up to 2 marks can be achieved for identifying elements of commonality as identified in the question, ie evidence of Joy's fear/anxiety about relating to other people. A further 2 marks can be achieved for reference to the extract given. 6 additional marks can be awarded for discussion of similar references from at least one other part of the text. In practice this means: Identification of commonality eg Fear/anxiety is ever-present in Joy's view of the world around her and how she relates to other people (1 mark) shown through a range of narrative techniques/descriptions of her experiences (1 mark). From the extract: 2 marks for detailed/insightful comment plus quotation/reference; 1 mark for more basic comment plus quotation/reference; 0 marks for quotation/reference alone. eg Health Visitor's clichéd comments reveal (Joy's perception of) her lack of understanding of the depth of Joy's problems and show that they cannot relate to one another (2 marks) **OR** Joy's direct statement ("Needing people … wearing me out") reveals her inability to cope with forming relationships which she, nevertheless, recognises she needs (2 marks) From at least one other part of the text: 2 marks for detailed/insightful comment plus quotation/reference; 1 mark for more basic comment plus quotation/reference; 0 marks for quotation/reference alone (Up to 6 marks). Possible references include: • Joy's attempts to distance herself from/avoid contact with her sister, Myra "Tell me where you live" (2) • Anxiety about visits from the Health Visitor — Joy refers to herself as a patient to distance herself from her illness and putting on a brave front by not being honest about how much she is struggling/how deep her depression is (2) • Anxiety about meeting doctors — eg referring to them by numbers, "Doctor 1, Doctor 2" which shows her refusal to engage with them on a personal level (2) • Fear of the phone — eg. after she self-harms she says "I can't face the phone tonight either" showing that, even when desperate, she cannot use the phone to seek help (2) • Fear/avoidance of communication — eg. despite having a landline, Joy prefers to use the phone box nearby because the landline represents people coming in/she can't control who is calling (2) Many other answers are possible.

Text 4 — Prose — *Sunset Song* by Lewis Grassic Gibbon

Question	Expected Answer(s)	Max Mark	Additional Guidance
25.	Candidates should explain how Chris is feeling in lines 1—8. 2 marks are awarded for detailed/ insightful comment plus quotation/ reference. 1 mark for more basic comment plus quotation/reference. 0 marks for quotation/reference alone.	2	Possible answers include: • Chris's desire to arrive at the Stones displays great mental strength like the strength of the metal iron; • the strength of Chris's will in her single-mindedness; • peace and restfulness of Chris lying down after her exertions; • sense of Chris's complete freedom from tension; Chris feels at peace with nature; • Physical symptoms indicative of exertion or distress
26.	Candidates should analyse how the writer conveys the impact her mother's death has had on Chris in lines 9—23. 2 marks are awarded for detailed/ insightful comment plus quotation/ reference. 1 mark for more basic comment plus quotation/reference. 0 marks for quotation/reference alone.	4	Possible answers include: • "as a dark cold pit" — the simile suggests Chris's misery and difficulty in escaping from so much sorrow; • "and the world went on … the world went on and you went with it" — repetition reinforces the fact that Chris has no choice but to carry on with her life, despite her personal tragedy; • "something died in your heart and went down with her to lie" — suggests that emotionally Chris has suffered a loss which will accompany her mother to her grave; • "the child in your heart died then" — shows Chris's acknowledgement of the abrupt end of childhood for her; • "hands ready to snatch you back … over-rough" — image conveys a past where Chris knew she would be rescued from harm; • "the Chris of the books and the dreams died with it" — all that might have been must be cast aside because reality has taken over from fantasy; • "the dark, quiet corpse that was your childhood" — stark image of death conveys the certainty of this childhood stage of Chris's life being over.
27.	Candidates should analyse how the writer conveys the horror of Chris's memory of her mother's death in lines *23—45*. 2 marks are awarded for detailed/ insightful comment plus quotation/ reference. 1 mark for more basic comment plus quotation/reference. 0 marks for quotation/reference alone.	4	Possible answers include: • Description of Mistress Munro as a terrifying presence: "uncaring", "black-eyed futret", "snapping", "terrified" • Pathetic fallacy showing Chris's despair: "awful night", "rain-soaked parks" • Chris's initial feelings of shock/numbness: "dazed and dull-eyed" • Description of mother's body as beautiful heightening the horrific nature of Chris's loss: "sweet to look at" • Chris's movement from denial to the agony of grief: "hot tears wrung from your eyes like drops of blood" • Chris's thoughts conveyed directly to show her utter despair, including repetition: "Oh mother, mother, why did you do it?"

Question	Expected Answer(s)	Max Mark	Additional Guidance
28.	Candidates should discuss how Grassic Gibbon presents Chris's growing to maturity in this and at least one other part of the novel. Candidates may choose to answer in bullet points in this final question, or write a number of linked statements.	10	Up to 2 marks can be achieved for identifying elements of commonality as identified in the question, ie Chris's growing to maturity. A further 2 marks can be achieved for reference to the extract given. 6 additional marks can be awarded for discussion of similar references to at least one other part of the text by the writer. In practice this means: Identification of commonality (theme, characterisation, use of imagery, setting, or any other key element …) Eg Her evolving identification with the land. (1 mark) This helps her to resolve her internal conflict and find her own identity at a time of personal and societal change. (1 mark) From the extract: 2 marks for detailed insightful comment plus quotation/ reference; 1 mark for more basic comment plus quotation/reference; 0 marks for quotation/reference alone. eg During a time of change she finds comfort in the permanence of the Standing Stones (2 marks) **OR** Mistress Munro's role in reminding Chris of her familial responsibilities leads to her leaving behind her childhood and assuming the role of mother: "you'll find little time for dreaming and dirt when you're keeping house at Blawearie" (2 marks) From at least one other part of the text: 2 marks for detailed/insightful comment plus quotation/ reference; 1 mark for more basic comment plus quotation/reference; 0 marks for quotation/reference alone (Up to 6 marks). Possible answers include: • Chris's loss of her father and decision to stay on the land which shows her increased sense of her identity being tied up with the land/taking responsibility for her own future (2) • Chris falling in love with and marrying Ewan further links her to the land as Ewan represents the agricultural way of life (2) • Her pregnancy and the birth of her son which shows her taking on responsibility and starting new life with her own family (2) • The return of Ewan as a soldier and the apparent destruction of their relationship when she displays resilience and determination to endure as an independent woman (2) • The death of Ewan which brings about redemption/ reconciliation in her eyes as he "went into the heart that was his forever" (2) Many other answers are possible.

Text 5 — Prose — *The Cone-Gatherers* by Robin Jenkins

Question	Expected Answer(s)	Max Mark	Additional Guidance
29.	Candidates should analyse how language is used to create a positive picture of Lady Runcie-Campbell in lines *1—19*. 2 marks are awarded for detailed/ insightful comment plus quotation/ reference. 1 mark for more basic comment plus quotation/reference. 0 marks for quotation/reference alone.	4	Possible answers include: • Her attractiveness: "clear courteous musical voice"/"charming" speaker/"loveliness"/"outstanding beauty of face" • Her sense of fairness and justice: "earnestness of spirit"/"almost mystical sense of responsibility"/"passion for justice, profound and intelligent"/"determination to see right done, even at the expense of rank or pride" • Her ability to bring out the best in people: "ability to exalt people out of their humdrum selves" • Her Christian beliefs/altruism/spirituality: "almost mystical sense of responsibility"/"associated religion ... with her perfume"/"her emulation of Christ"
30.	Candidates should analyse two instances of the use of language to convey the contrast between the two characters in lines *23—43*. 2 marks are awarded for detailed/ insightful comment plus quotation/ reference. 1 mark for more basic comment plus quotation/reference. 0 marks for quotation/reference alone.	4	Possible answers include: **Openness and duplicity:** Duror 's desire to corrupt Lady Runcie-Campbell' — "it would implicate her in his chosen evil"; in contrast she "looked at him frankly and sympathetically", suggesting her honesty and compassion **Beauty/Purity and ugliness:** Setting in the room suggests beauty — "sunny scented room" which contrasts with the evil thoughts in Duror's mind — "black filth" **Contrast in physical appearance** She is beautiful and "vital"; in contrast he is unkempt and ill-looking — "hadn't shaved". **Light and dark** Setting of the room suggests light/"glittering rings" contrasts with "black filth" **Good and evil:** Reference to the goodness of nature in the birdsong — "everywhere birds sang"-which contrasts with Duror's evil thought which "crept up until it entered his mouth, covered his ears, blinded his eyes, and so annihilated him"
31.	Candidates should explain why Lady Runcie-Campbell now feels more able to identify with Peggy's situation. 2 marks may be awarded for a detailed/ insightful explanation. 1 mark for a more basic explanation.	2	Possible answers include: • The war (and the fact she is separated from her husband as a result) has demonstrated to Lady Runcie-Campbell what it is like to miss a loved one — she links this to Peggy Duror's illness as her 'war' and understands how she and Duror must feel • The war has stopped Lady Runcie-Campbell being able to appreciate aspects of everyday life: "flowers ... friends", something Peggy has been deprived of for years • Word-choice such as "dreadful separations"/"cut off" may also be commented on, showing the hurt/pain caused by being apart • Candidates may also notice that her sympathies lie with Peggy rather than Duror — she empathises with a wife who is missing her husband (and perhaps fails to acknowledge his lack of emotion)

Question	Expected Answer(s)	Max Mark	Additional Guidance
32.	Candidates should discuss how Duror is presented not just as an evil character, but one who might be worthy of sympathy or understanding, and should refer to appropriate textual evidence to support their discussion. Candidates can answer in bullet points in this final question, or write a number of linked statements. For the full 6 marks on elsewhere in the text, both evil and sympathy must be covered, although coverage will not necessarily be balanced.	10	Up to 2 marks can be achieved for identifying elements of commonality as identified in the question, ie how Duror is presented not just as an evil character, but one who might be worthy of some sympathy. A further 2 marks can be achieved for reference to the extract given. 6 additional marks can be awarded for discussion of similar references from at least one other part of the text. In practice this means: Identification of commonality eg: Duror's evil character is primarily shown through his persecution of those whom he perceives as imperfect (1 mark) yet some sympathy can be felt because of personal circumstances (1 mark) From the extract: 2 marks for detailed/insightful comment plus quotation/reference; 1 mark for more basic comment plus quotation/reference; 0 marks for quotation/reference alone. eg His duplicitous behaviour towards Lady Runcie-Campbell, yet some sympathy could be evoked by awareness of his own immorality (2 marks). **OR** his intention in this extract is to damage the cone gatherers, but we have some sympathy for the burden he carries with his wife (2 marks). From at least one other part of the text: 2 marks for detailed/insightful comment plus quotation/reference; 1 mark for more basic comment plus quotation/reference; 0 marks for quotation/reference alone (Up to 6 marks). Possible answers include: Duror as evil: • Duror lurking in the wood, spying on the cone-gatherers/aiming his gun at them suggests that he sees them as animals/inferior beings to be hunted/suggests his devious nature (2) • His determination to drive them out of the wood shows selfish protection of his own territory in the face of their geuine need (2) • The lies he spreads about Calum (eg. with reference to the doll) shows his desire to crush his innocence and/or destroy others' views of him (2) Sympathy for Duror: • His nightmare about Peggy before the deer drive/his collapse at the end of the deer drive shows that he is mentally ill — reflected in many of his thoughts (2) • His mother-in-law accuses him of spending more time with his dogs than with his wife suggests his loneliness and isolation (2) Many other answers are possible.

SCOTTISH TEXT (POETRY)

Text 1 — Poetry — *To a Mouse, On turning her up in her Nest, with the Plough, November 1785* by Robert Burns

Question	Expected Answer(s)	Max Mark	Additional Guidance
33.	Candidates should analyse how at least two aspects of the speaker's personality are established. 2 marks awarded for detailed/insightful comment plus quotation/reference. 1 mark for more basic comment plus quotation/reference. 0 marks for quotation/reference alone.	4	Possible answers include: Sympathetic • shows awareness of mouse's vulnerability — "poor, earth — born companion,/An' fellow-mortal" • apologetic tone of "I'm truly sorry" • reflected in the language emphasising the mouse's vulnerability — "wee", "cowrin", "tim'rous", "poor", "panic" Understanding • of the mouse's need to live/the modest nature of its needs — "A daimen icker in a thrave" Affectionate • tone of diminutives — "beastie"/"breastie"; • reassurance in direct address: "Thou need na start …" Forgiving • the mouse's thieving put into the context of its need to "live" Reflective • his apologetic tone of "I'm truly sorry" suggests speaker's regret for man's destruction of the environment Generous • "'S a sma' request" suggests his willingness to share; "blessin" in allowing the mouse a living
34.	Candidates should analyse how the poet's language creates pity for the mouse and its predicament by dealing with at least two examples. These examples could be of the same, or of different technique(s). 2 marks awarded for detailed/insightful comment plus quotation/reference. 1 mark for more basic comment plus quotation/reference. 0 marks for quotation/reference alone.	4	**Possible answers include:** Word choice • "wee bit" or "wee bit heap" or "silly" underline the smallness and fragility of the mouse's nest • "housie" — as above; "house" (as opposed to nest) humanises the mouse • "strewin" — emphasises the power and harshness of the wind in the utter destruction of the nest; emphasises the fragility and flimsiness of the nest, so easily blown away • "bleak December's" — the harshness of the weather/season reinforces the desperation of the mouse's situation • "ensuing" — sense of inevitability, unavoidable harshness • "bare an' waste"; — emphasises/reinforces the devastation caused by winter and the hopelessness/harshness of the mouse's situation • "winds" or "snell" or "keen" or "blast" — (unrelenting) harshness of weather to emphasise vulnerability of mouse without its nest • "sleety dribble" — depicts the coldness and misery in store for the mouse without shelter • "cruel coulter" — harshness/malice of the plough; sense of a force set against the mouse • "thole" — underlines suffering in store for mouse Personification • "housie"/"house or hald" — compares the mouse's nest to a human habitation encouraging empathy from the reader • "Now thou's turn'd out" — suggests forced eviction, homelessness

Question	Expected Answer(s)	Max Mark	Additional Guidance
34.	*(continued)*	4	Alliteration • "weary Winter" — underlines the difficulty/hopelessness posed by the coming cold • "Beneath the blast" — emphasises the harshness of the elements and the shelter the mouse might have had • "crash! the cruel coulter" — harsh sounds mirror the harsh action • "But house or hald" — underlines the complete loss the mouse has suffered • "Cranreuch cauld" — underlines the harshness of the cold the mouse will have to endure Onomatopoeia • "crash!" — adds drama to the sudden destruction; relives the experience from the mouse's perspective to make us feel the disaster Contrast • "cozie here" with "blast" (and any of the other weather words) — reinforce pity for mouse; hope for warmth and safety replaced with coldness and vulnerability • "thought to dwell" with " now thou's turned out" — reversal of fortune creates pity Repetition • "An'" — used at the start of lines to emphasise sense of all the problems/difficulties piling up to add to the mouse's predicament • words to do with harshness of weather — reinforce the mouse's vulnerability in face of the remorseless elements • "December — winter — winter" — emphasises the inescapable nature of the elements and the vulnerable mouse Tone • emotional, empathetic tone underlined by frequent use of exclamation marks, underlining the pitiful nature of the mouse's situation • empathetic — in the speaker putting himself in mouse's • situation — "Til crash! the cruel coulter" — and relating what has happened as a disaster • sympathetic — towards the effort now destroyed without hope of mending — "has cost thee mony a weary nibble"
35.	Candidates should explain how the final two verses highlight the contrast between the speaker and the mouse. 2 marks awarded for detailed/ insightful comment plus quotation reference. 1 mark for more basic comment plus quotation/reference. 0 marks for quotation/reference alone.	2	Possible answers include: • the mouse is fortunate only living in the present whereas mankind must suffer the anxiety and trouble which come from being conscious of the past and the future • the penultimate verse deals with the mouse and the speaker's shared experience(s) whereas the final verse contrasts the emotions/feelings of the speaker and the mouse • the final verse starts with a direct comparison "Still thou are blest, compared wi'me!"

Question	Expected Answer(s)	Max Mark	Additional Guidance
36.	Candidates should discuss how Burns uses a distinctive narrative voice to convey the central concerns of *To a Mouse* and at least one *of* his other poems. Candidates can answer in bullet points in this final question, or write a number of linked statements.	10	Up to 2 marks can be achieved for identifying elements of commonality as identified in the question, ie how Burns uses a distinctive narrative voice to convey the central concerns in *To a Mouse* and at least one of his other poems. A further 2 marks can be achieved for the reference to the extract given. 6 additional marks can be awarded for discussion of similar references in at least one other poem by Burns. In practice this means: Identification of commonality eg the creation of a persona/speaker in a dramatic situation and/or communicating directly with reader (1 mark) allows Burns to explore a variety of themes — hypocrisy/social class/love religion/nature etc (1 mark) From the extract: 2 marks for detailed/insightful comment plus quotation/reference; 1 mark for more basic comment plus quotation/reference; 0 marks for quotation/reference alone. eg The regretful tone adopted by the persona allows Burns to reflect on man's destruction of nature and the impermanence of existence. (2 marks) **OR** The persona's compassion for the mouse allows Burns to comment on how even the "best laid plans" can be destroyed by fate. (2 marks) From at least one other text: 2 marks for detailed/insightful comment plus quotation/reference; 1 mark for more basic comment plus quotation/reference; 0 marks for quotation/reference alone (Up to 6 marks). Possible answers include: In comments on other poems by Burns, possible references include: • *A Poet's Welcome to his Love-Begotten Daughter* — the emotions of the defensive/combative speaker/persona are appropriate for the heartfelt challenge to contemporary religious and moral attitudes (2) • *Address to the Deil* — humorous, ironic speaker/persona is appropriate for poet's satirical critique of Calvinism (2) • *A Man's A Man For A' That* — a spokesman, champion of equality and fraternity speaking as the voice of a community/nation (2) • *Holy Willie* — creation of hypocritical character for dramatic monologue is an apt vehicle for poet's religious satire (2) • *Tam O'Shanter* — character of moralising, commentating narrator allows Burns to point out the vagaries of human nature/undermine the apparent moral 'message' of the poem (2) Many other answers are possible.

Text 3 — Poetry — *War Photographer* by Carol Ann Duffy

Question	Expected Answer(s)	Max Mark	Additional Guidance
37.	Candidates should analyse how imagery is used to create a serious atmosphere. A detailed/insightful comment on one example may be awarded 2 marks. More basic comments can be awarded 1 mark each. Identification of image alone = 0 marks	2	Possible answers include: • The metaphor "spools of suffering" links the content of the photographic images in the spools to the subjects of the photographs to highlight the awareness of the (on-going, cyclical) misery endured by the subjects. • The image "spools … ordered rows" compares the meticulous arrangement of the spools to the graves in a (war) cemetery to highlight the scale of deaths witnessed/ the violent nature of the deaths. • The image of the "dark room" with its red light as a "church" compares the interior lighting within the darkroom to that of a church to highlight the gloomy, funereal atmosphere of the darkroom. • Word choice of "red" suggests danger (of war zone/ pictures) or blood (represents the horror of the war zone) • The image of the photographer as "a priest … intone a Mass" suggests a similarity between the role of the photographer and the priest in terms of the seriousness of the processes they are involved in/the importance of their roles in spreading the word. • The image "All flesh is grass" compares human life to short lived "grass" to highlight the transient nature of human life (especially in times of conflict).
38.	Candidates should analyse how Duffy conveys the contrast between the photographer's perception of life in Britain and life in the war zones he covers. For full marks both sides of the contrast should be dealt with but not necessarily in equal measure. 2 marks awarded for detailed/insightful comment plus quotation/reference. 1 mark for more basic comment plus quotation/reference. 0 marks for quotation/reference alone.	4	Possible answers include: • The word choice of "Rural England" suggests the idealised view of England as predominantly countryside which is leafy, peaceful, natural, wholesome. • The juxtaposition of "ordinary pain" suggests how trivial and unimportant the problems faced in Britain are compared to those in war zones. • The word choice of "simple weather" and/or "dispel" suggests how shallow/easily addressed the problems faced in Britain are. • The word choice of "explode" suggests the unpredictability and danger of life in the war zone. • The word choice of "nightmare heat" suggests extreme climactic conditions endured (with suggestion of oppressive or threatening atmosphere). • An extended contrast could be drawn between the stereotypical feature of "rural England" — "fields" and "running children" and how this is contrasted with reality of life in the war zone — "exploded" and "nightmare heat". • The word choice of "hand, which did not tremble then"- emphasises contrast between his ability to cope with the job at the time and the impact on him now as he reflects on it
39.	Candidates should analyse how poetic technique is used to convey the distressing nature of the photographer's memories. 2 marks awarded for detailed/insightful comment plus quotation/reference; 1 mark for more basic comment plus quotation/reference. 0 marks for reference/quotation alone.	2	Possible answers include: • Word choice — "twist" suggests the subject's body distorted by pain/injury; writhing in agony. • Word choice — "half-formed ghost" suggests memories of death/being haunted by the memories. • Word choice of "cries" suggests the anguish of the man's wife. • Enjambement "cries/of this man's wife" suggests emotional turmoil, uncontained by ordinary line structure. • Word choice of "blood stained" suggests the scale of the violence remembered/the indelible nature of the memory. • use of sense words such as "blood stained" and "cries" suggests the vivacity of the memory. • Word choice of "foreign dust" suggests abandoned and forgotten.

Question	Expected Answer(s)	Max Mark	Additional Guidance
40.	Candidates should analyse how the poet's use of poetic technique conveys the indifference of the readership of the newspapers to the suffering shown in them. 2 marks awarded for detailed/insightful comment plus quotation/reference; 1 mark for more basic comment plus quotation/reference. 0 marks for reference/quotation alone.	2	Possible answers include: • Word choice — "A hundred agonies" suggests the emotional power/quantity of images that the public respond to in a limited way. • Word choice — "black and white" suggests the veracity of the images that the public respond to in a limited way. • The contrast in numbers, "hundred" with "five or six", illustrates the public's limited capacity for images of this horrific nature. • Word choice of "prick with tears" suggests the public's limited emotional response to the images • The juxtaposition/alliteration of "between the bath and the pre-lunch beers" suggests the brief impact of the suffering shown in the images. • The positioning/tone of "they do not care" reinforces sense of the British public's indifference to the suffering.
41.	Candidates should discuss the link between the past and present in this poem by Duffy and at least one other poem. Candidates may choose to answer in bullet points in this final question, or write a number of linked statements.	10	Up to 2 marks can be achieved for identifying elements of commonality as identified in the question, ie the way one's past influences one's present. A further 2 marks can be achieved for reference to the extract given. 6 additional marks can be awarded for discussion of similar references to at least one other poem by the poet. In practice this means: Identification of commonality eg Past exerts a powerful influence on the present (1 mark) this can be negative, haunting or add further complexity to life (1 mark). From the extract: 2 marks for detailed/insightful comment plus quotation/reference; 1 mark for more basic comment plus quotation/reference; 0 marks for quotation/reference alone. "half-formed ghost" suggests haunted by the memories of conflicts that he has witnessed (2 marks) From at least one other text: 2 marks for detailed/insightful comment plus quotation/reference; 1 mark for more basic comment plus quotation/reference; 0 marks for quotation/reference alone (Up to 6 marks).

Question	Expected Answer(s)	Max Mark	Additional Guidance
41.	*(continued)*	10	Possible answers include: • *Originally* — sense of childhood security lost in moving to unfamiliar environment still remembered vividly in adulthood shown in "big boys ... shouting words you don't understand" • *Anne Hathaway* — happy memories of the past with her late husband influencing her thoughts in the present "we would dive for pearls" (2) • *Mrs. Midas* — intimacy of past relationship intensifies pain of absolute separateness in present memory of "his hands, his warm hands on my skin" (2) • *Havisham* — pain of betrayal in youth has become the defining bitterness of age "ropes on the backs of my hands I could strangle with" (2) • *Havisham* "the dress yellowing" — wedding dress losing its bright whiteness symbolises the tarnishing/loss of her youthful dreams/ideals (2) Many other answers are possible.

Text 3 — Poetry — *My Rival's House* by Liz Lochhead

Question	Expected Answer(s)	Max Mark	Additional Guidance
42.	Candidates should explain why the speaker feels uncomfortable in her rival's house. 2 marks may be awarded for detailed/insightful comment. 1 mark for more basic comment. (Marks may be awarded 2 or 1+1.)	2	Possible answers may include: • the decorative materials look expensive but are cheap suggesting the rival's welcome is false/only superficial — "ormolu and gilt, slipper satin" • the furnishings seem luxurious at first glance but, in reality, are uncomfortable suggesting an unwelcoming atmosphere — "cushions so stiff ... can't sink in" • disconcerting reflections in polished surfaces suggest deceptive nature of rival/too perfect to be true — "polished clear enough to see distortions in" • rival's almost aggressive pride in the perfection of the house — "ormolu and gilt, slipper satin"
43.	Candidates should analyse how the poet conveys a tense atmosphere by referring to at least two examples from these lines. 2 marks awarded for detailed/insightful comment plus quotation/reference. 1 mark for more basic comment plus quotation/reference. 0 marks for reference/quotation alone.	4	Possible answers may include: • "Silver sugar-tongs ... salver" — suggests the rival is trying to intimidate the speaker with a display of wealth • "glosses over him and me" — gives the impression the rival thinks the speaker's relationship with the son is unimportant • "I am all edges ... shell — suggests the speaker's sense of her own fragility/anxiety • "squirms beneath her surface" — suggests the speaker is aware that she will never be able to get to grips with her rival's hidden nature • "tooth ... nail ... fight" suggests the animalistic/visceral nature of the rivalry • "Will fight, fight foul ..." — repetition of 'fight' emphasises the ongoing/intense nature of the rivalry • "Deferential, daughterly ..." — irony as she is well aware of her rival's true feelings and is also putting up a façade

Question	Expected Answer(s)	Max Mark	Additional Guidance
44.	Candidates should discuss how the speaker's resentment of her rival is made clear in at least two examples. 2 marks awarded for detailed/insightful comment plus quotation/reference. 1 mark for more basic comment plus quotation/reference. 0 marks for reference/quotation alone.	4	Possible answers may include: • "first blood to her" — grudging acknowledgement of mother's blood relationship/boxing imagery suggests speaker views this as a bitter match • "never, never can escape scot free" — repetition of "never" emphasises speaker's reluctant admission that she will never truly have her partner to herself • "sour potluck of family" suggests the speaker's bitter feelings about family ties • "And oh how close …" — mocking tone to suggest speaker's resentment • minor sentences "Lady of the house. Queen Bee." — suggest speaker's derogatory dismissal/summation of her rival's position • repetition of "far more" suggests the speaker's fearful view of the threat posed by her rival • "I was always my own worst enemy … taken even this from me" — speaker's sardonic comment reveals her awareness of her rival's power/destructive qualities • brevity of final two lines encapsulates the idea that the rivalry will never end
45.	Candidates should discuss how Lochhead uses descriptive and/or symbolic detail to explore personality in this and in at least one other poem. Candidates can answer in bullet points in this final question or write a number of detailed linked statements.	10	Up to 2 marks can be achieved for identifying elements of commonality as identified in the question, ie how Lochhead uses descriptive and/or detail to explore personality A further 2 marks can be achieved for the reference to the extract given. 6 additional marks can be awarded for discussion of similar references in at least one other poem by Lochhead. In practice this means: Identification of commonality eg details of description and/or symbolism of objects or activities (1 mark) can help to focus on key personality elements developed in the poem (1 mark). From the extract: 2 marks for detailed/insightful comment plus quotation/reference; 1 mark for more basic comment plus quotation/reference; 0 marks for quotation/reference alone. eg Process of the rival's making tea for the speaker in such a superficially proper way is both patronising and, she senses, a precursor for more open hostility (2 marks) From at least one other text: 2 marks for detailed/insightful comment plus quotation/reference; 1 mark for more basic comment plus quotation/reference; 0 marks for quotation/reference alone (Up to 6 marks).

Question	Expected Answer(s)	Max Mark	Additional Guidance
45.	*(continued)*	10	Possible answers include: • *Last Supper* — "So here she is, tearing foliage," reveals savagery of revenge underlying 'civilised' making of meal (2) • *Last Supper* — "cackling round the cauldron" in their desire to criticise the faithless boyfriend, the friends have become consumed by malice themselves (2) • *For my Grandmother Knitting* — "the needles still move/their rhythms" even though woman is old and frail, the need to provide for her family still defines her (2) • *For my Grandmother Knitting* — "deft and swift/ you slit the still-ticking quick silver fish." evokes the dexterity and skill as a young woman (2) • *View of Scotland/Love Poem* "Down on her hands and knees ... on Hogmanay" conveys mother's commitment to ritual, but not the spirit, of celebration (2) Many other answers are possible.

Text 4 — Poetry — *Visiting Hour* by Norman MacCaig

Question	Expected Answer(s)	Max Mark	Additional Guidance
46.	Candidates should analyse how the poet's use of language establishes his response to the surroundings. 2 marks awarded for detailed/insightful comment plus quotation/reference. 1 mark for more basic comment plus quotation/reference. 0 marks for quotation/reference alone.	2	Possible answers include: • Opening line of the poem "The hospital smell" is blunt and matter-of-fact defining the odour universal to all hospitals. • Unusual imagery of "combs my nostrils" combines the senses of touch and smell to convey the pungent nature of the odour. It is so strong it is almost palpable. • Quirky word choice of "bobbing" is designed to disguise his discomfort/shut out the unpleasant reality he is facing/The disembodied nature of "nostrils/bobbing" indicates how dislocated he feels at this point as he struggles to remain detached. • Reference to unpleasant colours "green/yellow" connote sickness and echo his inner turmoil as he prepares to face the reality of his situation. • Word choice of "corpse" hints at the seriousness of the patient's position/his preoccupation with death. The impersonal terminology creates a darker tone, thus foreshadowing the inevitable. • "Vanishes" has connotations of magic/make-believe/disappearing forever suggesting that there is no afterlife and that, for him, death is final. • Religious imagery of "vanishes heavenward" introduces the hoped for final destination for those, unlike him, who believe in an afterlife. Ironic imitation of the "soul's" final journey is an observation conveying his view that this visiting hour will not be about recovery.

Question	Expected Answer(s)	Max Mark	Additional Guidance
47.	Candidates should analyse how the poet's use of language conveys his sense of his own inadequacy. 2 marks awarded for detailed/insightful comment plus quotation/reference. 1 mark for more basic comment plus quotation/reference. 0 marks for quotation/reference alone.	4	Possible answers include: • Repetition in stanza 3 "I will not feel" emphasises the sharp contrast between the acuteness of his senses in his previous observations and his endeavours to keep his emotions entirely contained • "I" repeated three times illustrates the intensely personal difficulty he is experiencing in keeping his anguish in check. • Climax of "until I have to" shows his acknowledgement of his own avoidance. • Adverbs "lightly, swiftly" create a sense of immediacy and a change to a lighter tone. They suggest the tactful/sensitive/deliberate way in which the nurses work. This contrasts with his feelings of inadequacy. • Inversion of "here … there" echoes the busy and varied nature of the nurses' demanding jobs yet they remain focused. • Word choice of "slender waists" conveys their slight physical frames and sets up the contrast with the following expression — "miraculously … burden" — to highlight the poet's admiration for their dignified demeanour whilst working in this difficult environment whereas he is struggling to cope. • Word choice of "miraculously" has connotations of wonder and awe, suggesting he finds it inconceivable that the nurses could withstand so much emotional suffering. • Word choice of "burden/pain" echoes the emotional and physical responsibilities of their job highlighting its exacting nature. • Repetition of "so much/so many" illustrates his observations that a large proportion of a nurse's job is dealing with death and the dying ie it is a regular occurrence. • Word choice of "clear" shows their ability to remain professional and not form deep emotional attachments to their dying patients.

Question	Expected Answer(s)	Max Mark	Additional Guidance
48.	Candidates should analyse how the poet's use of language emphasises the painful nature of the situation for both patient and visitor. For full marks, both patient and visitor must be dealt with for full marks, although not necessarily in equal measure. 2 marks awarded for detailed/insightful comment plus quotation/reference. 1 mark for more basic comment plus quotation/reference. 0 marks for quotation/reference alone.	4	Possible answers include: **Patient** • Metaphor "white cave of forgetfulness" suggests that her reduced mental capacity offers her some protection/refuge from the horrors of her situation OR diminishes her insight into her own situations/lessens her ability to communicate • Imagery of a flower/plant "withered hand … stalk" suggests her weakness and helplessness. The image is ironic as flowers are traditional tokens of recovery for hospital patients. • The unconventional inverted vampire image "glass fang/guzzling/giving" emphasises the reality that the patient is being kept alive medically as her body is decaying and death is imminent. Candidates may choose to deal with this as word choice/alliteration/onomatopoeia. All are acceptable approaches and should be rewarded appropriately. • Imagery of "black figure/white cave" suggests the patient is dimly aware of her surroundings but the "black figure" who has now entered her environment symbolises her approaching death. • Word choice of "smiles a little" indicates that the patient has, perhaps, accepted the reality of her situation/does have a sense of the caring nature of the visit **Visitor** • Personal pronouns "her/me/she/I" indicate that both are suffering albeit in different ways. The patient suffers the physical agony of dying but the visitor has to face the emotional anguish of her loss. • Repetition of "distance" highlights that on a literal level he has arrived at her bedside but there is still a gulf between them as he cannot help her. • Word choice "neither … cross" conveys he is no longer an observer but a helpless participant who now feels acute emotional misery. • Word choice of "clumsily" highlights his feelings of inadequacy and ineptitude in the situation in which he finds himself. **Either/both:** • Symbolic reference to "books that … read" creates a tone of futility/despair as the pleasure to be gained from reading will never be experienced again. • Oxymoron/pun "fruitless fruits" effectively conveys the hopelessness of the situation for both patient and visitor. Just as fruits are traditional gifts brought to hospital to aid recuperation, "fruitless" ironically reveals that this patient will never recover so there is no hope. The agony of her loss is, therefore, laid bare.

Question	Expected Answer(s)	Max Mark	Additional Guidance
49.	Candidates should discuss the significance of loss in this poem and in at least one other by MacCaig and should refer to appropriate textual evidence to support their discussion. 0 marks for reference/quotation alone. Candidates can answer in bullet points in this final question, or write a number of linked statements.	10	Up to 2 marks can be achieved for identifying elements of commonality as identified in the question, ie MacCaig's presentation of the theme of loss. A further 2 marks can be achieved for reference to the extract given. 6 additional marks can be awarded for discussion of similar references to at least one other poem by the poet. In practice this means: Identification of commonality loss is a universal human experience(1 mark) Which can have a profound and long-lasting effect on the individual (1 mark) From the extract: 2 marks for detailed/insightful comment plus quotation/reference; 1 mark for more basic comment plus quotation/reference; 0 marks for quotation/reference alone. eg Fear of loss of the loved one influences the speaker's perception of everything in the hospital eg 'what seemed a corpse' (2 marks) OR Sense of despair at end of visit due loss of communication with the loved on- nothing has been achieved 'fruitless fruits; (2 marks) From at least one other text: 2 marks for detailed/insightful comment plus quotation/reference; 1 mark for more basic comment plus quotation/reference; 0 marks for quotation/reference alone (Up to 6 marks). Possible answers include: • *Sounds of the Day* — profound impact of loss when a relationship ends shown through contrast between sounds — meaning life — and the 'silence' after parting (2) • *Sounds of the Day* use of 'numb' as final word emphasizes finality and intensity of negative feelings associated with the relationship ending (2) • *Memorial* — all consuming, all pervading nature of loss in the death of a loved one shown in 'Everywhere she dies' (2) • *Memorial* — despite passage of time, his life is now a 'memorial' devoted to her memory 'I am her sad music' (2) • *Aunt Julia* loss of opportunity to communicate with his aunt shown in 'absolute silence' of her death/grave, by the time he could have spoken Gaelic to her (2) Many other answers are possible.

Text 5 — Poetry — *An Autumn Day* by Sorely Maclean

Question	Expected Answer(s)	Max Mark	Additional Guidance
50.	Candidates should analyse how the poet's use of language emphasises the impact of this experience. 2 marks awarded for detailed/insightful comment plus quotation/reference. 1 mark for more basic comment plus quotation/reference. 0 marks for quotation/reference alone.	4	Possible answers include: • Reference to "that slope" suggests that the specific place is imprinted on the mind of the persona • "soughing" is surprising, suggesting the deadly shells make a gentle noise • "six dead men at my shoulder" — a matter-of-fact tone, suggesting that the persona has become accustomed to the extraordinary and the traumatic. • "waiting … message" suggests a communication with a higher power, as if the dead soldiers are in a state of limbo • "screech" conveys the disturbing nature of the noise from shells • "throbbing" suggests pain and discomfort • "leaped … climbed … surged" makes clear the rapid spread of deadly fire • "blinding … splitting" shows how the shell robs the persona of his senses.
51.	Candidates should analyse how the poet uses at least two examples of language to emphasise the meaninglessness of the men's deaths. 2 marks awarded for detailed/insightful comment plus quotation/reference. 1 mark for more basic comment plus quotation/reference. 0 marks for quotation/reference alone.	4	Possible answers include: • "the whole day" suggests that their deaths have been ignored • "morning … midday … evening" emphasising the time continues as normal/is never-ending • "sun … so indifferent" — the sun, rather than being a primary life-force, is portrayed as being cold and lacking in nurturing qualities • juxtaposition of "painful" and "comfortable/kindly" highlights the ironic nature of the landscape ignoring the men's deaths • "In the sun … under the stars" highlight the starkness of death in the midst of the continuous nature of time/life's cycle • contrast of "six men dead" and "stars of Africa/jewelled and beautiful" emphasises the triviality of the men's deaths beside the greatness/majesty of nature
52.	Candidates should explain what the speaker finds puzzling when he reflects on the men's deaths. 2 marks may be awarded for detailed/insightful comment; 1 mark for more basic comment	2	Possible answers include: • he is puzzled by the random/indiscriminate nature of death —"took them and did not take me" • he is puzzled as these deaths seem to contradict the beliefs/religious teaching of his background — the notion of the Elect

Question	Expected Answer(s)	Max Mark	Additional Guidance
53.	Candidates should discuss how MacLean uses nature to convey the central concern(s) of this and at least one other poem. Candidates may choose to answer in bullet points in this final question, or write a number of linked statements.	10	Up to 2 marks can be achieved for identifying elements of commonality as identified in the question, ie how MacLean uses nature to convey the central concerns of his poetry A further 2 marks can be achieved for the reference to the extract given. 6 additional marks can be awarded for discussion of similar references from at least one other poem by MacLean. In practice this means: Identification of commonality eg vivid images from nature (1 mark) allow MacLean to explore a variety of themes — war/heritage and tradition/love/ relationships etc (1 mark) From the extract: 2 marks for detailed/insightful comment plus quotation/reference; 1 mark for more basic comment plus quotation/ reference; 0 marks for quotation/reference alone. eg The grandeur contained in the imagery of the "stars of Africa, jewelled and beautiful" highlights humanity's insignificance. (2 marks) **OR** Autumn is used to suggest the transience of life/ inevitability of death in the continuous cycle of nature. (2 marks) From at least one other text: 2 marks for detailed/insightful comment plus quotation/reference; 1 mark for more basic comment plus quotation/ reference; 0 marks for quotation/reference alone (Up to 6 marks). Possible answers include: • *Hallaig*: the native trees of Raasay are used to symbolise the traditional ways of life/ inhabitants who have been removed as a consequence of The Clearances (2) • *Screapadal*: the beauty of the natural setting allows the persona to reflect on his connection with the Hebrides (2) • *Screapadal*: the peaceful nature of the seal and basking shark is contrasted with the submarine/ threat of destruction from humans (2) • *Shores*: the sea coming into "Talisker bay forever" depicts the fulfilling qualities of love (2) • *I gave you Immortality*: **the permanence of nature symbolises his undying love for Eimhir** (2) Many other answers are possible.

Text 6 — Poetry — *Two Trees* by Don Paterson

Question	Expected Answer(s)	Max Mark	Additional Guidance
54.	Candidates should analyse how the poet's use of poetic technique in lines 1—12 emphasises the importance of the story of the trees. 2 marks are awarded for detailed/insightful comment plus quotation/reference. 1 mark for more basic comment plus quotation/reference. 0 marks for quotation/reference alone. (Marks may be awarded 2+2, 2+1+1, 1+1+1+1)	4	Possible answers include: • Temporal sequence of 'One morning ... Over the years ...' suggests the ever-present/universal nature of the story • Interest in character of Don Miguel as obsessive: 'one idea rooted' • Allegorical representation/characterisation/symbolism of trees: 'the magic tree' suggest powerful nature of the story • Impact of the tree on the villagers: 'not one kid in the village didn't know'
55.	Candidates should analyse how language is used to create an impression of 'the man'. 2 marks will be awarded for 1 detailed/insightful comment plus reference. 1 mark for more basic comment plus reference (2+2, 2+1+1, 1+1+1+1). 0 marks for reference/quotation alone.	4	Possible answers include: • "The man" is unnamed, remains faceless/anonymous • "had no dream" suggests lack of imagination or empathy • "dark" suggests sense of foreboding • "malicious" suggests evil intent • "whim" suggests casual, thoughtless act • "who can say" suggests his actions were inexplicable/unaccountable • "axe"/"split the bole" suggests a violence/brutality in his actions
56.	Candidates should explain the irony of the final two lines. 2 marks awarded for one detailed/insightful comment. 1 mark for more basic comment. (Marks may be awarded 2 or 1+1)	2	Possible answers: • Idea of trees having no human qualities despite earlier allusions • Trees are essentially prosaic with no magical qualities • The definitive statement that the poem is only about trees when it is clearly not
57.	Candidates should discuss how Paterson develops the theme of relationships. Candidates may choose to answer in bullet points in this final question, or write a number of linked statements	10	Up to 2 marks can be achieved for identifying elements of commonality as identified in the question, ie the theme of relationships. A further 2 marks can be achieved for reference to the extract given. 6 additional marks can be awarded for discussion of similar references to at least one other short story by the writer. In practice this means: Identification of commonality eg the profound and complex nature of intimate relationships on the individual (1 mark) and the potential fragility of human relationships (1 mark). From the extract: 2 marks for detailed/insightful comment plus quotation/reference; 1 mark for more basic comment plus quotation/reference; 0 marks for quotation/reference alone. eg "so tangled up" suggests complex mutual dependency which can be either damaging or productive (2 marks) **OR** "nor did their unhealed flanks weep every spring" suggests the resilience of the human spirit/the pain of separation/longing for intimacy (2 marks)

Question	Expected Answer(s)	Max Mark	Additional Guidance
57.	*(continued)*	10	From at least one other text:
			2 marks for detailed/insightful comment plus quotation/reference;
			1 mark for more basic comment plus quotation/reference;
			0 marks for quotation/reference alone
			(Up to 6 marks).
			Possible answers include:
			• *Waking with Russell* — father/son bond explored through transformative power of love showing it is unconditional — "pledged myself forever" (2)
			• *Waking with Russell* — "lit it as you ran" suggests love providing mutual benefit, enriching lives (2)
			• *The Ferryman's Arms* — relationship with self when he plays pool alone, suggesting the conflict between different aspects of the self (2)
			• *The Thread* — development of the thread image shows fragility of family relationship/resilience gained through trauma (2)
			• *The Thread* — "the great twin-engined wingspan of us" suggests the uplifting exhilaration of sharing experiences with loved ones (2)
			Many other answers are possible.

SECTION 2 – Critical Essay

Supplementary marking grid

	Marks 20–19	Marks 18–16	Marks 15–13	Marks 12–10	Marks 9–6	Marks 5–0
Knowledge and understanding The critical essay demonstrates:	thorough knowledge and understanding of the text	secure knowledge and understanding of the text	clear knowledge and understanding of the text	adequate knowledge and understanding of the text	limited evidence of knowledge and understanding of the text	very little knowledge and understanding of the text
	perceptive selection of textual evidence to support line of argument which is fluently structured and expressed	detailed textual evidence to support line of thought which is coherently structured and expressed	clear textual evidence to support line of thought which is clearly structured and expressed	adequate textual evidence to support line of thought, which is adequately structured and expressed	limited textual evidence to support line of thought which is structured and expressed in a limited way	very little textual evidence to support line of thought which shows very little structure or clarity of expression
	perceptive focus on the demands of the question	secure focus on the demands of the question	clear focus on the demands of the question	adequate focus on the demands of the question	limited focus on the demands of the question	very little focus on the demands of the question
Analysis The critical essay demonstrates:	perceptive analysis of the effect of features of language/filmic techniques	detailed analysis of the effect of features of language/filmic techniques	clear analysis of the effect of features of language/filmic techniques	an adequate analysis of the effect of features of language/filmic techniques	limited analysis of the effect of features of language/filmic techniques	very little analysis of features of language/filmic techniques
Evaluation The critical essay demonstrates:	committed evaluative stance with respect to the text and the task	engaged evaluative stance with respect to the text and the task	clear evaluative stance with respect to the text and the task	adequate evidence of an evaluative stance with respect to the text and the task	limited evidence of an evaluative stance with respect to the text and the task	very little evidence of an evaluative stance with respect to the text and the task
Technical accuracy The critical essay demonstrates:	few errors in spelling, grammar, sentence construction, punctuation and paragraphing; the ability to be understood at first reading				significant number of errors in spelling, grammar, sentence construction, punctuation and paragraphing which impedes understanding	

Acknowledgements

Permission has been sought from all relevant copyright holders and Hodder Gibson is grateful for the use of the following:

An extract from 'The Last Veteran' by Peter Parker, published by Fourth Estate, reprinted by permission of HarperCollins Publishers Ltd. © Peter Parker 2009 (Model Paper 1 Reading for Understanding, Analysis and Evaluation pages 2 & 3);

A passage adapted from 'Why World War I Resonates' by William Boyd from The New York Times, 21 January 2012 © The New York Times. All rights reserved. Used by permission and protected by the Copyright Laws of the United States. The printing, copying, redistribution, or retransmission of this Content without express written permission is prohibited (Model Paper 1 Reading for Understanding, Analysis and Evaluation pages 5 & 6);

An extract from 'The Slab Boys Trilogy' © John Byrne 2003, published by Faber & Faber Ltd. All rights whatsoever in this play are strictly reserved and application for performance etc. should be made to the Author's agent: Casarotto Ramsay & Associates Limited, Waverley House, 7–12 Noel Street, London W1F 8G (rights@casarotto.co.uk). No performance may be given unless a licence has been obtained. (Model Paper 1 Critical Reading pages 2 & 3);

An extract from 'The Cheviot, the Stag and the Black, Black Oil,' by John McGrath. Published by Methuen Drama, an imprint of Bloomsbury Publishing Ltd. © John McGrath (Model Paper 1 Critical Reading pages 4 & 5);

An extract from 'Men Should Weep' by Ena Lamont Stewart. Reproduced with permission of Alan Brodie Representation Ltd (Model Paper 1 Critical Reading page 6);

An extract from 'The Crater' by Iain Crichton Smith, taken from 'The Red Door: The Complete English Stories 1949–76', published by Birlinn. Reproduced by permission of Birlinn Ltd. www.birlinn.co.uk (Model Paper 1 Critical Reading page 8);

An extract from 'The Bright Spade' by George Mackay Brown taken from 'A Time To Keep' published by The Hogarth Press Ltd, 1969. Reproduced by permission of The Estate of George Mackay Brown/Jenny Brown Associates (Model Paper 1 Critical Reading page 10);

An extract from 'The Trick is to Keep Breathing' by Janice Galloway, published by Vintage, reprinted by permission of The Random House Group Limited (Model Paper 1 Critical Reading page 12);

An extract from 'Sunset Song' by Lewis Grassic Gibbon, published by Jarrold Publishing, 1932. Public domain. (Model Paper 1 Critical Reading page 14);

An extract from 'The Cone-Gatherers' by Robin Jenkins published by Canongate Books Ltd. (Model Paper 1 Critical Reading page 16);

The poem 'To a Mouse' by Robert Burns. Public domain. (Model Paper 1 Critical Reading page 18);

The poem 'Mrs Midas' by Carol Ann Duffy, taken from 'The World's Wife', published by Picador 1999. Reproduced by permission of Pan Macmillan © Carol Ann Duffy 1999 (Model Paper 1 Critical Reading page 20);

An extract from the poem 'Last Supper' by Liz Lochhead from 'A Choosing: Selected Poems', published by Polygon. Reproduced by permission of Birlinn Ltd. www.birlinn.co.uk (Model Paper 1 Critical Reading page 22);

The poem 'Assisi' by Norman MacCaig from 'The Many Days: Selected Poems of Norman MacCaig' published by Polygon. Reproduced by permission of Birlinn Ltd. www.birlinn.co.uk (Model Paper 1 Critical Reading page 24);

An extract from 'Hallaig' by Sorley MacLean, taken from 'Caoir Gheal Leumraich/White Leaping Flame: collected poems in Gaelic with English translations', edited by Christopher Whyte and Emma Dymock 2011. Reproduced by permission of Carcanet Press Ltd (Model Paper 1 Critical Reading page 26);

The poem 'The Thread' by Don Paterson from 'Landing Light' (Faber & Faber 2003). Reproduced by permission of the author c/o Rogers, Coleridge & White Ltd., 20 Powis Mews, London W11 1JN (Model Paper 1 Critical Reading page 28);

The article 'Buying Stuff is the Heroin of Human Happiness' by Carol Midgley, taken from The Times © The Times/News Syndication, 22 July 2009 (Model Paper 2 Reading for Understanding, Analysis and Evaluation pages 2 & 3);

The article 'Shopping and Tut-tutting' by Will Hutton, taken from The Observer 4 September 2005. Copyright Will Hutton (Model Paper 2 Reading for Understanding, Analysis and Evaluation pages 5 & 6);

An extract from 'The Slab Boys Trilogy' © John Byrne 2003, published by Faber & Faber Ltd. All rights whatsoever in this play are strictly reserved and application for performance etc. should be made to the Author's agent: Casarotto Ramsay & Associates Limited, Waverley House, 7–12 Noel Street, London W1F 8G (rights@casarotto.co.uk). No performance may be given unless a licence has been obtained. (Model Paper 2 Critical Reading pages 2 & 3);

An extract from 'The Cheviot, the Stag and the Black, Black Oil,' by John McGrath. Published by Methuen Drama, an imprint of Bloomsbury Publishing Ltd. © John McGrath (Model Paper 2 Critical Reading pages 4 & 5);

An extract from 'Men Should Weep' by Ena Lamont Stewart. Reproduced with permission of Alan Brodie Representation Ltd (Model Paper 2 Critical Reading page 6);

An extract from 'The Painter' by Iain Crichton Smith, taken from 'The Red Door: The Complete English Stories 1949–76', published by Birlinn. Reproduced by permission of Birlinn Ltd. www.birlinn.co.uk (Model Paper 2 Critical Reading pages 8 & 9);

An extract from 'The Eye of the Hurricane' by George Mackay Brown, taken from 'A Calendar of Love' published by Polygon. Reproduced by permission of Birlinn Ltd. www.birlinn.co.uk (Model Paper 2 Critical Reading page 10);

An extract from 'The Trick is to Keep Breathing' by Janice Galloway, published by Vintage, reprinted by permission of The Random House Group Limited (Model Paper 2 Critical Reading page 12);

An extract from 'Sunset Song' by Lewis Grassic Gibbon, published by Jarrold Publishing, 1932. Public domain. (Model Paper 2 Critical Reading page 14);

An extract from 'The Cone-Gatherers' by Robin Jenkins published by Canongate Books Ltd. (Model Paper 2 Critical Reading page 16);

The poem 'Tam o' Shanter' by Robert Burns. Public domain. (Model Paper 2 Critical Reading page 18);
The poem 'Anne Hathaway' by Carol Ann Duffy, taken from 'The World's Wife', published by Picador 1999. Reproduced by permission of Pan Macmillan © Carol Ann Duffy 1999 (Model Paper 2 Critical Reading page 20);
An extract from the poem 'Some Old Photographs' by Liz Lochhead from 'A Choosing: Selected Poems' published by Polygon. Reproduced by permission of Birlinn Ltd. www.birlinn.co.uk (Model Paper 2 Critical Reading page 22);
The poem 'Memorial' by Norman MacCaig from 'The Many Days: Selected Poems of Norman MacCaig' published by Polygon. Reproduced by permission of Birlinn Ltd. www.birlinn.co.uk (Model Paper 2 Critical Reading page 24);
An extract from 'Shores' by Sorley MacLean, taken from 'Caoir Gheal Leumraich/White Leaping Flame: collected poems in Gaelic with English translations', edited by Christopher Whyte and Emma Dymock 2011. Reproduced by permission of Carcanet Press Ltd (Model Paper 2 Critical Reading page 26);
The poem 'Two Trees' by Don Paterson taken from 'Rain' (Faber & Faber 2010). Reproduced by permission of the author c/o Rogers, Coleridge & White Ltd., 20 Powis Mews, London W11 1JN (Model Paper 2 Critical Reading page 28);
An extract from the article 'Want to exercise your mind? Try playstation' by Steven Johnson © The Times/News Syndication, 13 May 2005 (Model Paper 3 Reading for Understanding, Analysis and Evaluation pages 2 & 3);
The article 'The Writing Is On The Wall' by Boris Johnson, taken from The Daily Telegraph © Telegraph Media Group Limited (28 December 2006) (Model Paper 3 Reading for Understanding, Analysis and Evaluation page 5);
An extract adapted from the article 'Goodbye birds. Goodbye butterflies. Hello... farmageddon' by Isabel Oakeshott © The Times/News Syndication, 19 January 2014 (2015 Reading for Understanding, Analysis and Evaluation pages 2 & 3);
The article 'Pasture to the Plate', by Audrey Ayton, taken from The Observer Supplement, 10 July 1994. Copyright Guardian News & Media Ltd 2015 (2015 Reading for Understanding, Analysis and Evaluation pages 3 & 4);
An extract from 'The Slab Boys' © 1982 John Byrne. 'The Slab Boys' was first performed at the Traverse Theatre, Edinburgh, on 6 April 1978. All rights whatsoever in this play are strictly reserved and application for performance etc. should be made to the Author's agent: Casarotto Ramsay & Associates Limited, Waverley House, 7–12 Noel Street, London W1F 8G (rights@casarotto.co.uk). No performance may be given unless a licence has been obtained (2015 Critical Reading pages 2 & 3);
An extract from 'The Cheviot, the Stag and the Black, Black Oil,' by John McGrath. Published by Methuen Drama, an imprint of Bloomsbury Publishing Ltd. © John McGrath (2015 Critical Reading page 6);
An extract from 'Men Should Weep' © Ena Lamont Stewart, 1947. Reproduced by permission of Alan Brodie Representation Ltd (www.alanbrodie.com) (2015 Critical Reading pages 8 & 9);
An extract from 'Mother and Son' by Iain Crichton Smith, taken from 'The Red Door: The Complete English Stories 1949–76', published by Birlinn. Reproduced by permission of Birlinn Ltd. www.birlinn.co.uk (2015 Critical Reading pages 12 & 13);
An extract from 'The Wireless Set' by George Mackay Brown taken from the book 'A Time To Keep' published by Polygon. Reproduced by permission of Birlinn Ltd. www.birlinn.co.uk (2015 Critical Reading pages 14 & 15);
An extract from 'The Trick is to Keep Breathing' by Janice Galloway, published by Vintage, reprinted by permission of The Random House Group Limited (2015 Critical Reading page 16);
An extract from 'Sunset Song' by Lewis Grassic Gibbon, published by Jarrold Publishing, 1932. Public domain. (2015 Critical Reading pages 18 & 19);
An extract from 'The Cone-Gatherers' by Robin Jenkins published by Canongate Books Ltd. (2015 Critical Reading pages 20 & 21);
The poem 'To a Mouse' by Robert Burns. Public domain. (2015 Critical Reading pages 22 & 23);
The poem 'War Photographer' by Carol Ann Duffy from 'New Selected Poems 1984–2004' (Picador, 2004). Reproduced by permission of the author c/o Rogers, Coleridge & White Ltd., 20 Powis Mews, London W11 1JN (2015 Critical Reading page 24);
An extract from the poem 'My Rival's House' by Liz Lochhead from 'A Choosing: Selected Poems', published by Polygon. Reproduced by permission of Birlinn Ltd. www.birlinn.co.uk (2015 Critical Reading page 26);
The poem 'Visiting Hour' by Norman MacCaig from 'The Poems of Norman MacCaig' published by Polygon. Reproduced by permission of Birlinn Ltd. www.birlinn.co.uk (2015 Critical Reading page 28);
An extract from 'An Autumn Day' by Sorley MacLean, taken from 'Caoir Gheal Leumraich/White Leaping Flame: collected poems in Gaelic with English translations', edited by Christopher Whyte and Emma Dymock 2011. Reproduced by permission of Carcanet Press Ltd (2015 Critical Reading page 30);
The poem 'Two Trees' by Don Paterson taken from 'Rain' (Faber & Faber 2010). Reproduced by permission of the author c/o Rogers, Coleridge & White Ltd., 20 Powis Mews, London W11 1JN (2015 Critical Reading page 32).

Hodder Gibson would like to thank SQA for use of any past exam questions that may have been used in model papers, whether amended or in original form.